"Dion, Carey, and David have become family not only for themselves but for others. They are an example of the importance of adoptive parents being open to future needs of both children and birth parents."
—Most Reverend Anthony M. Pilla, Bishop of Cleveland

"If we are to build a better society, we must be responsible for children and their mothers. We all know this to be true. Dion Howells is one of the first with a simple plan for how to make it happen."
—Rabbi Bruce Abrams

"Dion, Carey, David, and Nancy are an example to us all and show us in the clearest possible way God's will for us. Open adoption and a close relationship between the birth parents and the adoptive parents are loving realities which must find expression in today's world."
—J. Clark Grew, II
The Episcopal Church in the Diocese of Ohio

THE
STORY
OF
DAVID

∽

DION HOWELLS
AND
KÄREN WILSON
PRITCHARD

Delacorte ▬ Press

Published by
Delacorte Press
Bantam Doubleday Dell Publishing Group, Inc.
1540 Broadway
New York, New York 10036

The trademark Delacorte Press® is registered in the U.S. Patent and Trademark Office.

Library of Congress Cataloging in Publication Data

Howells, Dion.
The story of David / by Dion Howells and Kären Wilson Pritchard.
p.   cm.
ISBN 0-385-31886-3
1. Open adoption—United States—Case studies.   2. Foster parents—United States—Case studies.   3. Adopted children—United States Case studies.
I. Pritchard, Kären Wilson.   II. Title.
HV875.55.H69   1997
362.73′4′092—dc21

[B]   96-49399
                                                                                               CIP

Manufactured in the United States of America

Published simultaneously in Canada

June 1997

10   9   8   7   6   5   4   3   2   1

BVG

This book is first and foremost dedicated to my son, David Evan. Where many adoptive children have to struggle with the loss of their heritage, you, my son, will never have to wonder. Your mother and I have not only recorded your biological heritage with the love and support of your birth mother, Nancy, we have also given you the greatest gift any child could hope for—your own heritage; one that will allow you to explore what life has to offer you. Your destiny and future belong to only you. The people who love you will forever support you in whatever endeavor you choose.

You were born in love, and have lived in love, and have allowed us to share your life. In that responsibility, with God's help, we shall try to never fail you.

This book is also for any parents who have experienced the loss of a child whether from death or traditional adoption, abandonment or abortion. It is my sincere hope that you will find help or comfort in experiencing and sharing in my son's life.

D.E.H.

For my children: Griffin, Annelise, Kai, Jameson, Kip, and Wilson.

—K.W.P.

In memory of: Karen Jean Howells, Edward William Howells, Sr., Thomas Augustin Flinn, Anne Brammer Wilson, and The Virgin Mary

Acknowledgments

Our sincere and endless thanks go to:

Mary Ellen O'Neill, our outstanding editor, who recognized a good story and expertly helped us turn it into a great book. We feel privileged to say that in working with Mary Ellen, we've worked with the best. Her wisdom, patience, understanding, and insight through our writing efforts and family commitments have been steadfast.

Dell/Delacorte as an organization deserves commendations. It sustains an environment that aspires to effect positive social change through creative means. Our appreciation goes to Virginia Van Dyk, director of sub-rights, who initially took the manuscript of *The Story of David* on the advice of her friend, Mimi Jones. Virginia launched us on our publishing journey at Dell/Delacorte. We are forever indebted to both Mimi and Virginia.

Leslie Schnur, associate publisher and editor-in-chief, Carisa Hays, director of publicity, and Karen Mender, director of marketing, did more than just meet with Dion. They embraced him as a friend and were committed to the success of *The Story of David*.

Marian Rees and Anne Hopkins of Marian Rees Associates, Inc., who listened to us and to our story when no one else would. Also to Jan Parkinson, who put us in contact with Marian and Anne.

To Peter Guzzardi who took Dion's cold call and gave generously of his experience and advice. Peter listened to David's story and put Dion in touch with a friend of his, Lynn Franklin, a literary and film agent.

Dion's first phone call to Lynn Franklin was not only productive but extraordinarily meaningful, as Lynn explained that she had been personally affected by the issue of adoption. Needless to say, she is an agent with both the outstanding professional capacity as well as the exceptional personal capacity, to see *The Story of David* as more than just a business project. Lynn exhibited great patience in dealing with a less-than-traditional author, who knows how to be a policeman but not very much about the business world.

Lynn Franklin and our attorney, Marc Krantz, navigated us through the legalities and business end of this heartfelt project.

If it takes a village to raise a child, the same is true for creating a project of this magnitude. Thanks go also to Dion's friends at the police station, who lent personal support: patrolman Dale Whitmer and dispatchers Irene Roseum and Debbie Murfello.

Dion would also like to thank James Mendlik, who tirelessly offered sound, fatherly advice.

Dion would like to express his gratitude to his family, Carey and David, for their understanding in completing this book. Without their support, this book would not have been possible. David's grandmothers Catherine J. Howells, Barbara B. Flinn, and Marilou Caneo have not only influenced the author but are responsible for guiding the family.

Dion would like to express a special acknowledgement to Kären who, while pregnant with triplets, finished the original book proposal, and after losing her mother, worked on deadline to complete the balance of the manuscript.

Several people and organizations were especially supportive as this project took shape. They deserve special thanks:

Betsie Norris and the Cleveland Adoption Network served as educators on issues of adoption and established our commitment to having an open adoption.

Our social workers and friends, Beth Brindo, Karen Anderson,

Lori Mekinda, Nancy Lahr, and Kate Feighan-Becca, who saw us through to what we are today.

Dr. R. D. Thompson, our family doctor, who quickly did physicals so we could become licensed foster parents to our son.

Also, the Lyndhurst Fire Department and Captain Mike DeLuca, for expediting the fire inspection and ordering commercial grade fire extinguishers for us.

Kären would like to thank Betsy and John Vulanich. Without their encouragement, adoption and parenthood would never have been part of her life. Thanks also to Judy Scarpelli-Dwyer who served as a friend and sounding board throughout this project.

Also, special thanks from Kären to her family: her father, Earl L. Wilson; her mother, Anne B. Wilson; her sister, Dr. Lise A. Wilson, and her brother, Kip B. Wilson. They have offered support and steadfast love always, but especially when they unconditionally opened their hearts and arms to the beautiful baby she and her husband were blessed with through adoption.

Last, but not least, is David, who inspired his dad to write a diary for him that became *The Story of David*.

CHAPTER

I

It was March 3, 1992, and still very much winter. The sky was gray and overcast—standard fare for a March afternoon in Cleveland. Outside, the air was cold, damp, and uninviting. The neighborhood was unusually tranquil. Glancing down the street, I saw a small child, bundled in thick winter clothes, riding his brightly colored tricycle down the sidewalk. His mother followed him a step or two behind, her hands ready to correct any mistakes in his naive navigation. The beauty of the scene cut through me, and I climbed quickly into my car.

I needn't have hurried. I had expected the bank to be crowded and slow this late in the afternoon. Instead it was nearly empty. I was able to sit down with a clerk and begin my business immediately.

"I want to open a mutual fund account," I told her. "I'd like to start with this," I said, and handed her the tax return check that my wife, Carey, and I had recently received. That was as much information as I volunteered. I didn't tell her that this account was to ensure my child's college education. I didn't tell her that I wasn't a father, that I had no child, and that I had watched my wife's heart sink into the deepest despair imaginable as the years had passed and we had not conceived the child she so desperately wanted.

As I waited for the account to be processed, I tried to ignore the subtle melancholy that crept over me. I knew all too well the risk of what I was doing. If things didn't turn out the way Carey and I were hoping, I was now creating yet another reminder of the loss we would live with forever.

The clerk worked efficiently. There were no glitches. The transaction was complete in less than fifteen minutes. I thanked the clerk, pocketed the paperwork, and left the bank.

Until David, my love for Carey was the single most powerful force in my life. She generated a loyalty and love so strong inside me that they debilitated and finally destroyed the irreverent rebel in me. I had grown up on the wild side, the proverbial angry young man. Carey changed everything for me.

We had grown up in the same suburban Cleveland neighborhood and had attended the same church. We had a lot of mutual friends, but we didn't meet each other until she was nineteen and I was twenty-one. I was a security guard in a department store. One afternoon a friend of mine was browsing in the store with her friend, Carey. We were introduced. As I stood in my uniform, hoping I looked impressive, I had a feeling about this woman, this Carey. The rest, as they say, is history.

Carey's calm composure crept over me and began transforming me from the moment I met her. Her beauty and personality were understatedly elegant. She captivated me. We were married in April 1982.

Our first years of marriage fit neatly into the profile of the American dream. My commitment to Carey propelled me through each day and instilled in me a newfound sense of ambition. I was accepted into a police training program, and I was able to channel my energies into being an outstanding husband to Carey and an outstanding police officer. For the first time, I felt a comfortable sense of balance and control in my life. Carey continued her career as the business manager of an ophthalmology practice at a local teaching hospital while also making our marriage work. Everything fit together perfectly, everything felt right.

In 1986 we bought a four-bedroom house in the suburbs. Our neighborhood was the epitome of what a neighborhood should be—nice people, low fences, and a sense of camaraderie and mutual respect. Our fledgling household consisted of Carey, myself, and two furry cats, Aggie and Elizabeth. On the wall in our back hallway hung a small framed print that I had bought for Carey. It showed a simple friendly house with large hearts puffing out of the chimney. To me, it was our house and our selves: humble and overflowing with love.

Having a yard, we soon decided it was time to add a dog to our suburban menagerie. Neither of us was big on the idea of paying a huge sum to buy a purebred. We put out feelers to find a puppy who was really in need of a good home. An advertisement led us to Sam, a six-week-old Lab-shepherd mix with tan fur and black triangular ears. He belonged to a family in our community who couldn't keep him. We took him home and he became a member of our family.

In 1987 we began to talk about having children. Carey had always loved children. She had been an avid baby-sitter since she was twelve years old. She was everybody's favorite baby-sitter—parents and kids alike. By the time she was nineteen, she had earned enough money from baby-sitting to buy herself a car. Loving and mothering children clearly came easily to her. She grew up with a plan to have five children of her own one day.

When Carey's sister, Jennie, had Emily, her first of two children, she asked Carey to be Emily's godmother. When Jennie had her second child, Paul, Aunty Carey became even more a part of their life. She was like a second mother to them. She was warm and loving, and always able to teach them something worthwhile without their knowing it.

Carey was meant to be a parent, and wanted nothing more. It was very important to her, something that was part of the "big plan" in her mind. I was quite the opposite. I had always leaned toward a "two's company" attitude. I now realize that my ambivalence came from fear that I wouldn't measure up to the awesome responsibility of parenthood. Back then I thought life would be just fine without children. But if Carey thought we should have children, that was enough for me. I was going to see to it that we had a family of our own.

So we opened ourselves to the possibility of conceiving a child. We were relaxed and comfortable with the idea and figured that in a matter of months Carey would be pregnant. The first month or two went by with no results. They were fairly easy to write off— we chalked it up to the statistical odds that Carey had read about: On average it takes a couple three months to conceive a child.

We had agreed to make this a "no pressure" situation, so we merely looked ahead each time Carey discovered she wasn't pregnant. As the months went on, Carey's disappointment began to surface, and we made a more concerted effort to get pregnant. Milestones passed: Carey's birthday, my birthday, Christmas— events we had imagined celebrating with the added joy of impending parenthood.

It's hard to pinpoint when things turned from relaxed to stressful, but we went from one extreme to another in a matter of months. As hard as we tried not to think about getting pregnant, we were in fact thinking about it all the time. It seemed as if eons were slipping by, yet we had made no progress toward starting the family we hoped to have. We began to wonder if something was wrong with us.

After six months it was getting hard to pretend things were okay. "I'm a little worried," Carey told me one night at dinner after yet another hoped-for pregnancy failed to materialize. "I'd like to look into this before too much more time goes by," she said quietly. I knew she was getting really discouraged, and it hurt me to see her pain. I agreed without hesitation. Her happiness was paramount to me.

We decided we should make arrangements to talk to a doctor about our situation as soon as possible. Looking back, I don't know how we survived the months that followed. Things became complex and invasive in record time. Within six months Carey underwent exploratory laparoscopic surgery and several other procedures with fairly encouraging results. Our hopes were raised temporarily. I went to a urologist to undergo my part of the work-up. I had test after test. Discouragement crept back into our hearts as I was told I should undergo surgery to correct a mild problem. We were told this might increase our chances of conceiving by improving my sperm count. I underwent the surgery and ended up spending a month in painful recuperation. It was an absolutely miserable procedure, and still Carey didn't get pregnant.

We moved on to infertility specialists, who urged us to move on to the next step, which involved Carey undergoing hormone injections and intrauterine inseminations every other month for a period of fourteen months. Like gamblers, we were playing out the odds.

Our marriage began to suffer as our every day was dictated by our infertility treatment. An insidious and poisonous stress accompanied the emotional roller coaster we were on. The hormones Carey was receiving were wreaking havoc on her state of mind. I hardly knew her anymore, and in fact I didn't especially *like* her hormone-induced personality. We avoided each other like the plague except for those times dictated by our carefully orchestrated treatments.

The months dragged on endlessly. Carey continued to receive injection after injection. With distaste and embarrassment, I continued to provide the lab with specimen after specimen. After a year and a half of treatments my doctor suggested I undergo another surgery. He didn't have to wait for an answer. It was the straw that broke the camel's back.

"Like hell I'll go through another surgery," I ranted. I told him he had to be out of his mind, and left his office in a rage.

I was sick and tired of waiting and wondering, sick and tired of disappointment. I was sick of my marriage being in shambles, and tired of watching Carey fall deeper and deeper into despair. I had had it with the infertility treatment. It was time to get on with life.

I thought long and hard about what the doctor had said and what Carey and I had endured. I would tell her what had happened later that night when she got home from work.

Over the months, she had frequently told me that she felt like a professional patient, like someone whose daily life and schedule were dependent upon doctors, medications, and procedures. Now, as she listened to me tell her that what the doctor had said about another surgery, she wavered back and forth between despair and fury. It was as though her emotions were hanging by a thread.

Suddenly the thread snapped. "That's it," she said. "No more." I felt a wave of relief come over me. It was as though the weight of the world was lifted from our shoulders. "We're taking back control," she said with conviction. We hugged each other long and hard and with real love in our hearts for the first time in over a year. Eighteen months and forty thousand dollars after we began, we threw in the towel on infertility treatments.

CHAPTER

2

Dinner that night was relaxed and leisurely for the first time in over a year, despite our emotional exhaustion. Our relief at giving up the fight was overwhelming. We were glad to have each other as dinner companions. Believing we were leaving the physical and emotional anguish behind us, we were able to talk again without resentment or irritation.

Later that night, as we got ready for bed, Carey turned to me and hugged me. "I feel like our stopping the treatments puts the ball back in our court. It means we're in charge of our lives again," she said.

"I know what you mean," I told her as I pulled back the bedspread. "It felt really good to 'just say no' today when he suggested another procedure. It was really liberating."

Carey sat down on her side of the bed. "But I guess it also means we have to face the fact that we might never be parents," she said quietly. "I think maybe I've finally come to the point where I can accept not having children." She paused and then went on. "After everything we've been through, I know our marriage is strong, and you're the most important person in the world to me. We could be happy by ourselves, without children."

She paused again. I waited patiently, not saying anything. I knew there was something more she needed to say. "But before I completely resign myself to that finality—to knowing I'll never be a mother—I'd like for us to consider adoption." She took a deep breath. "I guess what I'm saying is, let's close the door on the infertility treatments, but let's not completely close the door on the possibility of having a child. Let's keep it open, even if it's just a crack."

My love for Carey could sustain me through this lifetime all by itself. I felt that I didn't *need* to dilute this love by being a father. I had visions of Carey and me growing old together, glued in devotion to each other's side. I practically had our his-and-her rocking chairs picked out.

Adoption was an idea that had been lurking somewhere in the far, shadowy corners of my mind, but I had never truly given it much close thought. As always, Carey was several giant steps ahead of me. She had a plan. Without hesitation I agreed with her that we should try adoption.

I walked around the bed and sat down next to her. I held her tightly and stroked her hair. I breathed in the sweet smell that always surrounds Carey. She is everything to me. Her wish, as the genie says, is my command. Still, adoption was something that was a mystery to me. I had no idea, really, of what adoption entailed. As I sat with my arms around Carey, I had visions of strolling through a cheery baby nursery and pointing to the little bundle I wanted to bring home with me. It sounded easy enough, but it wasn't the way my male ego had envisioned arriving at parenthood. Nonetheless if Carey wanted it, I was behind her all the way.

"All right," I told her, "let's pursue adoption." She hugged me tighter. "I'll get on it tomorrow," I promised. Carey laughed softly. "What?" I asked her.

"When you make up your mind," she teased, "you don't waste any time."

So, with a hug and a promise, we agreed to pursue adoption. We also reestablished, without specifically saying so, our commitment to our marriage. Everything felt good and hopeful and controlled again. This was the way I liked things. I looked forward to the next day instead of dreading the anxiety to which we had become accustomed. In one short evening we managed to crawl out of the emotional pit we had dug ourselves into.

I tackled the next day as if I were connected to an adrenaline pump. It was my day off and I was up and in the shower as the sun began to tint the outside with its subtle light. I put on a huge pot of coffee, dug a fresh pad of paper and a ballpoint pen out of my desk, and sat down at the kitchen table with the Yellow Pages in front of me. I looked under "Adoption Services," "Counseling Services," and every other possible subject heading I could think of. As the coffee brewed, I scribbled notes and turned pages frantically. Finally, in frustration I tore the pages from the phone book and laid them out in front of me.

When I heard Carey coming down the stairs, I put everything aside and poured her a mug of coffee. As she sat down, she ran her hands through my hair and said, "Thank you."

"For what?" I asked.

"For everything," she said. "Just *everything*." She already knew that I wasn't going to lose at this. We were going to adopt a child.

As soon as Carey left for work, I began making phone calls. I asked question after question, and took notes while I talked. By lunchtime I had made considerable headway in finding and requesting information about adoption.

Within a week we were inundated with adoption application

packets arriving in the mail. I tore each one open with a vengeance. The paperwork was voluminous. The questions on the applications were endless. Often they asked what "type of child" we were "seeking." It was reminiscent of a shopping list: The options covered everything from race, religion, physical status, and emotional status, to age, siblings who came as a "set," and on and on and on.

I now know that a better tactic for matching adoptive parents with children would be to place any parentless child in the waiting arms of prospective parents and let the decision be made then and there. All the checklists in the world would lose their meaning as human bonding took place. It's easy to check off boxes on a form. It's impossible to say no to a small bundle who has no prejudices and one single, all-encompassing need: to be loved.

Carey's desire to pursue adoption became my pet project. Every morning before leaving for the afternoon shift I would sit down and tackle my to-do list. I would phone Carey at work every day and give her updates on whom I had called and what had transpired. My determination in getting an adoption launched resulted in us receiving reams of paperwork from every imaginable source, from religious organizations to private agencies to attorneys.

Carey and I were shocked as we read some of the information. In some cases there were elements of profiteering and prejudice. The costs involved ran the gamut all the way up to the twenty-five thousand dollars quoted by an agency that guaranteed us a child within three months. Several religious adoption agencies I spoke to told me that we were of the wrong faith, but that they could help us adopt a "special-needs" child.

Even then, in my state of relative naïveté, I could see the injustices that were part of the "adoption game" played by some of these agencies and individuals. In pursuing adoption Carey and I had one simple wish: to be parents. That wish was without exception. We looked at it the way we looked at pregnancy: There are lots of risks and no guarantees. "No matter how it happens, if we end up with a child," Carey once said to me, "then that's the child who was meant to be in our lives." And she meant it.

Carey's attitude was very open and very realistic. She gave much thought to the different circumstances we might face. She had a contingency plan for every scenario she could think of. If a special-needs child entered our lives, then Carey planned to stop working and stay at home to help that child. She scrutinized our front steps and our stairway, trying to envision how we could build a ramp or adapt them to make them wheelchair accessible. If our child needed special medical care, then Carey would find out who the leading authorities were. If the leading medical authorities were in a different city or state, we would simply move to that area. If a child came to us who for whatever reason was not accepted graciously by our neighborhood, then we would put our house on the market and find a different neighborhood.

Her clarity of purpose amazed me and inspired me. Together we agreed to assume the responsibility of any child who entered our life, regardless of his or her racial, ethnic, physical, emotional, or mental status.

As the days passed, I spent virtually all my free time furthering my research and filling out applications. There was one agency, located in Ohio, that seemed especially appealing and promising to Carey and me for several reasons. It was fairly close to us, so we didn't have to anticipate any out-of-state travel. The application itself stood apart from the rest. It was nicely printed, on quality paper; it didn't have the look of a mass mailing—no photocopies of photocopies stapled carelessly together. The questions posed to us as prospective adoptive parents probed into the nuances of our personalities and personal values instead of into our bank accounts and lines of credit. The philosophy of the agency felt right to us. We thought we had found "our" agency.

It was with high hopes and great confidence that we sent in our application along with the required seventy-five-dollar application fee. We waited anxiously to hear back from them. We believed ourselves to be strong candidates for an adoption, and expected they would contact us without much delay. I felt sure that when they did, it would be the clincher, a firm assurance that they could and would provide us with a child.

Retrieving and sorting through the mail became an obsession for me. It got to the point where I could eyeball the pile of mail as I picked it up and instantly single out the pieces that were part of our quest. Each time I received an envelope from an adoption organization, it was like receiving a letter from home while stationed overseas. I opened every envelope with a jittery sense of hope and excitement. Each envelope held the potential for being the first tangible step toward finding our child and fulfilling Carey's fondest dream.

I returned home from work one day to a particularly large pile of mail. I scooped it up from the floor of the foyer where it landed after falling through the slot in the front door. I flipped through the stack in my hand and saw the return address of the agency we had been waiting to hear from. I walked to the kitchen and tore open the white envelope.

After reading the first paragraph, my ears and neck began to burn. I read it over again, and once again. I couldn't believe what it said. It was a form letter stating that for unspecified reasons we were rejected as candidates. *Rejected.* The word hit me like a ton of bricks. There was no explanation, no mention of returning our application fee, and furthermore the letter stated that the agency would not accept any telephone calls concerning the rejection.

I was livid. All my angers and frustrations of the past year and a half were brought bubbling and boiling right back up to the surface in less than a minute. I thought about Carey. She was going to be devastated. My mind and heart raced as I clutched the one-page letter of dismissal. The whole thing was an insult, a slap in the face. It was a rude setback I didn't want us to have to contend with. They had *rejected* the wrong people, I thought angrily.

I went to the kitchen phone and called the agency. I insisted on speaking immediately to the director. When she got on the phone, I told her my name. She clearly had no idea of who I was or why I was calling. When I explained what had happened, she merely recited the agency's policy of not discussing rejections with applicants. Her tone was cold and callous. As my anger escalated, she maintained her stony reticence. Finally I reminded her that I was a police officer and that her refusal to talk to me clearly constituted theft by deception on the part of the agency. I could feel the angry, defiant me of yesteryear stepping up to bat. The conversation ended with me threatening to call my attorney, and her responding with an arrogant "You do what you have to do, Mr. Howells."

Carey called me from work later that day. I didn't tell her about the letter or the phone call. I knew it would be difficult for her, and it seemed better to wait to tell her in person. I am a strong-willed man, and very few things intimidate or unnerve me. But when Carey's happiness is involved, it's a different story. I have never been able to maintain my inner composure when her happiness is at stake. I can hold myself together on the outside, but inside I turn to jelly. This rejection was going to hurt her, and I was going to be the messenger. It was not something I wanted to do.

When she got home, we sat down in the living room and I showed her the letter. I told her about my phone conversation with the agency's director. As I had anticipated, she was devastated. But I had never imagined what the extent of her devastation would be. It was like watching someone flick a switch. Her face lost its soft, gentle expression and went almost blank. Her contagious energy seemed to fade right before my eyes. I don't think she even cried. She just sort of shut down. My Carey was suddenly lost and totally defeated.

I watched as Carey slowly stood up, almost as if she were in a trance. She went to the basement door and walked down the stairs. I heard the sound of the ironing board as she took it from the closet and set it up. When I checked on her a little while later, she was ironing methodically and meticulously, an empty look frozen on her face. I knew she was searching for a way to keep going.

Our neighbor was our attorney. Early the next morning I got up, showered, dressed, and stormed out the door and across the road to her house. I wanted to catch her before she left for work. I knocked on the door and she answered, still in her bathrobe, mug of coffee in hand. She let me in and, my emotions running high, I told her what had transpired. I paced around her kitchen like a bull in a pen. She told me to calm down and take a few deep breaths. She said she would fire off several letters, including one to the office of the state attorney general, with a copy to the agency informing them that we would be contacting several government agencies regarding this incident. She grabbed a legal pad, a red pen, and together we wrote the main drafts of the letters.

Three days later a Federal Express package arrived with a refund check from the agency. It was small consolation for the travesty that had occurred. Seventy-five dollars back in our pocket was a long, hard way from bringing Carey back to the optimistic, joyful person she had been. We had miles to go.

CHAPTER

3

Weeks and then months went by. I still followed any promising adoption leads that came my way, but it was no longer a full-tilt project for me. Carey and I took things as they came instead of aggressively trying to make things happen. It was hard for me to admit, but my determination had suffered a slight setback when the Ohio agency rejected us. For me it was a case of "once bitten, twice shy."

For Carey it went deeper than that. She functioned in her various roles, but with a hollowness that could come only from a deep and debilitating loss. Not only had she faced the loss that came from our inability to conceive a child, but she faced another loss, a loss of hope, when the agency rejected us. She withdrew herself from my sporadic efforts to find another way to adopt a child, and sank into a deep depression. I felt helpless and confused by her anguish, and very worried about how or when she was going to come out of it. She never spoke of it, but it was clear to me that she was suffering.

The emptiness Carey felt became so painful that she began avoiding friends who had small children. Our neighborhood, which we had once cherished, became too much for her to bear— the hordes of children served as a reminder of what we were missing. We began seriously looking for another home, something out in the country with enough acreage to ensure that we wouldn't have to look out our window and gaze upon someone else's children. Each weekend we went with our realtor to see what was on the market. Our life felt unsettled and uncertain.

The fall of 1990 brought added sadness for Carey. Her father, to whom she had been very close, died in September. She was really struggling through all the loss that life was heaping on her.

One bitterly cold evening in the fall of 1990, Carey and I sat together in the living room. We had a fire in the fireplace, and Sam was stretched out on the rug in front of it. I was on the floor next to Sam, feeling peaceful. Carey sat on the couch, with a stack of paperwork at her side. I looked over at her and winked. She instantly fell apart. She covered her face with her hands and leaned forward so that she was almost doubled over. It scared the hell out of me. I moved to her side instantly and begged her to tell me what was wrong. It was difficult for her to catch her breath to talk. Her voice came out in deep, long sobs.

"I'm never going to be a mother," she cried, "and that's all I've ever wanted to be."

My heart broke. The loss she was feeling was tremendous, indeed it was probably incomprehensible to me. I knew I had to stay calm, or she was going to fall deeper into this frightening depression she had been battling. I took her hands and held them in mine. I looked directly into her eyes and held her gaze.

"I promise you," I told her solemnly and with the utmost sincerity, "I *promise* you that you will be a mother."

To my amazement she stopped crying. Her depression seemed to lift spontaneously. "Okay," she said. "Thank you." And that was all.

I was no longer just someone hoping to adopt a child. Carey depended on me to keep my word. From that moment on I was a man with a mission like no other. Wild horses couldn't hold me back. If I died in the effort, I was going to see to it that Carey had the baby she so desperately wanted. Carey was never going to face misery of this magnitude again. I was going to make it all better for her. And she believed in me enough to know that if I said it, it was going to happen. She became the happy Carey I knew and loved once again.

But I had to admit, I was running out of options and ideas. I spent the final months of that fall and the early months of 1991 trying to rally some more possibilities. Nothing materialized, or even held promise of materializing. By February I felt as though I had exhausted all the obvious options. My promise to Carey was still the driving force behind my efforts. As I followed the maze of adoption leads, it was without giving thought to fatherhood. My focus was on achieving motherhood for Carey.

In complete frustration one afternoon I phoned Bishop Anthony Pilla of the Cleveland Catholic Diocese. Although I was Episcopal, which is part of the Anglican Church, I thought he wouldn't mind hearing from me.

I sat at the dining-room table with the portable phone in my hand and a cup of coffee and my pad of notes in front of me. I punched the main number for the Catholic diocese. The bishop's executive assistant took my phone call immediately. I spent about an hour telling him of our experiences and our disappointments. I told him how frustrated we had become and asked him if he could help us or give us any advice. I told him that we were Episcopalians and asked him if that mattered. I wasn't prepared for the deep compassion and help I received. Little did I know that this was the phone call that was going to set the wheels in motion. This call turned out to be the first step in bringing us together with our son.

"A child doesn't care about denomination," he replied. "A child cares about love and having a family." With that he offered to make some inquiries on our behalf. Within the hour he called me back with a recommendation. He advised me to call Lake County Catholic Service Bureau and speak with the head social worker there, Beth Brindo. He told me she was expecting my call.

I hung up with him and phoned her right away. Despite the gentle response I had received from Bishop Pilla's assistant, I was still struggling with a defensive attitude. I'm afraid my tone conveyed my attitude. "Is there an application fee?" I asked Beth. She managed to cool me off, saying that the agency accepted no money until the prospective parents were starting the home-study process. Due to my frame of mind at the time, and to my past experiences as a police officer, I was still wary of Beth's motives. I was looking for the bait and switch.

I was mistaken. I had been introduced to the finest, most caring group of professionals I had ever met. This was an organization who saw their first priority as the preservation of family. Their second priority was upholding the belief that adoption is a lifelong process. She told me she would send us the necessary applications and paperwork right away.

I had a fire in the fireplace and dinner on the table for Carey when she arrived home from work that day. As we ate the spaghetti dinner I had prepared, I told her all about my talk with the bishop's assistant and with Beth. My excitement was contagious. Carey listened closely to every word I said, and then made me repeat my phone conversations all over again.

We were excited that our introduction to the agency had been through the church instead of through a blind phone call. The fact that our phone call was taken right away by the director, and treated with sincere courtesy and patience, was a far cry from our past experiences with adoption agencies. I told Carey that I felt really good about this connection. Carey, too, could sense that maybe, just maybe, this time it was going to be different. Maybe we had finally gotten a foothold in this long, hard climb to parenthood.

After talking with Beth we realized that an adoption was something we were going to have to wait patiently for. Five years was what the agency suggested we expect to be our waiting period. By now Carey was thirty and I was thirty-three. We had been married for nine years. Our friends had already started families. We were definitely standing out among our crowd as late bloomers. When we added five years to the picture, we realized we'd really be trailing the general trend.

Five years. It sounded light-years away, but when Beth said it, it sounded promising. Beth herself was so accessible and she sounded so knowledgeable and so on top of things that we thought if anyone was dealing us a fair hand, a hand that held some promise, it was she. Yes, five years sounded like a long time, but somehow the bigger picture was beginning to feel right. I asked Carey if she felt discouraged by the possibility of having to wait five years to adopt. "I've waited this long, I can wait some more," she told me without hesitation. "If it's meant to happen that way, then so be it," she added. She was much better than I was at being patient, and much better at accepting that fate or God would see us through.

We decided to play those five years for all they were worth. We were going to celebrate our marriage, indulge ourselves, and pamper ourselves silly after all we had been through.

Over the next several months Carey and I fell in love again. We were able to relax and enjoy our time together. We went out to dinner on the slightest whim, took in movies when the mood hit us, and made plans with friends. Instead of following an all-consuming infertility treatment protocol or searching endlessly for new adoption leads, we came to terms with the fact that it was okay to just do *nothing* if that was what we felt like.

We decided to plan some vacations. I phoned our travel agent and asked her to make some suggestions about trips we could take. We arranged a trip to Florida and a Caribbean cruise. We were excited about our plans and reveled in at last having something really special to look forward to. Time slipped by happily and with no sense of pressure. Nonetheless I made a point of phoning Beth Brindo at the agency every other week or so. I didn't want her to forget about us, and I wanted to make sure that the wheels kept turning. She was always kind and open, and told me to call her anytime.

Early in the summer of 1991 we took a summer trip to Richmond, Virginia, to see my mother. The long drive down was leisurely. Sam sat in the backseat and listened in on our road-trip babble. We talked about everything but fertility and babies. We had a wonderful trip together. Carey had regained her natural radiance. She was once again my friend, my wife, my lover. I took her out for a romantic dinner at an upscale Italian restaurant. She no longer had to worry about the infertility drugs or the wait-and-wonder limbo of hoping the treatment had succeeded. She was free to have a glass of red wine, which she sipped slowly and contentedly.

We were open with our friends and families about our hope to adopt a child. Our families were supportive of our decision, although in retrospect I don't think they truly understood the magnitude or ramifications of what we were proposing to do. Nonetheless I'm sure that they could sense the change in our attitudes and could see that we were much more at peace with ourselves. We were undoubtedly much easier to be around. Parenthood was no longer a taboo topic. Other people's children and pregnancies no longer sent us running in the other direction.

One night while we were at my mother's, my brother and his wife joined us for dinner. My sister-in-law was quite pregnant with their first child. Carey was very accepting and very at ease with it all. As we sat at my mother's dining-room table eating a casual dinner, Carey asked with genuine interest if they had thought of names for the child. My sister-in-law, a dyed-in-the-wool southerner, jokingly told Carey that if the baby were a girl, they were going to name her Scarlett. Carey immediately appreciated her humor. I, on the other hand, didn't realize it was a joke.

"What?" I asked. "Are you crazy? You're going to name her Scarlett if it's a girl?"

"Oh yes, Dion," Carey said with a poker face. "It's such a beautiful, traditional southern name. I think it would be perfect. What's the matter, don't you like it?"

They really got me going. After a few minutes Carey told me, with feigned sympathy for my gullibility, that they were only kidding around. I joined in the laughter. It was such a relief to see that Carey and I could finally be relaxed and free of our envy over someone else's impending parenthood.

CHAPTER

4

The summer of 1991 unfolded. Cleveland continued its descent into its familiar hot, humid, sticky doldrums. We filled our pool, bought some new inflatable rafts, and became serious poolside groupies when we weren't at our jobs. We spent much of our free time stretched out on the rafts or on lounge chairs, tall glasses of iced tea in hand, or swimming in the cool, refreshing water. Friends dropped by to visit and swim almost every day. Our barbecue grill seemed to be in constant use, and the smell of grilling meat was part of the vacationlike ambience of our backyard. The summer had a sort of relaxed rhythm to it.

In late June I put in a call to Beth at Lake County Catholic Service Bureau. "What a coincidence!" Beth said when she got on the phone to take my call. "I was just thinking and talking about you. I was going to call you to see if you and your wife could stop in for an informal chat."

It was reassuring to hear that we had been on their minds. It had been four months since I initially contacted them, and I was glad to hear that we were more than just another set of names to them. I told Beth that we would love to come by to chat, and we chose a date and time a couple of weeks away. Carey and I were excited at the prospect of the proposed meeting. It felt like a step, albeit a very small one, in the right direction. As we understood it, it was to be a put-a-face-to-the-name kind of meeting.

Our meeting occurred on a simmering afternoon in July. We found our way to the agency's offices, arriving somewhat wilted but well before our designated time. The agency was in a modern office building, with windows that offered a bird's-eye view of the old-fashioned town square below. We were relieved to discover that the office was air-conditioned. Beth Brindo greeted us in the agency waiting room. She introduced herself to us and then asked us to follow her to her office.

We were quickly joined by another woman, whom Beth introduced to us as Nan Lahr. She didn't make it clear to us exactly who Nan was. She looked very young, and seemed to be there to observe rather than to participate. We thought she was a student. In fact she was a social worker, who was there to help Beth assess us as prospective adoptive parents. She would go on to play a major role in bringing us together with our son.

We had wondered how the meeting would transpire, but we definitely had not anticipated the endless stream of general questions about ourselves, our professions, and our home life. We had believed it would be a preliminary information meeting, a pass/fail kind of litmus test—nothing as in-depth as what it turned out to be. Beth's questions were very probing, and yet they were surprisingly diplomatic and "neutral" in nature and subject matter.

Much later and farther down the road, when we knew each other well, Beth and Nan told us that they had been a little skeptical about me at first, having heard how strongly and aggressively

I had reacted to the treatment we received from the other adoption agency. They had privately agreed between themselves that if they felt they couldn't help us, they would have to let us know up front and tactfully lest I let loose on them as I had on the other agency.

We answered all their questions with the open, innocent honesty of children. As naive as we still were about adoption, we had no idea where things were headed. Then came a question that really threw us for a loop. Beth asked us to talk to her about our feelings on open adoption. "I'd like to find out where you stand on this," she said, looking first at Carey and then at me. "I'd like to know whether you'd consider knowing the birth parents of your child. Think about it carefully and let's discuss your ideas."

For the first time in the meeting Carey and I physically turned to each other as if searching for our real feelings. We had never even heard the term *open adoption,* and so we were unclear about what she was really asking us. At the same time I think we both felt a surge of adrenaline and incredible excitement when we heard Beth say the words *your child.* It was as if her question held some promise for us merely by unhesitatingly stating these words. They were words we had never really heard, and by now were afraid to say to each other. As we hesitated in giving her a response, she clarified what she meant.

"What I'm talking about is *not* coparenting," she assured us. "I'm talking about the possibility of having limited to full knowledge of your child's birth parents." She looked at us closely and could see that we were still confused. "It can mean anything from meeting the birth parents of your child one time, to exchanging occasional pictures and letters, to setting up a yearly meeting. It means that the adoption is not *closed.*"

I could see that Carey was still not entirely comfortable or clear on the whole concept. "Well," Carey said with hesitation, "I can tell you that I'm not real hot about some woman coming in to tour my house and check my corners for cobwebs."

Beth smiled with patience and tried to explain some more to us.

"It doesn't mean that the birth mother has unlimited and discretionary access to you, your child, your house, or anything about your lives at all. Open adoption is only as open as you and the birth mother choose to make it."

As the conversation continued, we began to sort out our answer to this bombshell question. After several minutes we found our way to our answer. Strangely enough, a key to the answer lay with our dog, Sam. Carey explained to Beth, "When we adopted our dog, Sam, we found him by answering an ad in the paper that offered puppies from a litter for thirty-five dollars. When we got to the house, the woman grilled us for an hour about our house, what we knew about taking care of dogs, and how we'd be raising and caring for this puppy. Finally she seemed satisfied and told us to go ahead and pick the puppy we wanted. When we went to pay her, she refused the money. She told us she had advertised the puppies for a price simply to weed out anyone who wasn't serious about undertaking the care of a dog. The only thing she asked for was our name and phone number so that she could call to check in and see how he was doing in a month or two."

Beth listened with obvious interest to what Carey was saying. Carey continued. "It didn't strike me as strange at all that this woman was so concerned with the long-term welfare of the puppy she was giving away. I totally understood that she just needed to know he was going to a good family and that he would be well cared for and have a nice life. She couldn't just blindly hand him over to someone. It makes complete sense to me that a mother giving up a child would want no less than what that woman wanted. In fact I can't see how a birth mother could possibly do it any other way."

Beth and Nan had exchanged short glances throughout the meeting. Now they seemed to almost nod at one another. Beth told us they would like to invite us to join their group home-study program, which was starting the following week. (A home study is a state-dictated process that is necessary for any prospective adoptive parents to undergo.) We told her absolutely, we could and would join the program whenever she wanted us to. It was with soaring hopes and enthusiasm that we approached any kind of concrete steps toward adoption. Since this was a mandatory step, we figured we were lucky to be able to get it done and out of the way. She told us that the group would meet there next Thursday, from seven-thirty to nine-thirty P.M., and we told her she would see us then.

The warm summer air blew in the open windows of our car as we drove down the highway toward home. As we cruised down the highway, we reviewed our meeting with Beth and Nan. In excitement we recalled and dissected fragments of the conversation, giving each other our impressions of what had been said and how we had responded. Question after question from the meeting popped back into our minds, and we worked our way backward and forward through each ensuing dialogue. Carey, who was keenly observant of people, offered up commentary on Beth's and Nan's facial expressions and "body language" in relation to our conversation. We hoped we had left them with a good impression. We agreed that we had done our best, and had answered as honestly as possible.

"Did you see all the pictures of the kids and families on the bulletin board?" Carey asked me. I told her that I had noticed them. "I kept looking at them," she said, "all those babies and kids. There were so many of them! While I sat there, I kept thinking . . ." She paused.

"What?" I prodded her.

"I kept thinking that if this works, if it really happens, then our child's picture will be up there. That's all. I guess it gave me a vicarious thrill to see all those pictures of success." I hadn't thought of it that way. I had merely been impressed by the fact that there were so *many* pictures up on the bulletin board, that so many people had been there before us.

"The invitation to join the home-study group is a good sign, don't you think?" I asked Carey as I pulled the car into our driveway.

"Oh, yeah, *definitely* a good sign," she answered. There was a pause. "Wait a minute," she said.

"What?" I asked.

"I just realized something," she said as she opened the car door. She had a look of complete amazement on her face. "Being asked to join the home-study group means we're actually *starting* our home study. Beth said they only accept a certain number of people into their program, because those people are hand-selected as strong candidates for becoming adoptive parents."

I looked blankly at her. "It *means*," she said with a squeal, "that we're starting the process of adoption! It means that we're on our way to becoming parents!"

I thought for a moment and realized that what she said made sense. The agency did indeed accept only a given number of applicants at a time, and only a given number matriculated into the rigorous home-study program at a given time. As a general rule a home study could be requested by *anyone* considering adoption. But in and of itself a home study was in no way an indicator of the likelihood that an adoption would occur. It was merely an unavoidable prerequisite for anyone applying to adopt. But in our case, because of the way the agency orchestrated its group home-study process, rather than the state, it was in fact similar to passing "Go" on the Monopoly board.

CHAPTER

5

The night of our first home-study meeting was upon us. It was a hot, steamy August evening. We both made a point of getting home from work on the early side, and we began our preparation for attending the meeting.

We picked outfits that we thought would fit the "just-so image" we thought we should project. I put on sport slacks, loafers, and a freshly pressed shirt. Carey chose a simple summer dress. Today we laugh about it: at that point we approached every detail of our adoption quest with weighty consideration, and our personal presentation was no exception. We agonized over every item of clothing we would be seen in, how our hair should be combed, what kind of aftershave or perfume to wear.

The home-study meeting started at seven o'clock. We left the house at five-thirty, leaving a giant margin for error in our travels. Nothing was going to get in our way. We took some back roads and then a short stint of highway so that we could avoid rush-hour traffic. We made good time. By six-fifteen we were a block away from the agency. Carey spotted a Taco Bell, and with forty-five minutes to kill we decided to grab some dinner. Prior to that night I had never seen Carey unable to do justice to a heaping plate of Taco Bell delicacies. Our stomachs were in knots, though, and we both picked at our food. Our nerves silenced us and there was very little dinner conversation. Nonetheless dinner at Taco Bell became a home-study-meeting-night ritual.

The meeting was held in the conference room of the agency. We were the third set of people to arrive. There was a semicircle of chairs set up. We sat down and waited nervously for Beth and Nan to get things started. We watched with focused interest as six other couples came into the room and sat down. While there were obvious differences among us, we knew there was a critical common thread: We were all there for the same reason—to become parents by adopting a child.

It was difficult not to view the other couples as "competition." After all, we were all there in the hope of being chosen by a birth mother to adopt her child. It wasn't something that was merely luck of the draw. Each adoption would occur only after a birth mother made her informed decision about which, if any, of the waiting couples she wanted to relinquish her child to. One couple's gain might very well feel like another couple's loss. Everyone had the same look of uncertainty, nervousness, and anticipation.

Beth Brindo introduced herself and Nan Lahr to the group and then asked each couple to introduce themselves and talk about their infertility or reasons for seeking adoptions. When it came our turn, I introduced Carey and myself and thanked the social workers for including us. Together Carey and I told the group of our years of medical intervention and failure to conceive a child. We expressed our feelings of emptiness and frustration. As each couple introduced themselves, it became obvious that we had all been through a similar battle.

Beth pointed out the recurring theme of emptiness and loss and told us that our own sense of loss would serve to help us understand the emotions involved on all sides when an adoption takes place. She told us to stay in touch with that feeling, as it would teach us a great deal in the process we were undertaking.

She then explained to us our objectives. "You should know," she told us solemnly, "that many people are envious of you and would give a great deal to be included in this group. Not only are you embarking on your home-study process, but you have been hand-picked to participate in our first open adoption home-study program." She paused and looked around the table at each couple. "This doesn't necessarily mean that you will get an open adoption, but it means that you are being trained for that possibility."

Carey and I looked at each other. Our initial meeting with Beth and Nan now made complete sense to us. We had indeed been in a screening process, and we had "made the grade." Despite our conversations with Beth and Nan about open adoption, we hadn't understood what the agency was undertaking. When we listened to Beth now, we were overcome with pride and tremendous excitement. This was a groundbreaking program, and we were privileged to be part of it.

Beth continued to talk to us. She reminded us that the agency's creed was preservation of family. Their top priority was to give birth mothers the resources to keep and raise their children. They viewed adoption as the last resort in the preservation of family: By creating a new family through adoption, a family unit could be maintained in the face of a very painful set of circumstances. Hearing her say this tempered our elation. We had a fleeting insight into the sometimes conflicting emotions that lay ahead.

We hung on every word that Beth and Nan spoke. Everyone else in the room was doing the same. As the meeting drew to a close, Beth and Nan passed out form after form that we would have to fill in as the home-study process continued. The forms ranged from questionnaires about our backgrounds, beliefs, and expectations to requests for personal-credit and bank-account reports. The paperwork was voluminous and we knew that completing it was going to be a project in itself.

As we were driving home from the meeting, I noticed that Carey was kind of quiet. "Is something bothering you?" I asked her.

"Not at all," she answered lightly.

"Then why are you so quiet?"

"I'm just mulling over everything they said to us. And I'm making mental lists of things I need to get done quickly."

"Like what?" I asked her, wondering what was so pressing.

"Dion, I can't believe you! Think of everything that has to be done! I need to research pediatricians, buy an infant car seat, think about getting the baby's room ready, where to buy a crib. We really need to do some planning or we could get caught totally off guard and unprepared."

The tide had turned. Now that we were part of the program at the agency, we didn't have to avoid thinking about becoming parents, we had to start focusing on it. Carey's doubts were gone at last. For her it was no longer a question of if we would become parents. It was now just a question of how soon.

Over the course of the eight-week home-study program, we were introduced to issue after issue regarding adoption. There were adoptive parents who had been contacted by a biological mother after years of a closed adoption. There were adoptees; some had searched for and found their birth parents, others were lost in a confusing and devastating maze of mystery. Many birth mothers were brought in to speak to us. Some were searching for their children, others had found their children. All had one thing in common: They ached from the loss they had suffered.

I can still remember the first time the group was introduced to two birth mothers. They were both in their early twenties and each had given up a child for adoption. These were the first birth

mothers Carey and I had ever met. The same probably held true
for most of us in the group. Their presence was like having cold
water thrown in our wide-eyed faces. Outwardly, at first glance,
they looked like any other young women. After they began speaking to us, however, their pain became clearer and clearer to us
until we could no longer look at them without seeing in their
young faces a pain that could come only from the worst kind of
human suffering—the loss of a child.

These young women talked open with us about what they had
been through. More important they talked about what they were
still going through. As they sat at the table with us, just a few feet
away, they were strikingly real to us. They removed the enigmatic
mental picture of a birth mother that had been painting itself in
our minds.

Their children were still very much a part of them. They told
us about an overwhelming sense of loss and emptiness that was
unshakable. "Sometimes a few hours will pass and something dis-
tracts me," one of the women told us. "But even if my thoughts
turn off, it's only temporary, and the hollowness is still there underneath everything." She stopped and took a deep breath. "It's
always with me," she said slowly and sadly. "The hollowness is
always, always with me." *Hollowness.* It was a word that would
come back over and over again as our story unfolded.

As part of our home-study requirements, we had to attend group
meetings of a local organization called the Cleveland Adoption
Network. This group is dedicated to helping participants of adoption. They work tirelessly and selflessly to help anyone involved
in adoption with search and relinquishment issues. They lobby to
change laws relating to adoption and they conduct searches to
help individuals trying to locate their biological family members.
The Adoption Network is a source of great hope and help to

anyone who walks through their door or picks up the phone to call them.

The meetings were held at a nearby community library, upstairs in one of the large meeting rooms. Attendance was phenomenal. There were usually about seventy-five people gathered. The attendees were always seated in a large circle of chairs so that each person could see everyone else's face. Personally I have never felt so much intense human pain as I felt when attending these meetings. Each person at these meetings had stories of personal anguish, from mothers who had given up their children, to adoptees struggling to establish their heritage and identity, to adoptive parents who lived in fear of birth parents trying to establish a relationship with their children or interfering with their family.

We attended the meeting naively. We were totally unprepared for the intensity of the issues and the individuals. Since the meetings were a mandatory part of our home-study process, we thought we'd be able to attend, have our slip of paper signed, and get home in time to have a bowl of ice cream and watch the evening news.

At our first meeting we sat with some other couples from our home-study group as if there was strength in our numbers. Looking around the circle, we saw all kinds of people, from young children to gray-haired grandparents. As I looked closer at the people seated in the circle, I recognized the face of one man. He was about my age, with red hair and the look of a dyed-in-the-wool Irishman. After a moment or two I realized that he worked at the car wash where I had my squad car cleaned once a week. His presence at the meeting was a complete surprise. I wondered if he had seen me and whether he recognized me out of uniform.

The format of the meeting was "open mike." Anyone could talk for as long as they wanted about whatever they wanted. My friend from the car wash turned out to be an active participant. He introduced himself as Steven, and launched into a long monologue about why he was there. I was transfixed. His story was fascinating, and deeply sad. He told the group he had been adopted thirty-five years ago. A redheaded Irishman by heritage, he had been adopted into a devout Jewish family. He had struggled his whole life with a sense of displacement, of not belonging, which had crippled him emotionally. The details of his biological heritage were unknown to him, and it was a mystery that haunted him constantly. His adoption experience had overwhelmed his ability to carry on a fruitful, functional life. To this day I keep him in my prayers.

As the meeting broke up, Steven came over and we shook hands. We chatted for a few minutes and quickly came to realize that not only did we know each other from the car wash, we had known each other as children. His grandmother (through adoption) was an immigrant from Russia and had lived upstairs from my family's apartment. She used to baby-sit me and had taught me some Yiddish.

The coincidence amazed us both, but it probably affected me much more profoundly than it did him. It had never occurred to me that someone I knew—whether intimately or in passing—might not only be adopted but might very well be harboring the deep emotional scars that can result from being part of an adoption triad. His presence at the meeting taught me that "adoption" or being adopted is not necessarily glaringly apparent from the outside, but can be overwhelming from the inside.

Our first Adoption Network meeting felt to Carey and me like some kind of debriefing. We emerged changed people, almost shell-shocked by the emotions with which we had been confronted. As soon as Carey and I walked out the door, we turned to each other. "I don't know, Dion," Carey said to me. "This meeting really frightened me. If adoption creates this much emotional pain, I'm not sure I want to pursue it." I told her I felt the same way.

As we drove the short way home, we talked in more detail about our impressions from the meeting. "I don't want to raise a child who has to deal with those horribly painful issues, the way Steven does," Carey told me. "I can't subject a child to that kind of deception and secrecy," she said with conviction. "And those birth mothers who have no contact with their child are suffering terribly too. They must feel as if their heart has been torn out of them. There's so much pain involved, on every side. It's so sad." I told her I agreed with her wholeheartedly. "I know I want a child," she said. "But I also know I don't want it at that kind of emotional cost for anyone. If we adopt, it has to be in a way that promotes the emotional well-being of everyone involved."

Again, I told her she had my full agreement. "I don't know what that way is exactly, but I do know it can't be a closed adoption," Carey said. "In my heart I know I couldn't do that. I would have to turn down a closed adoption. Do you agree with me?"

"I agree."

"Good," she said, sounding much relieved. "I know that an open adoption isn't a cure-all, but it's the best way I can think of to try to avoid all that pain." I reached over and took her hand. As always she had a plan. We made an out-loud, mutual commitment to each other: We were going to do an adoption our way or we weren't going to do it at all.

CHAPTER

6

The weeks clicked by, and we pushed past the halfway mark of our home-study program. It was late September, and this year we were having some good runs of Indian summer. From time to time, in the early morning or the late evening, there was a fall crispness in the air. It didn't seem possible that another season was coming to an end. I knew Carey would be thinking about the holidays soon. She had always thrown herself into the holidays, but the past couple of years I had watched her spirit fizzle as our disappointment grew. I wondered if the holidays would be easier for us this year, now that we had come this far in our work with Lake County Catholic Service Bureau.

Before Carey and I had been accepted into the home-study program, we had made plans to go on a Caribbean cruise. It had been another one of our attempts to embrace life as a childless couple, to prove that life was still worth living, that there was still fun to be had. We were going to sail in the lap of luxury, eat like royalty, shop like crazy people, and completely indulge ourselves. Instead of moping, we had decided to spend our way to happiness.

But then came our unanticipated acceptance into the home-study group. We had undertaken the program with total commitment. We had been so excited at the honor and promise of being accepted into the group that it hadn't even dawned on us that we faced a scheduling conflict. When our travel agent phoned one day to iron out a small detail, we started to reconsider our trip.

It didn't take much discussion for us to decide that despite the nonrefundable payment we had made on the cruise, we would forgo it to complete our home-study program. We weren't about to mess things up now. In talking to Beth Brindo one day I mentioned the situation offhandedly. With her customary compassion and kindness Beth told us that after everything we had been through the past couple years, we deserved such a luxurious getaway. She told us it would be all right if we missed the one meeting that conflicted with the cruise schedule. She amazed us. We felt like the luckiest people in the world: We were going on a Caribbean cruise, and down another long path somewhere we were going to find our way to parenthood.

We thanked Beth over and over again for being so open-minded and supportive. We knew how important each home-study meeting was. But we, too, viewed this cruise as a well-deserved break from the roller-coaster ride we had been on. Moreover, having gotten almost all the way through the home-study process, we now knew the cruise might be the last getaway we would undertake as the carefree dual-income-no-kids people we were. We felt certain that parenthood was at long, long last coming to us, whether it was sooner or later.

We packed our bags and prepared to leave our routines behind. Sam went to stay across the street with his buddy, Ozzie, so he was on vacation too, enjoying himself. Sam, our jobs, and our home-study group were our only responsibilities, and we had taken care of each. We were free to go without looking back.

When the ship left port in Miami, we set sail with a personal determination. We were going to whoop it up and celebrate the astounding happenings of our lives.

We took one of Carey's friends from childhood, Kit, on the trip with us. Together the three of us were like the Three Stooges. We each got to do what we wanted to do. Carey and Kit enjoyed shopping and exploring together each time we docked. I focused on my favorite pastime: eating.

We had unbelievable fun together that week. The ambience of the ship seemed to dissolve our worries and our stresses. We purposely avoided talking about anything related to adoption. We ate delicious food, relaxed by the pool, and baked in the sun. Although we had sworn we were going to put all adoption-related thoughts to rest for the trip, Carey and I saw an opportunity we didn't dare pass up. We wanted to get deep tropical-looking tans—a healthy glow that would show off well in photographs. Then we planned to have the ship's photographer take some professional photos of us at the end of the trip to include in our autobiographical profile.

By the last day of the cruise we looked like an ad for suntan oil. We found the ship photographer and told him we needed some photos for a very special reason, but we didn't tell him why. He was kind and accommodating. Kit laughed at us and then helped us choose our outfits, some backdrops, and the final print we would use. We were pleased with the results. We selected a close-up portrait of Carey and me standing side by side. Today when Carey and I look at that picture, we laugh at how unspontaneous it is. But we always remember the sincerity with which we did it. It was all part of our heartfelt effort to find our child.

The trip home was miserable. We docked back in Miami. As we prepared to debark, a sort of melancholy came over us. It was sad to leave behind the relaxation and good times we had found on board the ship. On top of the sense of letdown I had developed a horrendous sinus infection and was suffering from severe vertigo, which made me a walking mess. As we left the ship, Carey and

Kit had to stand on either side of me and hold me to keep me from falling down. When we got to the airport, they practically carried me as we walked down the concourse and onto the plane. I sat between them. As soon as we reached cruising altitude, I dropped my seat back as far as it would go and tried to close my eyes to the pain in my head.

As we sped through the skies, misery set in. My sinuses ached relentlessly. Kit and Carey fell into a heated argument about whose fault it was that one of their books had been left behind on the ship. Back and forth they would send nagging, accusatory comments until finally I told them they had to stop or they'd be getting off the plane at our layover and not coming back on board. My head felt like it was going to explode. They quieted down and we landed safely in Cleveland. When we walked out the door to the parking garage, we were hit by cold, damp air. We threw our bags in the trunk, climbed quickly into the car, and hit the highway. We picked Sam up at the neighbor's and went home.

As soon as we got back home on Saturday, we began to think about our upcoming home-study meetings. The last meeting, when we would have to turn in our personal portfolios, including our autobiographical essays, loomed ahead of us. It was time to get to work. This autobiographical profile would be given to all birth mothers to review. Then each birth mother could choose, based on the profile, with which couple, if any, she wanted to place her baby. We had known all along that we were going to have to do this. But now the heat was on. Its creation had loomed over us dauntingly, something that was going to drain the very lifeblood out of us. We felt as if everything hinged on this one tangible thing. For the first time we could feel an undeniable sense of competition in ourselves as we tried to imagine what the other couples in our group were preparing.

Carey had to go to work on Monday, so I had the morning to

myself. I had gone to the doctor and gotten antibiotics to treat my sinus infection. I felt better and needed something on which to focus my postvacation restlessness. I had been thinking about the profile off and on for the past couple of days. We had picked out photographs of ourselves (including our on-ship portrait) and of Sam, Aggie, and Elizabeth to include in our packet. But we hadn't done anything about writing the profile itself. This morning it was heavily on my mind.

I began my usual morning routine. I put on a pot of coffee, retrieved the paper from the front walk, and let Sam outside. When I came back into the kitchen, I poured myself a mug of coffee and stood looking out the window. Usually I sat down at the kitchen table and read the sports page. Today I felt lost in my own house. It was the strangest feeling. I found myself grabbing a notepad and pen, and then I headed into the dining room and sat down at the table.

A tingly kind of rush crept over me as I picked up the ballpoint pen. It was as though I was suddenly and rapidly coming out of a fog or a deep sleep. I felt a sense of clarity and insight wrapping itself around me. I looked down at the paper and began to write.

Ten minutes later I had written two pages. They were a letter to our birth mother. I hadn't imagined the profile as a letter to our birth mother. I had imagined it as a glowing report about Carey and me and our lives together. Some unknown part of me—a part I had never tapped into before—had taken over. I flashed back to all the faces—birth mothers, adoptees, adoptive parents—we had encountered, and all the emotions they had shared. What I had written was from the heart, and as such I thought it might touch the heart of a birth mother. I knew I had written what we needed to say.

Dear Birth Mother,

As difficult as it is for us to write this profile objectively, it pales in comparison to what you must be feeling. Before we tell you about ourselves, we would like to say a few things first. We cannot pretend to say we know how you feel, for you are making an ultimate and unselfish decision. We do, however, applaud your courage and we pray sincerely not only for you and your child but for anyone faced with such a decision. The fact that you did not terminate your pregnancy says a great deal about you and your love of life. Our thoughts and prayers will be with you, not only through the adoption process but for a lifetime because we recognize that you will always be the biological mother of this child.

We have included pictures of ourselves and our pets. We have been married for almost ten years. Since we are unable to have children, in many ways our dog, Sam, and two cats, Aggie and Elizabeth, have become our kids—yes, they are spoiled!

Our home was purchased with the idea of having a family. We have lived in our current house for almost six years. It is a four-bedroom colonial in the eastern suburbs. We have a nice-size fenced-in yard with an inground pool and enough room to play volleyball. Our home is located within two blocks of the elementary, junior high, and senior high schools. We can use the playgrounds, baseball fields, track and tennis courts. We are also within walking distance of the YMCA and public library.

Together we share a very large extended family. We visit often, as well as on holidays and family reunions. We have traveled extensively and really enjoy it. Some of the enclosed photos were taken on our most recent vacation—a cruise to the Caribbean. We expect to continue traveling after becoming parents, and plan on taking our child(ren) with us.

We belong to an Episcopal church, where we were both confirmed and married. Due to work conflicts we are unable to attend every Sunday, however we are committed to raising our child(ren) as Christians. We are active in the youth program at church and plan to be chaperones on some trips, possibly out of the country. We were both raised in the same community and attended the same schools and church. We also had many of the same friends, although we did not meet until we were twenty-one and nineteen, respectively. We were married two years later and we still have many of the same friends we had as children.

We are both professionals in stable careers. Dion, age thirty-three, is a police officer and has been in the same community for eleven years. Since he started his career at an early age, he will be eligible for full retirement in fourteen more years. Carey, age thirty, is in management at a large teaching hospital and plans to work part-time, mostly at home, after adopting.

We do hope that with your permission we can exchange more information. It is our belief that you should have as much or as little information as you would want. We are willing to try to meet with your expectations now, as well as in the future. Really, it is what you are comfortable with. We will respect whatever decision you make.

Love,
Dion and Carey

I waited eagerly for Carey to come home that night. I had made a salad and put some spaghetti on so that she wouldn't have to worry about making dinner. I wanted to show her what I had written; I couldn't stop thinking about it. It wasn't that I was so impressed with myself, it was more that I had a *feeling* about what I had written.

We kissed hello, and I asked her how her day had been. "It was fine," she said as she headed upstairs to change out of her business clothes. "I'll be right back down so that we can get dinner going and then I want to take a look at the instructions for our profile. I think we need to get going on that," she yelled down the stairwell.

When she came back down, the table was set and dinner was on our plates. She was surprised. "Wow!" she said. "This looks great. You didn't have to do this, D. I know how busy you are at work these days. Thank you so much. This is such a treat," she said.

Carey sat down. Before she had a chance to say anything, I spoke. "I wrote the profile today."

"You did?" she asked. "You didn't want to do it together?"

"It just came to me," I told her. "I didn't really have a choice. I sat down at the dining-room table and it just poured out of me onto the paper."

"May I read it?"

"Of course you may read it," I told her. "I've been waiting all day for you to come home so that I could show it to you. I'll get it." I went into the dining room and took it from the side buffet, where I had left it. Bashfully I put it in her hands and walked out of the kitchen. I was too self-conscious to watch her as she read it.

I went out to the living room and sat in a chair in the bay window. It was already dark outside. The streetlights were on and the wind was blowing lightly, so I could see the flickering shadows of leaves on the sidewalk. Soon the leaves would change to the deep yellows and oranges I had loved since I was a child. I wondered if Carey and I were going to have a child who would love the changing seasons too. I imagined raking piles of leaves with a small child at my side, then jumping in them. My vision included Sam, too, who I knew would protect any child who came into our lives.

Carey walked quietly across the living room and knelt down in front of me. I wondered if she might be upset that I had written it without her. She put the pages I had written in my lap. "It's beautiful," she said softly. "You said everything perfectly." She reached out and touched the pages. "Thank you for writing this. This is how we're going to find our child. There is a birth mother out there who this was written for. She's waiting to read this letter. It was meant only for her. It's okay that we don't know who she is right now. Maybe she's not even ready yet, maybe there isn't a baby yet. But after reading this, I know she's out there."

We attended our last meeting of the home-study program. It had the bittersweet feeling of a college graduation. We had entered the program together and we were leaving together. We had shared our lives' most intimate details, given of ourselves completely and without inhibition. We had sat there week after week baring our souls, and in the process had become very close to one another.

We all turned in our personal profiles. Carey had put ours together. She had transcribed the letter to our birth mother that I had authored. At my suggestion she wrote it out longhand. I told her she should put it in her beautiful, flowing handwriting because that in itself said so much about Carey. She included pictures of Sam, Aggie, and Elizabeth as well as some more pictures of us. She had matted them and done a wonderful layout. For the front page of our packet, Carey chose a copy of the house print—the small, simple house with heart-shaped puffs of smoke coming from the chimney. The profile was the last major entry for our agency file. We were proud of how it had turned out. We gave it to Beth feeling that we had done our best all the way around.

It was time to say good-bye to our fellow group members. We had undergone an intense, panoramic learning process together. We all saw the world differently now. Even the most jaded and skeptical among us had been humbled by the experience.

For Carey this last meeting signaled the beginning of waiting. The work was over, and now our modus operandi would be to keep busy against a backdrop of waiting. Finally, though, it was "good waiting," as Carey described it. It no longer had the open-endedness we had struggled to control for so long.

As we stood having coffee together at the end of the last meeting, we all agreed to send one another birth announcements when our children came to us. We each had an address and telephone list of our group, so we knew we could stay in touch if we chose to. Some of us had laid the foundations of friendship over the course of the program and would remain in touch with one another. Carey and I would maintain our friendship with Bob and Lori. Others we would say a fond farewell to and pass out of one another's lives. From this point on, our lives would return to their own individual directions. We believed that we would probably all become parents sooner or later, but there was no guarantee about who would be chosen first. As we ended our time together and hugged good-bye, we could almost read in one another's eyes the question: Will it be *you* who is blessed first with a child?

CHAPTER

7

Five months passed since our last home-study group meeting. Carey and I continued to go to Adoption Network meetings from time to time. We knew that if we were going to be involved in an adoption, we were going to go into it with our eyes and hearts open. Each of these meetings affected us profoundly. Each time we left, after hearing an array of compelling firsthand experiences from adoption-triad members, we had a deeper and more realistic impression of the forces and emotions that were a part of every adoption, whether they were limited by secrecy or kept out in the open.

However, we came to realize through these meetings that the heartaches could often be alleviated by openness. Through openness no member of an adoption triad had to live with unanswered questions and unanswerable loss. While we understood that openness was not necessarily right for everyone, it was something that should be considered by everyone.

We fell back into the routine of our lives. Talk of our hoped-for adoption was kept to a minimum, although we both knew it was always in the back of our minds. With the hope that we would be adopting someday in the not-too-distant future, we gave up our hunt for another house.

We had enjoyed Thanksgiving and Christmas of 1991 with quiet, traditional celebration rituals. Just before Christmas the dispatcher at my police station was selling a special line of children's toys. I was drawn to them and asked her to help me pick out three toys suitable for an infant. I told her that Carey and I were hoping to adopt a child and that these would be for her or him. She selected a blue and yellow rattle in the shape of an elephant, an accordion-folded vinyl panel that had simple black-on-white drawings of faces, and a colorful little gizmo that intrigued me because it had several different little knobs and handles that a baby could push, pull, twist, and slide.

On Christmas Eve I wrapped the toys and put them under the tree, trusting that they would serve as reminders of our impending gain instead of reminders of everything we might lose. When Carey opened them on Christmas morning, she grinned from ear to ear while tears of emotion filled her eyes. "Oh, Dion! Thank you, honey," she said as she hugged me. "These mean more to me than anything else here. I know we're in this together, and I know it's going to happen."

As our weekly meetings had drawn to a finish, Beth Brindo and Nan Lahr had both suggested to our home-study group that we give some thought to making some preparations in case we were chosen for an adoption that was set to happen quickly. They had told us that some couples even set up a nursery before being chosen by a birth mother so that they wouldn't have to worry about it in the frenzy of an adoption-in-the-making.

Between Thanksgiving and Christmas Carey and her friend, Kit, had gone to work stripping the stubborn, dated wallpaper in our smallest guest room. When they finally got the paper peeled, Carey chose a very neutral cream-colored paint for the walls, and the two of them did a beautiful job painting the room. After opening the small toys on Christmas Carey put them in a basket and took them up to the otherwise empty nursery. There they sat awaiting the child who would play with them.

In January the New Year's sales got the better of us. Not only did we shop wildly for ourselves but we succumbed to another temptation. One of the local baby stores advertised its "giant, once-a-year sale" on all baby furniture. We debated whether it was smarter to buy now (at a big savings) what we hoped we would eventually need or whether it was smarter to wait and not set ourselves up for sad reminders just in case things didn't happen the way we hoped they would.

We threw caution to the wind, and Carey picked out a beautiful oak nursery set that included a crib, a dresser, and a changing table. Knowing nothing would be too good for our child once we had one, we bought the top-of-the-line mattress too. One weekend we spent the better part of a day setting up the nursery. After it was up and ready, Carey put the baby toys in the dresser drawer, covered the mattress with a sheet, and closed the door.

The phone rang in Carey's office, lighting up the button for line two. Carey looked up from the paperwork in front of her, punched the button, and picked up the receiver. "Carey Howells," she said.

"Carey?"

"Yes?"

"Hi, Carey, this is Nan Lahr from Lake County Catholic Service Bureau."

"Nan! Hi! What's up?" Carey asked as she paper-clipped a pile of papers.

"Carey, listen to me. I have something to tell you. Get ready for the roller-coaster ride of your life." She paused. "You've been chosen."

The squabble from my radio was a constant background noise as I drove my squad car. It was as familiar and soothing to me as the constant ticking of a clock. I listened to the radio with one ear and to the outside world with the other. I performed a constant surveillance of everything going on around me. I prided myself on not missing a beat.

I turned left onto a long stretch of road. It was a route I had driven probably a thousand times and it had a familiarity about it I had grown to appreciate. Evergreen trees grew on the properties off the road. Soon the rest of the trees would get their leaves, so by the time summer rolled around, the road would be shady.

My radio hissed and the dispatcher's voice came over with a message for me. "Ten-nineteen, contact your wife. Ten-nineteen, contact your wife." Carey and I touched base once a day. It was a habit we had started when we first dated, and we had never given it up. Even if we didn't have any particular reason to speak to each other, we put a call in. I responded to the dispatcher and began a circle back toward the station so that I could get a cup of coffee and call Carey.

Fifteen minutes later I pulled up to the station, parked my car, and walked inside. I exchanged greetings with a few of my fellow officers as we passed in the hallway. The coffee machine was just dripping the final drops of a fresh pot of coffee. I poured myself a cup and walked into a squad room to call Carey.

She answered her office phone on the first ring. "Carey Howells," she said briskly.

"Hi, honey," I said, pausing a moment first to swallow a sip of coffee. "It's just me."

"We've been chosen." She said it deliberately and slowly.

I drew a blank. "What do you mean?"

"*We've been chosen,*" she said again, slowly and emphatically.

"We've been chosen . . . we've been chosen," I chanted back, still at a loss for what she meant. Then it hit me like a thousand volts of electricity right through my heart. "Oh my God, we've been chosen? Carey, we've been chosen by a birth mother?"

"Yes! Yes! Yes! Yes!" Carey was triumphant. "Nan Lahr called me a while ago and told me a birth mother has chosen our profile! She told me she's an eighteen-year-old girl, and Dion, she's due in three weeks! She wants to meet us, so we're going to arrange a meeting with her and her social worker!"

My heart was racing out of control. I leaned over and put my head down on the desk. Physical waves of fear shot through my body. My eyes closed and I gripped the telephone receiver tightly. My thoughts were in wild disarray, and my mouth was dry.

"Dion, are you there?" Carey asked.

"I'm here," I mumbled.

"Is something wrong?" Carey asked. I could hear the hurt in her voice. I wasn't responding the way she had hoped.

I took a deep breath and tried to bring the wild beating of my heart under control. "Wow," I said slowly. "This is unbelievable. It's beginning to sink in now. You really threw me a curve ball there. Let me think . . . Wow . . . We got chosen. *Wow.* Carey, this is incredible."

"Isn't it? It's outrageously incredible. It's a miracle. In three weeks we're going to be parents!" She sounded like she was floating on air.

"Tell me exactly what Nan said," I urged. "I want to hear every detail of your conversation."

Carey filled me in on the details that Nan Lahr had been able to share with her. The birth mother was an eighteen-year-old high school student, an average student, about five feet two inches tall, and was due in three weeks. We were given just her first name, which was Nancy. I listened carefully and memorized what Carey was saying to me. It was still a lot for me to grasp. I had never stopped to think that we would someday get a phone call like this one, one that would change our lives instantly. Carey not only knew it would happen this way, she had anticipated it. So this bombshell had blown me away much more than it had her.

When we were finished talking, Carey, far too excited to work, left the office and went home. She phoned her mother to tell her that we had been chosen for an adoption, carefully reminding her at the same time that it was in no way guaranteed to happen. Her mother was cautiously excited and asked for all details. When they were done talking, Carey nervously fussed around the house, cleaning up, picking up, trying to stay busy.

I got home from work midafternoon. Carey and I reviewed her conversation with Nan again. I called my mother to tell her the news, and like Carey's mother she was delighted. Carey and I talked some more. The more we talked, the harder it was to contain our excitement. Still, it was impossible to forget that everything could fall through at any time. As we talked some more, it dawned on us that we really wanted to know more than the few pertinent facts Nan had shared with us. The mystery and suspense were thrilling and at the same time nearly unbearable.

We ordered a pizza delivery and went to sit down on the couch in the living room. Sam, picking up on our nervousness, followed on our heels. He lay down in the middle of the floor facing us and kept his worried gaze focused directly on us. His very serious look of concern contrasted with the euphoria we felt. Sam's relentless stare made us laugh.

The pizza arrived and we absentmindedly ate it between bits of animated discussion. The news of "being chosen" was too big to keep to ourselves. We phoned our closest friends and told them what had happened. They were so excited for us that it made us even more excited ourselves. We would have called every friend and relative we had if not for that small, somber voice in the back of our minds that reminded us of what the social workers had emphasized over and over again: *Not all adoptions transpire as expected, and some do not transpire at all.*

CHAPTER

8

We had a nine-day wait from the day of the phone call until the day we would meet Nancy. That was the first date that was doable for all involved. Initially a nine-day wait sounded like nothing to us. We had already endured years of waiting for the chance to become parents—years filled with physical and emotional pain and sacrifices. What was another week or so of simple waiting in the big scheme of things? We would float through time in a comfortable reverie, having been told what every prospective adoptive couple prays to hear: *We had been chosen.*

The reverie wore off quickly and was replaced by nail-biting angst. Those nine days felt like forever and a day and then some. Time became thick and slow moving. What was worse was that each day was excruciatingly slower than the previous one.

The day before the meeting Carey went to work as usual. I had the day off. I'm not sure which one of us had it harder. Carey found it difficult to focus on her work, yet she had things to do and people to distract her. Flying solo at home as I was, time hung over me like a dead weight. I puttered around the house, scratching items off the endless to-do list of household tasks. My momentum and concentration quickly wore off.

I wandered into the kitchen, opened the well-stocked fridge, and poured myself a tall glass of milk. Carey had baked brownies the night before, and they sat invitingly in a pan on the counter. By lunchtime I had eaten the entire batch, and my stomach felt like I had swallowed a cannonball. My fatigue was suddenly overwhelming. I stretched out on the living-room couch and took an afternoon nap to sleep off my brownie hangover and to pass time.

At work Carey shared her anticipation of meeting the birth mother with some close friends. "I want to bring her a gift," she told them, "something small, but something that she can keep forever." In her infinite capacity for compassion and empathy, Carey was very focused on how Nancy—as a birth mother—must be feeling. Carey was very concerned about her, knowing she was going through an extremely physically and emotionally demanding time.

Carey had been profoundly affected by the sorrow expressed by the birth mothers we had met at our home-study and Adoption Network meetings. It was painfully clear to her that for many birth mothers in traditional adoptions, the only thing they were left with was a legacy of sadness. Carey was determined that this was not what was going to happen to Nancy. We were going to make the best of a very painful situation. Our "best," we knew, would be far from perfect, but it would be better than simply following the precedent that had been set by others.

Carey talked with her friend Kathy about finding a gift for Nancy. "I don't want it to seem like we're saying, 'Here, you take this and we'll take the baby,' because that's not it at all." Kathy understood what she meant. Suddenly Carey had an idea. "I've got it! How about a religious medallion? How about a medallion with the patron saint of children on it?" It was a great idea, Kathy told her enthusiastically.

There was a catch. "Who *is* the patron saint of children?" Carey asked. Kathy didn't know, but phoned a nearby convent and soon got the answer easily. The patron saint of children was Saint Nicholas. On her lunch hour Carey stopped by a religious book-store to look for a Saint Nicholas medallion. They had one left. Carey bought it immediately.

I didn't wake up until Carey got home from work. She showed me the medallion. We agreed that it was a humble but appropriate offering for someone who was preparing to give up so much. It would also help us to feel that Nancy, the birth mother, was some-how being watched over. Over the past week or so we had both begun to feel protective of Nancy despite the fact that we hadn't even met her yet. An unanticipated feeling of compassion and tenderness toward this enigmatic "birth mother" had crept its way into the exhilaration we felt at the thought of having our prayers answered. Already, this early in the big scheme of things, we were both aware that our miraculous gain could come only as Nancy experienced a profound loss.

Carey in particular was aware of how important Nancy was in this adoption triad. Carey was excited for herself that she would meet the birth mother of our child, and she was excited that she would be able to tell our child about his or her birth mom. But at the same time she knew that Nancy was feeling, and would con-tinue to feel, a great deal of emotional anguish.

We didn't know if our impending meeting with Nancy would be our one and only face-to-face encounter with her. Carey went into the whole thing with a "photographic memory" attitude. Carey was going to remember every detail, because it was going to be part of her child's legacy, and it might be the only part he had that included his birth mother.

That night we were tired from anticipation and decided to eat an early dinner. When it was all prepared and on the table, we realized we had no interest in eating. Carey's nerves had ruined her appetite, and I could have survived for the next two weeks on the reserve of brownies filling my stomach. We cleared and washed the dinner dishes and spent the rest of the evening watching—or should I say staring blankly at—the TV.

We barely slept that night. We tossed and turned with the anticipation of coming face-to-face with this woman who was known to us only as "Nancy" and "our birth mother." We faced the next day as though it were Judgment Day. It felt as if our lives hung in limbo, swinging and swaying just out of our reach and way out of our control. We had made it through those endless nine days, but the hardest part still lay ahead.

I thought about Nancy (whose face I tried to imagine but came up only with a fuzzy image of Carey's face), and wondered if she, too, were having a restless night. No doubt she was. *Of course* she was. What she was facing, it suddenly dawned on me at about two-fifteen A.M., was far beyond anything Carey and I might be facing or could even begin to truly comprehend. Nancy's future, her past, and her present were all at stake, and she herself was in charge of dictating the outcome.

The lessons taught in our preadoption classes came back to me, and a stark, vivid revelation hit me: This girl was probably lying in her bed trying to envision the people to whom she had said she would give her baby. *Give her baby.* Give up a little human being who—no matter how bad the timing and how unplanned the pregnancy—was flesh of her flesh and blood of her blood. This little person was still inside of her, physically attached to her, tossing and turning just like the rest of us, completely trusting in his or her surroundings and his or her existence.

With every kick and movement of this tiny human being, Nancy must be reminded of the life, the *miraculous life*, that grew inside of her. Her reality was so different from ours. We were waiting for a gift, a blessing, a miracle, a new dimension and purpose in our life. She was waiting for the culmination of nine months during which her life and body had nurtured the small, budding, helpless life inside her. She knew that soon there would be loss and emptiness where there had been fullness of the most physical and emotional kind.

Clearly she loved this baby dearly, or she would never have made the choice she had made. She had undertaken a course of action that was extraordinarily complex from a personal, emotional, and legal standpoint. The gravity and enormity of the situation swept over me like a wave of nausea.

In fact it occurred to me that as I tossed and turned and hoped and waited, she might very well be lying awake somewhere having second (or third, fourth, fifth) thoughts or even a complete change of heart. We had been counseled in our classes that adoptions don't always transpire as hoped and that we must always remember that the most natural (and therefore sometimes the best) outcome was for a mother to choose to keep and parent her baby.

The precariousness of the equation loomed gigantically over me. In the space of one moment Nancy (who would then remain forever in our minds as just a name) could change her mind, and our dream-about-to-become-a-reality could be gone forever. We might never be "chosen" again, might never have a child to love and care for, and might feel for a lifetime that very real ache that came from unrequited love for a child. All Nancy had to do was step back over the line she had drawn in her heart and her mind, and all of our lives would go back to the way they were nine days ago.

Above all I was acutely aware that this baby was Nancy's baby. That was reality. That was the undeniable. No one in the world had the right to try to persuade her, or even to wish, otherwise. The only thing that could change or rearrange that biological and emotional connection was Nancy's own personal conviction. If in her heart she knew she needed to be with her baby, then that was something we had to accept as the right thing. But, I thought, our hearts would never be the same.

Morning finally arrived. March 12th was a cool, sunny day. I watched out our living-room window as the neighborhood woke up and began its daily routine. In some ways I envied the rote activity everyone else seemed to be consumed with. I watched as our neighbor across the street stepped out of his front door, picked up the paper, and stretched. From where I stood, I could see the condensation of his breath. I watched as he turned around and went back in his house, presumably to a cup of hot coffee and the daily news.

I opened our front door and retrieved our newspaper, trying to assume a normal start to my day just like everyone else. Inside, the coffeemaker was hissing as it finished brewing a large pot of coffee. I poured myself a cup, unrolled the paper, and tried to focus on the news at hand. Carey sat down next to me with her mug of coffee and took a section of the paper. We sat for several minutes in silence.

Carey stood up. "I can't concentrate on anything!" she said urgently and yet almost sadly. "Six o'clock is hours away, and I can't think of anything but how our meeting is going to go and how Nancy is feeling this morning." She poured the rest of her coffee down the drain.

I told her I knew exactly what she meant. I looked down at the paper lying on the table. I had read the same headline over and over and couldn't get past the first paragraph of the top story. I kept focusing on the date at the top of the page. March 12th had been looming ahead of us, locked mysteriously in the future. Now, suddenly, here it was. The anticipation was unbearable, and all we could do was push through the rest of the day and keep our excitement at least a little at bay. Carey pulled on her coat, grabbed her briefcase, and gave me a quick kiss good-bye. Like me, she was trying to diminish her anxiety with routine. I was out the door shortly after her and embarked on another day on the job.

By four o'clock that afternoon we were both home from work and I was in a total frenzy. Carey, always organized, had laid out her chosen outfit the night before. I, on the other hand, was pulling items of clothing out of my dresser and closet as if I were hunting for a hidden bomb. My clothes were everywhere but on my body. Carey finally told me to sit down on the bed and take a deep breath. She pieced together an outfit for me and ordered me to get dressed. It was already well past five o'clock and we needed to leave. The more we rushed, the slower we moved. Now that the meeting was upon us, it felt so unreal. It was as if we were watching ourselves in a movie.

As we walked out the door to go to our car, I stopped to have a word with Sam. "Wish us luck," I said to him quietly as I stroked his ears. Then, realizing that I was being somewhat selfish, I changed my request: "Wish that whatever happens, happens for the best." He gave my hand what must have been a good-luck lick, and with that I stepped outside and pulled the door closed.

Our meeting was to be held at a former seminary where the agency maintained some office space. The car ride to the seminary was noticeably quiet. Small talk was out of the question, and we had had all the big talk either of us could handle for the time being. We sat in silence. At a seemingly endless red light we both looked down at the gift-wrapped box containing the Saint Nicholas medallion. "So you're sure we should give it to her?" I asked Carey. With our meeting just minutes away I was beginning to get cold feet about giving Nancy this small token. I didn't want her to think we were being pushy or mercenary. After thinking for a moment Carey suggested that we wait to give it to her until we were a little farther along in the adoption process. I agreed.

Despite our sensitivity to what Nancy was feeling, our anxieties, hopes, and fears were escalating exponentially. Would she show up for the meeting? What if she simply decided not to come? Would she sense our nervousness? Would she like us? Would we like her? What would she look like? Would she have red hair, brown hair, blond hair? Who was the baby's father? Would we ever know anything about him or ever get to meet him? How was Nancy feeling? How pregnant would she look? Who *was* that baby inside of her anyway? A boy? A girl? A child who would grow up with her, or a child who was going to become the central focus of our lives? Would I say the right thing? The wrong thing? Would words even form in my mind? Would Carey and I meet her expectations? Question after question raced through my mind.

Our anticipation grew as we parked the car and then, holding hands like two kids on the first day of school, entered the seminary through the front door. The building itself helped to calm us. Its quiet, long hallways and its aura of religious wisdom and peace made us feel we were safe and secure and that what was meant to be was what would happen.

Our social worker, Nan Lahr, greeted us as soon as we entered the building. She told us to be calm and relaxed (easy for her to say!), and led us to the room where we would meet Nancy. She opened the door and ushered us in, and left to go greet Nancy when she arrived. The room, while somewhat dated in its decor, was comfortable and inviting. There were various couches and chairs, well-worn and unpretentious, scattered almost haphazardly about the room.

My frazzled nerves were taking a toll. I went out quickly in search of a men's room. Unable to find one, and figuring that the seminary building was probably empty except for us that late in the day, I ducked into the ladies' room. When I was done and reached for the door handle, I was surprised when the door opened without me! A young lady stepped inside, and as our eyes met, she smiled a broad, warm smile at me. I smiled back and excused myself. As I passed her, I noticed that she was very pregnant. Walking back to the meeting room, I realized that I had probably just had my first glimpse of Nancy. Not exactly what I had in mind for first impressions—crossing paths in a ladies' bathroom.

A couple of minutes later the door to the room opened, and our social worker came in with Nancy and her mother. Indeed it had been Nancy who had been in the ladies' room with me. Instead of feeling embarrassed, I was touched by the quick smile she flashed at me, as if to acknowledge that we had already happily overcome an obstacle in this awkward and momentous occasion.

As Nancy stepped into the room, Carey, who was standing closest to the door, instinctively hugged her and then her mother. It seemed totally natural, and both mother and daughter seemed to appreciate Carey's genuine emotion.

Carey and I watched in fascination as Nancy and her mother sat down in the chairs opposite us. Seated before us was a truly beautiful young girl, with long, thick brown hair and grayish blue eyes. She wore a gray oversized Ohio State University sweatshirt, which added to the softness she exuded. I found myself looking at her rounded belly and back again at her face. She looked at us with great composure and smiled again, first at me and then at Carey. I felt an instant liking for her.

Her mother, like Nancy, was the picture of kindness and gentleness. She was dressed for the meeting in a tailored business suit. In one hand she clutched her pocketbook and in the other was a fistful of tissues. Her eyes were reddened and puffy from crying. I looked to catch Carey's attention, but she, too, was absorbed in taking in the scene that was before us. Our social worker made the formal introductions and suggested that she leave the room so that we could get to know one another in our own private forum. We all agreed.

As soon as the door closed behind the social worker, Nancy began to speak. Before she got halfway through her first sentence, her composure shattered and she broke into tears. Her emotional pain was obvious.

For a brief moment Nancy's pain commanded silence in the room. But then her mother, who had been introduced to us as Marilou, spoke. "Thank you so much for agreeing to meet us," she said as she dabbed at her eyes with a tissue. "We're both so grateful to you for your understanding. And, please, I want you to know that Nancy is a wonderful, good girl."

The magnitude of Marilou's feelings was obvious to both Carey and me. She deeply loved not only her daughter but her unborn grandchild as well. It was clear in the few minutes we had spent with her that her heart was being torn apart by the situation.

Nancy regained her composure, dried her eyes, and with the most extraordinary courage I've ever witnessed, began to tell us of her pregnancy, her reasons for giving the baby up for adoption, and her reasons for choosing us.

Nancy told us that a few months into her pregnancy she had telephoned several other agencies, but none of them had felt right to her. Most of the agencies not only didn't support the concept of open adoption, but didn't present it as an option. Nancy's hospital social worker had put her in touch with Lake County Catholic Service Bureau. By then, it was so late in her pregnancy that she was beginning to worry. She was afraid that she had waited too long, that it was too late to arrange for a loving, open adoption for her child.

Nancy explained to us that the birth father of her child was a friend of hers. It had happened one evening as they were spending time together as friends. She had been with him willingly but had not consented to having sex with him. He had held her down and forced himself on her, hurting her wrists as he held them tightly. She said her social worker had told Nancy that that was considered to be date rape. It was a term that Nancy had not heard.

Nancy explained that Jim, the birth father, had wanted her to have an abortion. It was something Nancy couldn't do. Her focus was on her child. Abortion, she explained, had never been an option in her mind. For Nancy, from the outset this pregnancy was about another human being for whom she had complete and full responsibility. She didn't view it as a correctable mistake or an inconvenience.

She took her pregnancy very seriously and dealt with it forthrightly and in the best way she knew how. She had sought prenatal care as soon as she discovered that she was pregnant. She was eating right, getting rest, and doing everything in her power to ensure that this baby would be born healthy. What she couldn't do, she said, was offer this baby what every child deserves: the chance to have a stable life, with a real family.

She knew she couldn't terminate the pregnancy, but she was also mature enough to realize that she would be unable to provide the things in life she wanted her child to have. She was aware that adoption was a strong option, but she knew how difficult it would be to give up her child.

Her mother, Nancy told us, had also given up a child when she was a teenager. As Nancy spoke, her mother cried quietly in the chair next to her. With great compassion and insight Nancy told us how she had witnessed her mother's anguish through the years as she lived with the emptiness that followed her relinquishment of her baby. August, the month the baby had been born, and Christmas were terribly painful times for her mother. It was a pain that had only increased over the years. Nancy knew she could never live with such a terrible, lifelong anguish and emptiness. For Marilou, watching Nancy experience an unplanned pregnancy was almost more than she could bear. And, we suspected, the mere thought of giving up a grandchild after having relinquished her own child was tearing her apart.

Nancy told us she had received very negative reactions from many of her peers at school when they found out she planned to give her baby up for adoption. When they taunted her, she stood her ground and reminded them that they didn't know the whole story. She was strong and brave enough to tell them that her child had been conceived in a date rape. She told them the baby's father would never be a part of her life, and she had to consider the possibility that if she kept her baby, she might raise the child with resentment because of what had happened. Then her classmates went on to gossip about the fact that the baby wasn't Todd's, Nancy's boyfriend.

The peer pressure had mounted as her due date approached. Winter had arrived, and she could no longer easily do the twenty-five-minute walk to school. She was growing increasingly fatigued from the pregnancy, and tired of the way she was treated at school. She told us she had recently taken a leave from school and was being tutored at home.

Nancy told us that she had been doing her vocational training at school in child care. As part of that training she had worked in the child-care facility located on-site at her school. The child-care facility served three high schools and was set up so that teenage students could leave their children in on-site day care while they attended school. She had seen other high school students decide to keep their babies when they got pregnant. She had all too sadly been witness to the disastrous outcomes of these situations. These girls, Nancy told us, ended up destroying not only their own lives but their children's lives by not giving them a chance to grow up in a home with a real family and financial and emotional stability. Nancy's decision was to pursue an open adoption.

Nancy told us that Jim, the father, was not opposed to her decision, but on the other hand was not particularly supportive. He had certainly given no financial assistance to Nancy and her mother, who had to pay for Nancy's prenatal care themselves. Jim's family was well-to-do, Nancy said, and until she had been counseled by her social worker at Lake County Catholic Service Bureau, she had been concerned that the family might try to take the baby from her at the last minute.

Her social worker had contacted Jim and gotten his consent for the proposed adoption. Nancy was dating her longtime sweetheart, Todd, and he was a great deal more supportive of Nancy and this baby than the birth father was. Todd had offered to get an apartment and help Nancy raise the baby. But that would mean

Nancy would have to go on welfare, and she didn't believe in doing that.

As Nancy spoke, Carey and I simply fell in love with her. She was intelligent and articulate in her reasoning, and direct in her thoughts to the point of being blunt (a quality we came to appreciate, as we have never had to wonder what Nancy's thoughts or objectives are).

She went on to tell us that she needed to meet the people who were going to be her baby's parents. She knew, above all else, that she did not want her child to fall victim to the foster-care system. She couldn't bear the thought of her child being shuffled around from hand to hand and suffering the consequences. She would not allow that to happen at any cost. She had her own standards and expectations, all of which were noble, well thought out, and valid.

She told us that the adoption agency had given her twenty-eight profiles of prospective parents to review. Ours, she said, was the third one she read, and she knew after the first paragraph that we were going to be the parents of her child. She explained that our profile addressed her feelings and needs first instead of boasting about what could be offered to the child financially and materially.

"You should have seen her plow through that stack of profiles," Marilou chimed in with obvious pride. "She looked like someone who was researching a term paper. She read every word of every profile." Marilou dabbed at her eyes with a tissue.

Carey looked straight at Marilou and smiled. "You've raised a bright and very caring daughter," she said. Marilou nodded.

Nancy said she wanted her child to grow up in a household filled with love, with pets and friends and open-mindedness. She didn't care about money or cars or swimming pools. She knew that what mattered was what came from the heart. The more she read and saw, the more she knew that we would be the parents of her baby.

Our pictures, she said with a mischievous grin, had reinforced her decision. We looked short in stature like her, she said, so her child would feel like he or she fit in well with us. She said she had caught glimpses of the inside of our house in the backgrounds of the pictures. Carey's taste in putting together a home was just like hers—simple and homey. Our house, she told us, looked like a home.

Finally, she said, the photo of our dog, Sam, touched her heart. She fell in love with his goofy, muttly face and knew that she was looking at the family with whom her baby belonged. As she told us this, I thought back to my nervous anticipation of the past nine days and then the lick that Sam had given me as I left the house that afternoon.

As she spoke, Nancy absentmindedly rubbed her hands lightly over her belly. I found myself watching her hands and envying the closeness she already had with this baby. I envied her position of responsibility and I admired, almost jealously, the extent of her devotion to caring for this unborn child. She was an amazing girl; in her quiet but steadfast demeanor she commanded and deserved the utmost respect and appreciation.

Nancy's candor and courage astounded us. What she said next to us nearly brought both Carey and me to tears. She told us that her life was just beginning and that she knew she didn't have the resources to provide well for this child. She told us she was working at a fast-food restaurant and, looking down at her belly, she said quietly, "What am I going to feed a baby? Hamburgers and fries?" She paused. "I want better than that for my child. I don't want my baby having to wear shoes from Goodwill."

Next we talked about the issue of openness in the adoption. Nancy was very clear in stating that she wanted an annual photograph and letter. "Is there anything else?" Carey asked her. "Is there anything more that we could do for you, now or later?" I knew Carey was thinking of how Nancy must be feeling, and I also knew she was speculating with some certainty that Nancy might find with time that she craved more knowledge of her child. Carey was giving her leeway to expand on her requests. Nancy said she thought that was all she needed.

I knew exactly what Carey was thinking. Earlier that week Carey had told me that she planned to keep a journal about the child for Nancy, and document his or her childhood with photographs for Nancy as well as for us. "If I were Nancy," Carey had told me, "I wouldn't just want to know, I would _have_ to know. I would have to know about his first step, his first tooth, his first birthday party, what his bedroom looked like. I would need to know that he had a warm jacket for winter, and the right medicine when he was sick, and what his first day of school was like. All those kinds of details would be so vital to me. I would want his adoptive parents to let me know, on a regular basis, that my child was healthy and doing well." I remember being astounded by the depth and insight of Carey's compassion for Nancy.

Again Carey tried to let Nancy know that she understood that Nancy not only would need to know but deserved to know that, as the years went on, her child was happy, healthy, and well cared for. She tried to express to her that she would do her best for Nancy too. "If I wait to send you a letter just once a year," Carey said warmly to Nancy, "it'll probably end up being a book-length letter attached to a phone-book-size photo album. So be fairly warned!"

The meeting felt very intimate. We were all sitting very close to one another, speaking candidly and comfortably, and we knew that we were forming a strong and permanent connection with Nancy, regardless of the outcome. Yet at the same time it was a very delicate situation. None of us had been through this before. Only Marilou had a firsthand understanding of the implications of what was happening. Still, she hadn't done it this way. Nancy, Carey, and I were all trying to follow the rules as we understood them from our social workers, while trying to make sure that no one's needs went unmet.

We offered to give Nancy our phone number and address so that she could reach us at any time if she had questions or needed to talk about anything. Nancy was clearly surprised by this and answered, "Aren't you afraid I might show up at your door one day?" My immediate reaction was to tell her, "If you did, we'd invite you in for dinner."

I tried to express to her that Carey and I considered her importance and feelings as a birth mother to be priorities. I told her that it was obvious to us by virtue of her actions and decisions that she must truly love this baby. Her love for this child, I explained, wasn't a threat to us, but a blessing. It was this strong love she had for the child that left us completely confident that she would never do anything to hurt this child or us as a family.

Our social worker tapped on the door. Nancy asked her if we could have more time to spend together. The social worker agreed and left us alone again. Carey pulled out some photographs we had brought of our home and family, and Marilou proudly took family photos out of her wallet to show us.

We all ended up on the floor, with our pictures spread out in front of us, telling one another about our families, friends, and lives. We listened in mutual fascination as small details were revealed back and forth between us. Nancy topped us all by showing us ultrasound photographs of the baby. We all had tears in our eyes as we looked at the fuzzy black-and-white image of a tiny body. Nancy told us she still didn't know if it was a boy or a girl, because they hadn't been able to tell by the ultrasound. But, she said, she knew in her heart that it was a boy. We noticed then that she always referred to the baby as a boy.

It didn't matter to us. Boy, girl, it didn't matter. We were awestruck by the reality of the situation captured right there, on those small Polaroid-type prints. Little arms and hands, little legs and feet, a little head with distinct facial features. This was the small being whose fate was being decided as we sat there together. A sense of familiarity warmed us as we unabashedly sniffled and wiped away our tears.

After a while of looking at the pictures, we agreed that it was getting late and we should let the social workers head home. If it had only been us, I felt, we might have talked well into the night.

Nancy decided to give us her phone number so that we could

contact her, but she stood by her decision not to take our number for fear that her temptation to call us after the baby was placed would get the better of her. Her maturity and insight were amazing to us. She was disciplining herself to make things easy and secure for us and the baby, despite the anguish it would inevitably cause her.

"There's one last thing," Nancy added as we got ready to leave. She looked at Carey and me. "If you'd like to be at the hospital when the baby's born, that's fine with me. That way you'd be able to tell him one day all about his birth." We told her we thought that would be incredible, and if she still felt okay with it when it was time, we'd be there for sure.

As we turned to leave, we all reached out to hug one another. Nancy began to cry again. Without even thinking I put my arms around her. Her emotions were so raw, and her confusion so great that they were almost palpable. I was strangely aware, even in the overwhelming emotion of the moment, that as I hugged and comforted her, I was hugging and comforting the baby inside of her.

As Nancy began to calm down, I took her hands in mine and said to her, "Thank you for this precious opportunity to meet you. When this child is old enough to understand, I'll be able to tell him or her that I met his mother and hugged and comforted her. Carey and I will be able to tell this baby how much you love him, and what a special person you are." Nancy's simple response: "Yes, please tell my baby all of that."

Our meeting had lasted almost two hours. Carey and I talked at length with our social worker after Nancy and Marilou had left the building. She was quite surprised, but pleasantly so, that we had exchanged so much identifying information with Nancy. In the aftermath of the meeting Carey and I were in a state of awe, and it was difficult to try to relate to our social worker the content and emotion of the meeting we had just had. We agreed that we would be in close touch in the following days.

On our way home Carey again demonstrated her uncanny insight and compassion for others. Upon hearing, nine days ago, that we had been chosen by a birth mother, our close friends had deluged us with a bounty of gifts for our child-to-be. As we drove home from the meeting, Carey looked at the road ahead of us and said, "Everything in the nursery belongs to this baby, no matter what Nancy decides."

It took a moment or two before I realized what she was actually saying: that even if this baby were not to be ours, even if Nancy decided against the adoption, we were going to pass all these gifts along to the child for whom they had been intended. I agreed fully. There was no way we could keep them for another child, or even give them back to the givers. These gifts were meant for that miraculous baby whose small image had cut through all our defenses and brought us to tears.

CHAPTER

9

Going home was a letdown. To say we were overwhelmed with emotion after meeting Nancy would be to radically understate the point. Nancy had so profoundly affected us that we didn't know how to interpret the change we felt within ourselves. She had broken our hearts and, at the same time, filled us with joy as we witnessed her devotion to her child, her radiant love, and her physical beauty.

Soon after we arrived home, Carey and I found ourselves wanting to phone our parents to share the experience and our emotions with them. We each spent a good half hour or more on the phone with our families, animatedly giving them a detailed summary of the meeting. When we were finished, we felt somehow satiated and content enough that we could relax and get ready for bed.

We quickly realized the irony of what this said: Even as adults we had a very real need to share life's ups and downs with our parents. For an adopted child, Carey speculated, this need to share might be doublefold: a need to share with the adoptive parents as well as the birth parents.

"But what if that child has no interest in knowing his or her birth parents, or what if the birth parents want no contact from their child, or what if the child isn't adopted in an open adoption?" I asked her. It didn't seem quite as clear-cut at first glance to me as it did to her.

"Even if it's a closed adoption, and the child doesn't find out until later in life that he or she is adopted, I can't help but believe that child would still feel a strong need or desire to communicate with his or her birth parents," Carey said to me, reflecting on how important it was to us to be in close touch with our respective parents. "It just doesn't seem natural to *deny* a child the right to know his birth parents, to share whatever part of his life he chooses or chooses not to, even if they aren't the ones who raise him. That connection is real too," she said, trying to sort through the complexities of emotions involved in the adoption triad. "And it certainly doesn't seem right to deny a birth parent the right to know how his or her child is doing. That seems to me to be a fundamental parental right, whether you're a birth parent or an adoptive parent."

Nancy never left our mind from the moment we met her. As Carey and I lay in bed the night we met her, we talked about her tirelessly. "I can hardly believe she's just a teenager," Carey said. "She's so pulled together about this. It's obvious that she's thought this through on the deepest level and has it clear in her own head, or as clear as she can have it without having given birth and held her baby yet. She's determined that everything is going to be just right for this baby, exactly right, with nothing overlooked. It has to be so painful for her to face all the facts, and so overwhelming. And yet she's been able to sift through all of that and decide what her priorities are for this child. She has a few simple requirements that she's focusing on, and she's going to make it happen. Nothing's going to stop her. Really, she's taking on a system that isn't set up to achieve what she's bound and determined to achieve. It's hard to believe she's only eighteen." We were both silent as we contemplated what we were all taking on.

"And yet," Carey said, "I keep remembering that look in her eyes."

"What look?" I asked.

"That look of need, of asking for help. It's as though behind her strength there's a vulnerability. Her eyes said a lot. I could see her strength in them, but there was also a plea for help. She was looking at us and telling us what she needed. What she didn't say, and what her eyes said, was that she needs us to help her do what's best for her baby."

We talked that night until we fell asleep midsentence. As soon as we got up the next morning, we picked up where we had left off. She was all we could talk about and all we could think about. We were dying to find out more, to have more contact with her, to hear her voice and listen to what she had to say. She became even more to us than a potential birth mother.

The real openness of our adoption began that next night, March 13th, when we decided to phone Nancy at home. The decision to call her was a big one. It came after much debate. We spent our entire dinner examining and reexamining the issue. Should we call her? Should we give her more time and space? What time should we call her? What should we say? How much should we tell? How willing would she be to talk to us? Would we know how to start the conversation? Would we know when and how to end the conversation? We looked at every question from every angle, and in the end it didn't make any difference. We *had* to call her. We simply *had* to call her.

We cleared the dinner table and did the dishes. When we were done, Carey got her purse and pulled out the slip of paper with Nancy's phone number on it. "Here goes," she said, taking a deep breath, and punched the buttons on the phone. I watched, my gaze fixed on Carey's face so that I wouldn't miss a cue.

"Hi, this is Carey calling. May I speak with Nancy, please?"

Carey has always had a soothing phone voice. She has the voice that gets past the receptionist and into the inner offices pronto. I felt myself holding my breath as Carey paused and looked over at me.

It turned out that Nancy had gone shopping with her mother. It was her older sister, Vickie, who answered the phone. She knew who Carey and I were. "I read a copy of your profile, and the beautiful letter you wrote," she told Carey. "And Nancy and my mother told me about meeting you. They think you're wonderful. And I want to thank you so much for helping my sister."

"No, no, not at all," Carey answered her. "We think *Nancy* is wonderful. She's so strong . . . and so brave. Dion and I just fell in love with her at the meeting last night. She's an amazing person. In fact I think we want to adopt her too," Carey said.

Vickie told Carey that Nancy was going to be very disappointed that she had missed our phone call. She urged Carey repeatedly to call back in a little while, and Carey promised that we would.

After she hung up, Carey opened the freezer door and pulled out a carton of ice cream. "Want some?" she asked, holding it up for me to see. "I need to do something to kill the time until we can call back again."

"Sure, what the heck," I answered.

We made ourselves two generous bowls of chocolate chip ice cream and sat down at the kitchen table together. The clock was on the wall behind Carey. I watched the minute hand's slow, almost imperceptible movement.

We talked more about our meeting with Nancy and what she needed and wanted from this adoption. We had entered into it with the intention of meeting our birth mother's needs as best we could, but after meeting Nancy herself, we knew we were committed to both her and the baby completely. We agreed that we could not have predicted the emotion that would be generated not only by the situation but by Nancy as a person in her own right. Even with Carey's insight and foresight, we had not imagined that we would be drawn so immediately, and without reservation, into the whole thing.

We began to realize that openness in adoption is at best a precarious experiment at the outset. "It almost has to unfold itself," Carey reflected. "It's one side waiting for a signal, or a request or an offering from the other side, not wanting to overstep any boundaries but then again not wanting to be inhibited or frightened by preconceived boundaries."

We weren't frightened by the skeptics' suggestions that openness would bring parenting confusion to the child, or to us and the birth mother. Each step we took would be only after assessing whether or not we were comfortable with how far the boundaries were being pushed. We felt that in the end we would rather confront the issues that might result from openness rather than the issues that we knew accompanied secrecy and reticence in adoption. Already we could see that trying to attain the appropriate degree of openness would require great trust, great patience, and great open-mindedness from both sides. And perhaps most importantly it required a great deal of mutual respect.

We spooned and sipped and swirled and talked. When we were done with our ice cream, thirty minutes had gone by. Carey suggested we put the dishes away and put the call in to Nancy again.

This time Nancy answered the phone. Carey's face lit up with happiness at the sound of Nancy's voice. She gave me a thumbs-up sign, and I sat transfixed. Carey and Nancy talked for a couple of minutes as though they were old friends. They talked about Nancy's shopping trip, how much we had all enjoyed meeting one another, how right everything felt. Finally I had to join in. I went upstairs and got on the extension in the bedroom.

"Hi, Nancy, this is Dion."

"Dion, hi! Thanks for calling. It's so good to hear your voices. I've been thinking about you two constantly since we met last night. My mom and I can't stop talking about you. I was hoping you guys would have called me last night after the meeting. I really wanted to talk to you some more."

Our hearts sank at the thought that we had already let her down in some small way. We felt so strongly connected to her, and so concerned about her well-being. Carey and I apologized simultaneously, and Nancy laughed at our synchronization. "Do you two always talk in stereo?" she joked.

"You really should be able to talk to us whenever you want, Nancy," I told her. "Please, won't you take our phone number so that you can call whenever you need to or want to?"

"No, I don't think so," Nancy answered. "I'm afraid I would be too tempted to call you after the baby goes home with you, and I don't want to interfere or make things hard for you and the baby." She paused for a moment. "Maybe you could give the phone number to my mother, and she can keep it. Then if I really need to get ahold of you, she can dial the number for me. That way the temptation isn't so great, but I know I can reach you if something urgent comes up."

"Nancy, honey," I said. "Don't wait for something urgent to come up. Call us anytime you want, even if it's to tell us you just sneezed. We want to know everything about you. We want you to know everything about us. Carey and I feel so connected to you already, and yet we really know nothing. There's so much we're curious about."

Nancy laughed. "Like what?"

"Like . . . well, for example, what do you like to eat? What are your favorite foods?"

She laughed again. "Um, let me think. Well, I love homemade pierogis, chicken paprikash, Burger King Whoppers. . . ."

Carey and I laughed. It felt so good and so easy to be talking to Nancy. There is a common sort of belief or phenomenon that seems to affect many adoptions. That is, oftentimes there seems to be a sort of serendipity in the way lives are brought together. It's as though there is a divine plan, and when the plan is enacted, everyone can see the rightness of it and how it was "meant to be." Carey and I could already sense that there was something far bigger than us working on this adoption. We could feel an almost spiritual force carrying us along. It was very comforting, and at times a little scary. For two people who had almost given up on the goodness of life, our newfound relationship with Nancy was nothing short of a miracle.

Nancy had an openness about her that was captivating. She sweetly and happily answered all of our questions, and unhesitatingly asked questions herself. She wanted to know what we liked to do in our spare time. She asked all about Sam, and reminded us of how his picture in our profile packet had captured her heart. (Thank you, Sam.)

With no prompting, she talked about her relationship with her father. She told us it was strained after he and her mother had divorced eight years ago. We could sense that this was an especially painful topic for her. She was living with her mother, her stepfather, and her older sister and younger brother. Her father and she had had virtually no contact for months at a time.

She easily talked about the baby. Her openness astounded us. He was a real active one, she said, a strong kicker, who gave her belly very little rest. One night, she said, she had woken up to find that he had positioned himself painfully high under her ribs. Laughing, she told us she had practically crawled into her mother's room, begging her mother to massage her belly and work this mischievous little being out from under her rib cage.

With great aplomb she assured us that she had been taking good care of the baby. She had revealed her pregnancy to her mother very early on, she said. Together they had seen to it that she received proper care from the start. We were amazed by the trust and love Nancy and her mother had for each other. Moreover we were astounded by Nancy's honesty and maturity.

She volunteered the details of her prenatal care. The health of her baby was top priority for her. After hearing that drinking water was good not only for her but for the baby, she had started drinking eight glasses of water a day. She had heard that this would also help the baby to have a healthy complexion, so she was adamant about her water intake. We smiled at her devotion to her unborn child, and her desire to do what was best and right in her situation. Everything about Nancy impressed us.

Carey and I found it easier to focus on Nancy and her well-being rather than to focus on the baby and the possibility of parenthood. Not only were we drawn to Nancy as a person but our preadoption training had taught us that quite often in unplanned pregnancies the birth mother maintains a strong denial well into the pregnancy or even past delivery. Even though it appeared that Nancy was in anything but denial, Carey felt strongly that any discussion of the baby should be initiated by Nancy rather than us.

In addition Carey had been let down so many times by the possibility of parenthood that she wasn't ready yet to let her defenses down totally. She simply didn't allow herself to think too much about the baby. She knew that the more emotion she invested, the more she stood to suffer if the adoption fell through. By really giving our hearts to this baby this early, then we were upping our own emotional ante and the extent of our potential emotional loss. It felt safer for us and safer for Nancy if we kept our attention focused on Nancy as an expectant mother and friend rather than on the baby she was carrying.

We talked for an hour and a half, and the conversation wound down easily. We were all getting tired, Nancy especially. Before we hung up, Nancy said, "By the way, it feels funny that I know your last name but you don't know mine. It's Miller. I'm Nancy Miller." Carey thanked her for sharing her name with us.

We said fond good-byes, and assured one another that we'd be talking very soon. Over the next week we spoke to Nancy almost every night, and we truly got to know one another. We talked about anything and everything, without inhibition. The conversations formed a bond and a friendship in an extremely short period of time.

Each time after we hung up, the three of us realized with increasing certainty that this adoption was going to be handled one way only: our own way.

CHAPTER

10

About a week after our initial meeting with Nancy, and about a week and a half from her due date, she phoned us in great distress. She had had a meeting with her social worker and had been told that if for any reason the baby was released from the hospital before three days, the child would have to be placed into foster care.

This was totally unacceptable to Nancy, and totally unacceptable to us as well. None of us could bear the thought of the baby being taken out of the close-knit circle we had formed, and put into the arms of strangers. The very thought sent a chill through all of us.

So when Nancy asked us if we would serve as the foster parents if the need arose, we immediately agreed. Ironically our social workers had mentioned to us early in our training that sometimes a short foster-care "layover" was necessary in adoptions. At that point in our education about adoption Carey and I agreed that we could never serve as foster parents. The risk of heartbreak was too great should the birth mother decide to keep her baby. We didn't think we could handle the pain of having a baby taken right out of our arms.

However, when our Nancy asked us to help her baby by serving as his or her foster parents, we agreed without a moment of hesitation. Her vulnerability was so apparent that despite our fears we knew we had to help her. We were so touched by her plea for help that we were willing to take the risk of fostering in order to help Nancy and to minimize her pain.

It practically takes an act of Congress to become foster parents. For us the red tape was especially sticky because we needed the licensing process to occur in record time, given Nancy's imminent due date. We could never have done it without the right kind of help. Our social worker, Nan Lahr, arranged for the foster-care social worker, Lori, to go right to work with us on our foster license. What normally takes weeks to accomplish was done in days.

The process was overwhelming. In two days we had to complete all the required state forms, which were at least equal in number to those required for our home study. In fact some of the requirements were duplicates of what we had already accomplished for our home study, yet the information had to be completely redone from scratch.

In addition to the reams of papers we had to gather about our finances, personal references, criminal checks, credit checks, and so forth, we had to each have yet another medical exam done to prove we were of healthy mind and body. We also had to have a thorough house inspection, including passing stringent fire codes. We had to purchase commercial-grade fire extinguishers and submit a detailed fire-escape plan for our home.

It was a nearly impossible task to accomplish all of this in such a short time. Once again, some greater power took over and things fell into place. Our friends rallied for us and turned in heartfelt, glowing references within twenty-four hours. Our family doctor rearranged his schedule so that he could fit us in for full physicals.

When I phoned the fire station, I was told that it would be four to six weeks before they could schedule an inspection. I talked directly with the fire captain and told him why our need for an inspection was so urgent. He astonished us by coming to our house that day and doing the inspection himself. He then phoned in an order for commercial-grade extinguishers and had them delivered to our house for us. All he asked for in exchange for his kindness was a photo of the baby when we had the time. Captain DeLuca remains a close friend to this day.

Lori, our foster-care social worker, came to our home for a preapproval visit. She was careful to remind us that what we would initially be undertaking was fostering. She was very clear and very specific that fostering—even fostering-to-adopt as we were doing—did not guarantee adoption. In explicit terms she told us that she would have to come to our house and remove the baby from our care should Nancy change her mind and decide to keep the baby. Nonetheless she was very supportive of our open adoption and, knowing the baby was due so soon, was graciously accommodating in granting us an interview almost immediately. In sum Muhammad moved the mountain, and we became licensed foster parents.

In addition to working with Lori we were still also working with Nan Lahr, our social worker from Lake County Catholic Social Services. In addition we had interactions with Kate, the social worker who was assigned to our birth mother, Nancy. The whole thing became very confusing.

It was difficult to understand who was in charge of what aspect of what part of the overall process. We were pulled in different directions by this network of social workers and the parameters of their individual jobs. It wasn't that they weren't good at doing their jobs, it's just that their jobs overlapped in places, diverged in others, and it was difficult to determine where each line was drawn.

Communication was complicated by this triple filter of people. One morning Nan Lahr called us and said Nancy was doing fine, the pregnancy was going well, she wasn't dilated yet and she had a doctor's appointment that day. I told her we had talked to Nancy the previous night and she had been feeling ill. Within minutes of getting off the phone with Nan Lahr, Nancy called and said she had a doctor's appointment and was dilated but—not wanting to anticipate her labor until it was definitely imminent— she didn't want the doctor to tell her how much. Shortly after getting off the phone with Nancy, Lori called and said she had spoken with Kate and that Nancy wasn't dilated yet. I told her yes she was and that I had just gotten off the phone with Nancy, who told me so herself.

Carey, Nancy, and I were totally frustrated by the complexities of dealing with the social workers and levels of authority at work here. Sometimes we felt as though everyone else was trying to control Nancy's and our lives, and we were merely to roll with the punches and see how it all turned out. What was worse was that these mandated complexities of power, combined with the openness established by Nancy, Carey, and me, seemed at times to be confusing and frustrating to the social workers themselves.

The candid openness upheld by Nancy, Carey, and me seemed to cause the social workers to feel that the situation was slightly out of their direct control. I believe, with no criticism intended, that this caused them to feel less than comfortable with the way things were working at some points in the process. What Nancy, Carey, and I felt was more than a relationship meant to achieve an end. We had bonded, and bonded deeply. Nancy was like a daughter and a friend to us. We felt very protective of her and her baby.

Even with the foster-care arrangements in place, we either couldn't or wouldn't allow ourselves to take the possibility of our impending parenthood as a probability. Carey especially tried to maintain a distance from the excitement that goes with impending parenthood. The potential for things to fall apart had been reiterated to us in our preadoption groups, and we took that potential seriously.

Soon after meeting Nancy our social worker phoned us and said she'd like to put us in touch with another couple who had recently undertaken an open-adoption situation. She gave us their telephone number, and Carey dutifully phoned them one evening.

After talking with them Carey told me their story. This couple had been chosen by a birth mother for an open adoption. They had met with the birth mother prior to the delivery, much as we had met with Nancy. They had been at the hospital for the birth and had even named the baby. But when they went to the hospital to pick up the baby, diaper bag and infant car seat in hand, they were told that the birth mother had changed her mind and was going to keep the baby. As unsettling and disappointing as the experience had been, they emphasized to us that they would undertake the process again and in fact were on the verge of embarking upon another potential open adoption. They were very committed to openness despite what had happened.

Their story sealed Carey's determination to view this adoption as tentative until proven otherwise. We both acknowledged yet again that there was a huge potential for an unpredictable ending to any adoption story, ours included.

Carey managed to keep her emotions in check most of the time. Still, there were those moments when the thought of becoming a mother carried her to lofty heights. One evening after dinner Carey disappeared upstairs and returned a couple of minutes later with a large shopping bag and a slightly sheepish look on her face.

"I went shopping today," she said, putting the bag down on the coffee table in front of me.

"Oh yeah?" I replied. "What'd you buy?"

She hesitated. "I don't know if I should have done this, Dion."

"What did you do?" I asked her, curious now.

"Well . . . I got tons of work done today, so I decided to duck out of the office a little early. I don't know exactly what was going on in my head, but I do know that for some reason as I was driving home I just got so excited at the thought that this little baby is about to be born and that I might get to be a mom at last. The excitement hit me, and I just couldn't fight it." She sounded almost apologetic about what she was saying, and I felt a rush of sadness at seeing the emotional battle she was fighting.

"That's okay, sweetie," I said as encouragingly as I could. "You deserve to be excited. That's part of this whole emotional roller coaster."

"I was just feeling so hopeful and so happy. I even started picturing myself taking care of a newborn baby. I couldn't help it, I just let go and gave in to the happiness."

"That's all right," I assured her again. "You can't hide from those feelings all the time."

"Oh, well, that's not all," she said, pointing to the bag. "I drove by the mall and remembered that there was a big sale at Horne's. Before I knew it, I had pulled in, parked, and found my way to the baby department." She began to pull items out of the bag. "I got these blankets, and some little sleepers, and these onesies." She piled the items on top of each other, one by one. She looked at me. "But the way I see it, even if we're only going to be foster parents to this baby, we'll need these. We can't agree to foster a baby and then not be prepared."

I could see that she had already brought herself back around to being guarded and cautious, and she maintained this control most of the time. Nonetheless a couple of days later I noticed that she had bought a special mild laundry detergent and had washed and folded the baby clothes meticulously. She carried them up to the nursery and laid them in the dresser drawer next to the three baby toys I had given her at Christmas. Once again she turned the light off and closed the door behind her.

CHAPTER

11

Carey and I looked forward to our phone conversations with Nancy. Each tidbit we found out about her was logged in Carey's mind as well as jotted down in the journal she had decided to keep for our child. But the better acquainted we got with Nancy, the more we longed to know about her. Our direct communication with one another was so rewarding; it contrasted sharply with the secondhand-news feeling we got when we communicated via the maze of social workers. As we gained familiarity with Nancy directly on the phone, Carey began to wonder if we might be able to take it one small step farther.

"At this point," Carey told me one night before we put in a call to Nancy, "we're talking so openly with one another on the phone that I don't see why we couldn't be doing it face-to-face. She wants to get to know us, and we want to get to know her, and the one who will ultimately benefit from it is this baby. Time is running out. If she wants to throttle back to her initial request for a yearly letter and picture after the baby's born, then we only have a week or so left to try to capture what we can about Nancy for posterity."

"So what are you saying?" I asked. "That we should try to arrange another meeting with Nancy?"

"I'm saying that I feel comfortable enough to ask her if she'd be up for another meeting. What do you think?"

"I think we should ask her," I answered. "She's strong enough to tell us no if she doesn't like the idea. And on the other hand maybe she'd like to see us again but is hesitant to come right out and ask. I don't see how it would hurt to ask."

Carey's face lit up at my approval of her suggestion. I could see that this proposed meeting was extremely important to Carey. The more we could learn about Nancy, the better we would be able to provide a realistic picture of his complete heritage for this child. That, driven also by our genuine fondness for Nancy, was as much investment as our hearts were willing to make at this point. We still felt that we were at arm's length from parenthood and from this baby, and for the time being we felt safe that way. And we felt safe acting as a support system for Nancy. But caution aside, Carey definitely wanted to acquire and preserve as many memories of Nancy as possible. I hoped Nancy would agree to the meeting.

Carey dialed Nancy's number and almost immediately put the question to her when Nancy got on the phone. Nancy was thrilled at Carey's invitation. The three of us decided that we definitely wanted to meet again face-to-face, away from the agency. We set a date to meet one another for dinner. We settled on March 30th, the earliest mutually doable date we could come up with. Even though the thirty-first was her due date, we predicted that the baby would probably be late, since this was her first pregnancy.

Nancy seemed excited at the prospect of seeing us again and asked if she might bring Marilou along again. Carey and I told her that would be perfect and that we could hardly wait to see both of them again.

The baby had his own plans.

On Sunday, March 29, 1992, I worked the four P.M.-to-midnight shift. It was one of the last frosty nights of winter. I drove carefully through the streets, noting how slippery the road was becoming as night set in. At eleven o'clock I was called to the scene of a horrendous single-car crash in which the driver, a middle-aged man, was crushed to death. There was a rumor that the accident had been preceded by the sound of gunshots.

I had to go to the hospital to examine the body for bullet holes. The dead man was lying faceup on a table, and I had to put my hands under him and tilt him over slightly so that I could look for any signs of bullet entry or exit on his back. As I moved him, I could hear a sickening crunch of bone.

After examining him I went to talk to his wife. I had to tell her that her husband was dead. I spared her the horrendous details, but they were vivid in my own mind. It was one of the most gruesome nights of my career.

I arrived home at two-thirty A.M. and got into bed. I couldn't shake the feeling of unease that followed me home from the hospital. For the first time death actually frightened me and completely threw off my sense of control. I lay in bed next to Carey, wide awake and shaken. My mind raced in circles as I thought about the man who had died so horribly. His bones were fragments in his lifeless body.

I remembered my own sense of despair as I had to tell this woman that her husband was gone. She had been devastated. For the first time I had a realization about how deep a loss the death of a loved one was for the survivors. This woman would never see her husband again. She had no choice. There was no changing the facts, no turning back.

My thoughts of the woman dovetailed with thoughts about Nancy and the baby. For a moment I felt relieved that I could change my focus. But then it hit me. I wasn't really changing the tenor of my thoughts, just the context of them. The parallels between death and adoption suddenly became frighteningly clear to me.

When a birth mother gives up her child, I realized, it had to feel at least in part like a death to her. That child was suddenly gone from his or her birth mother's life. And in a traditional adoption it could very well mean that the child was gone from her life forever, no changing the facts, no opening closed files, no turning back. Just as in death, the loss of a loved one was there, the emptiness was there, the finality was there. For the birth mother—the "survivor"—all that was left behind after relinquishing a child was what we had heard the birth mothers talk about repeatedly: the hollowness.

The realization sent a wave of doubt through me. Were Carey and I ready to be party to a loss this enormous and enduring? I tried to rationalize it for a moment. Nancy had decided not to raise this child herself. That was a fact, independent of us. She had chosen adoption as the best alternative. That was also a fact, independent of us. Therefore, I thought, we weren't necessarily a part of the chain of pain involved. With relief I thought that we were providing something she and the baby needed from *someone;* we weren't just serving as vehicles for Nancy's loss.

If this was what Nancy and her baby needed, and Carey and I could provide it lovingly and with compassion, and at the same time fulfill our desire to be parents, then didn't everyone come out a winner? For a very brief, very fleeting moment I bought in to my own rationalization. But then the reality of loss hit me again. No matter how the adoption transpired, the loss would still be there for the birth mother, and for the child, too, on a different level. It was undeniable, even in the most favorable of circumstances. It was undeniable.

I was exhausted, but sleep did not come easily. The last time I looked at the clock before falling asleep, it was four A.M.

Two hours later. Monday, March 30, 1992. Six A.M. The telephone rang. Carey dragged herself out of sleep, and reached for the phone.

"Hello?" she mumbled. It was Nancy.

"Carey, it's Nancy! My water broke!" Carey woke up instantly.

"Nancy! Are you all right?" Carey asked her.

The worry in Carey's voice brought me out of my sleep on the other side of the bed. I rolled over and listened.

"I'm fine," Nancy assured Carey. "I'm not having contractions yet. But I'm going to wake my mother up and then get ready to head for the hospital. Can you guys meet me at the hospital? I want you to be there."

"Okay, of course. We'll get up right now and get ready," Carey told her without hesitation.

"All right, good. You're the first people I've called. I wanted you guys to be the first to know. So don't forget, I can't let Kate know that I called you first. When she calls you to tell you I'm in labor, pretend I didn't talk to you already."

Carey laughed lightly. "All right. Don't worry, we'll be there. Be careful. See you soon. We love you." Her voice was very reassuring. She hung up the phone and filled me in on the details.

"She wants us to pretend that we haven't heard from her when her social worker calls us. She makes me laugh. It feels like such a teenage ruse, but then again she *is* a teenager. Anyway you answer the phone when it rings," she told me. "I'm no good at pretending."

The phone rang again after a couple of minutes. I answered it right away. It was, as predicted, Kate, Nancy's social worker. She told us that Nancy was in labor. I feigned surprise and asked her what we should do. She told us to go to the hospital, but to keep a low profile. She said she had advised the social workers at the hospital that we were coming. She told us we would be able to see the baby directly after birth and have visitation in the nursery.

We went on automatic pilot. It was as if we were in a play, following stage directions. Enter stage right, exit stage left. We raced out of bed and took turns in the shower. While Carey showered, I let Sam out and made coffee. I poured a mug of coffee for Carey and then raced back upstairs with it so that she could drink it while she got dressed. In a mad dash we pulled on clothes, grabbed our coats and car keys. We let Sam back in, jumped in the car, and took off.

The hospital where Nancy was going to deliver was some distance from our house. It would take us probably forty-five minutes on the road. We had never had any reason to go there before that morning. Knowing that Nancy could go into labor at any time, Carey had had the foresight to call the hospital for directions the day after we first met her. She had written the directions out in detail and had kept them in her purse, ready and waiting for this exact moment.

It was dark outside, and the streetlights were still on. I drove with tunnel vision, nervous that I would take too long and we'd arrive too late to be of any help to Nancy. After we got on the highway, Carey pulled out her meticulous directions and guided me to the right exit and then through the baffling backstreets that led finally to the hospital entrance. The drive seemed to take forever as we read directions and looked for street signs.

Other than our navigations, the ride was quiet and uneventful. We were still going on automatic pilot, just trying to get to the hospital on time while trying to wake up fully. The news of Nancy's labor still seemed surreal. It wasn't sinking in at all yet that we were on our way to the birth of our child. It felt more like we were watching someone else go through these motions. We arrived at the hospital just before eight, parked the car, and with fierce determination, went up to the labor and delivery floor.

The nurses' station was through a large set of double doors.

Side by side we marched up to the desk. "We're here to see Nancy Miller," I announced. There was a young nurse sitting at the desk. She looked up at us blankly. I repeated myself. Still she had no idea of Nancy's whereabouts. Time seemed to be slipping away while we waited for some acknowledgment that we were in the right place. Carey repeated Nancy's name and said she had probably arrived quite recently. "I'm sorry, I just came on shift," the nurse said, "let me look her up." She turned to the computer and typed something in. "Oh yes," she said, "she's here. She's in Room Five-twenty-three." She pointed the way to the room. We thanked her and charged off in the direction she had indicated.

The door to Nancy's room was open. We tapped gently and Carey called her name softly.

"Hello? Come in!" came the reply.

We walked into the room. Nancy was in bed, her thick brown hair pulled back, an expression of peacefulness on her face. Despite the sterile environment of a hospital room she looked beautiful—white sheets, glaring lights, and a hospital gown couldn't take that away from her. Marilou sat in a large armchair on the left side of Nancy's bed. Another young woman was seated near Marilou.

A dazzling smile lit up Nancy's face. "Hi, guys!" she said, reaching out her arms. Carey hugged her first, and then I hugged her. We greeted Marilou, and Nancy introduced us to the other woman as her older sister, Vickie. Vickie stood up and hugged us each and thanked us for being there for her sister. We were touched by her warmth and graciousness and told her we would do anything for Nancy.

Carey asked Nancy how she was doing. She told us she wasn't in a lot of pain yet and that she still wasn't really having contractions. Nonetheless we could see that she kept shifting her position, trying to get comfortable. Each time she started to move, her mother jumped out of her chair to help her. She fluffed Nancy's pillow, propped extra pillows behind and beside her, and stroked her hair.

We stood on the opposite side of the bed, wanting to be of some help. "Can we do anything for you?" Carey asked Nancy.

"I'm just glad you're here," she said. "Look at this," she said proudly, and pointed to a fetal heart monitor on the bedside table. We watched the steady pattern of the baby's heartbeat and heard the quick, swooshing beating of his heart. Although his birth was imminent, and we could hear the reassuring rhythm of his tiny heart, he still seemed unreal to us. He was the unknown.

We—Carey in particular—were working hard to stay in the moment as we progressed through this whole adoption endeavor. To jump too far forward was to anticipate an outcome that might not happen, and to borrow trouble or happiness. We knew Nancy's intention, but we also knew everything might change once she saw and held her baby.

So we made a conscious effort to stay in the here and now with Nancy. Her welfare was still our priority. Beyond that, everything was still uncertain, a bridge to be crossed. Nancy was important to us, and she needed us now.

"My back is aching," Nancy said as she tried to adjust her position in the bed again. "I hope I'm not going to have back labor."

Her mother was at her side again, moving pillows, arranging support for Nancy's back. "Well, I hope not," she told Nancy. "I had to go through that with your sister. It's not much fun. Here, does this help at all?" Her devotion to her daughter was obvious and kept her busy at Nancy's side. She picked up on all of Nancy's facial expressions, no matter how subtle. She knew how to read each of her daughter's body movements. Nancy listened patiently as her mother and Vickie spoke back and forth between themselves and to Nancy, offering advice and encouragement.

Even with her growing discomfort there was a great sense of calm about Nancy. I had imagined that by now everything would be in a state of high intensity. Instead Nancy was very peaceful, very much focused on what was happening. It was clear that she knew what she wanted to do, what she had to do, and that that was her focus. We were surprised when she turned to us and told us she was nervous. "I guess I'm still not sure exactly what to expect," she said.

"Everything's going to be fine," Carey told her. "You're in good hands here. Are you sure there's nothing we can do for you?"

Nancy ran her hands over her stomach and thought for a moment. "You know," she said, "my mouth is really dry. Some hard candy would help, I think."

A nurse came striding through the door and over to Nancy. She asked Nancy how she was doing as she checked the fetal monitor. Nancy said she was doing fine and that she was just waiting for things to get going. "Well," the nurse said as she looked over the strip of paper from the fetal monitor, "maybe this means you're going to have a boy. They seem to take their time being born, and they sometimes have a faster heart rate, like this."

I thought about what she was saying and wondered if she was right. I remembered that Nancy had said she knew all along in her heart that she was carrying a boy. She had always referred to the baby as "him." Carey, though, predicted a girl. It didn't matter. What mattered to us now was seeing Nancy through this birth.

A doctor came into the room, and breezed over to Nancy's bed. He greeted Nancy and picked up her chart. He was young and dressed casually underneath his open white coat. He looked busy, engrossed in his work, seemingly unaware of those of us who were gathered and waiting anxiously. This was all in a day's work for him. For us the world was contained in the four walls of that room.

"Dr. Jones," Nancy said.

"Yes?" he said without breaking his concentration on what he was doing.

"This is Dion and Carey Howells. They're the parents of my baby."

His reaction preempted any reaction we might have had to Nancy's declaration of our parenthood. The doctor came to an abrupt halt; he simply stopped short in the middle of what he was doing. There was a look of astonishment on his face. He was obviously completely thrown by what she had said. We could see him searching for his own reaction.

He looked closer at us, then back again at Nancy and back again at us. "It's nice to meet you," he said, his gaze fixed on us, studying us, sizing up the situation. "This is a wonderful thing," he pronounced slowly, making a sweeping motion with his hand in our direction. "Nancy is an amazing person." We knew Nancy had been frank with him during her prenatal care, so he had prior knowledge of the circumstances of the birth and Nancy's plans. Still, our physical presence in the room had jolted him, and his disapproval was thinly disguised by his gratuitous pronouncement that this was "a wonderful thing."

Behind him the nurse stopped what she was doing. She did her best to hide her bewilderment, but it was obvious to us that she had not had any idea of what was going on. There was no question that she, too, had been caught completely off guard, even more so than Nancy's doctor. The nurse, too, had a distinct look of disapproval on her face.

Carey and I looked quickly at one another. We could feel that there was a change in the air, cast by the reactions of the doctor and nurse. An element of awkwardness had been forced upon us. I wondered if Nancy picked up on it, and how quickly it would dissipate. I could see Carey refusing to be affected by their unspoken reactions. She accepted the inquisitive focus of the doctor and the nurse, and even managed to return their gazes with a slightly forced smile.

Now, with the doctor and nurse hovering around Nancy's bed, the room was full of people, almost crowded. There were no seats for Carey and me. I wondered if Nancy might want a little less commotion around her right now. I remembered the hard candy she had mentioned. I volunteered to leave and find some for her. Carey wanted to stay and be with Nancy a bit longer.

I set off down the maze of hallways and found my way down to the cafeteria. There was already a breakfast crowd, and the smell of coffee and bacon was in the air. I found a candy machine and bought two packs of Life Savers. I decided to bring coffee back for those of us who were waiting with Nancy.

The elevator brought me back to the fifth floor. I walked carefully with my tray of coffee, heading back toward Nancy's room. Carey waved to me from a seat in the waiting area. I detoured and went to sit with her. She told me that the doctor was examining Nancy, so she had left the crowded room to give Nancy some privacy. We each took a cup of coffee and tried to relax in the large cushioned chairs. We were tired. It was still early morning and we felt as if we'd been waiting for hours already. It felt good to sit down.

"I found Nancy some Life Savers," I told Carey, showing her the packs of candy.

"We can give them to her when we go back in the room," she told me. "I'll peek back in in a few minutes to see if things have settled down at all." She stopped for a moment and then continued. "Did you notice the reactions of the doctor and nurse?"

"That nurse was pretty intense," I responded.

"Pretty intense?" she gasped. "You mean she was pretty blatant about her disapproval of the situation. I felt bad for Nancy. I hope she didn't pick up on it. And I hope that isn't her nurse for the duration of this birth. Nancy seems nervous enough about the delivery without having a Nurse Hatchett hovering over her. And I certainly don't relish being the focus of her sour gaze."

Marilou walked briskly into the waiting area. She had a yellow hospital gown pulled over her clothes, and I wondered if the delivery had begun. As she got closer to us, we could see she was upset. Carey asked her if something was wrong.

"I don't know how to say this, so I'm just going to tell you what happened," she said. We could tell by the way her voice trembled that she was very angry. "The hospital social worker came up to the room a few minutes ago. She told us that you're not allowed to go in to visit Nancy. She says you're there for selfish reasons—for the baby—and not for Nancy's benefit." We could see that Marilou was really agitated by what the social worker had dictated. She told us that the woman had dashed into the room unannounced, with no introductions or courtesies. "Basically," Marilou told us, "she tried to tell Nancy that it's wrong that you're here. She tried to make Nancy believe that you're here only for the baby."

I felt as though I had been punched. Our intentions had been completely misinterpreted. This social worker obviously had no idea about why we were there, and moreover hadn't bothered to speak directly to us before coming to such a coldhearted and incorrect conclusion. If she had had any concept of what was really going on, she would have known that we were there for Nancy. After everything we had already been through with her, we considered ourselves to be her family too. We loved her as if we were family. The baby was still unknown to us, still secondary to Nancy and her well-being, although he would be our family if the adoption happened. But we knew and loved Nancy, and she, too, would be family if we adopted this child. We were there to help her in any way we could.

Marilou assured us that both she and Nancy knew we had every right to be there, that Nancy wanted us there, and that we were there for all the right reasons. They felt, for the time being, that they didn't have any recourse in the face of the hospital administration. She clearly felt terrible about what had happened.

Carey and I found ourselves consoling Marilou, trying to convince her that everything was going to be all right despite this wrench that had been thrown into our plans. "It's okay," Carey told her, "don't worry about it. You have enough on your mind without agonizing over this too. Dion and I will be here in whatever capacity we can. We'll be fine. We'll just take things as they happen. Let's just make sure Nancy's all right." Marilou looked grateful for Carey's heartfelt diplomacy.

Not wanting to make things any harder for Marilou by keeping her away from Nancy, I gave her a hug and asked her to bring a message to Nancy for us. "Please tell Nancy that we love her and we're praying for her," I told Marilou. "Tell her we'll stay right here in the waiting room."

"Okay," Marilou answered, still with worry in her voice. "I'm so sorry."

"Listen, Marilou," I told her, "you have nothing to be sorry about. We'll be fine. Don't worry about us at all. Let's keep our focus on Nancy. You go back and take care of her. Tell her we're rooting for her." Marilou still looked very distressed. "Tell her we won't go anyplace but the bathroom," I joked, trying to lighten the mood. I gave her the Life Savers for Nancy and some coffee, and she went back to the room.

We waited until Marilou had disappeared down the hall before turning to each other and letting our real reactions surface.

"I just don't think that's right," Carey said. "I can't believe they can forbid us from visiting Nancy. Who are they to decide whom she can and can't see? It's just not right," Carey repeated. She sounded both hurt and outraged. I could tell that she was taking it personally, and in fact so was I. How could we not?

What Carey said was true: It just didn't seem right. We were being singled out and dealt with in a punitive way by some part of the hospital "powers that be." The fact that she had tried to undermine Nancy's trust in us made us very angry. We were astounded that she would propagandize to Nancy at such a critical time. She had enough to contend with as she went through labor and delivery.

Marilou's support made us feel a little bit better, but we felt like we had driven into a brick wall. We felt cut off from the one person we were truly connected with. It was hard to believe that just hours ago we had been able to communicate with one another directly. How ironic, I thought, that we had been the first people she called as she got ready to head to the hospital, and now we were the only people she couldn't be with.

Despite our frustration we felt we were caught between a rock and a hard place. We didn't want to make any waves that would adversely affect Nancy's situation or cause her more stress. On the other hand if Nancy needed us, we didn't want anything to keep us from her.

We sat in our chairs in the waiting room, trying to rebound from the blow and assess our options. In the room with us were several teenagers, fifteen- or sixteen-year-olds, dressed in "street-smart" clothes, all with beepers clipped to their waistbands. They seemed to know one another, or at least recognize and approve of one another. We watched as they came and went. There appeared to be two couples, with a friend or two in tow, speaking loudly to one another in exaggerated tones of defiance.

They acted as if they owned the waiting area. We couldn't quite figure out why they were there. From the way they were acknowledged by the various hospital personnel who passed by, they were apparently allowed to be there. They were definitely receiving more attention from the staff than we were. Carey and I were the oldest couple in the room, and the only people not part of this bigger group. We began to feel more conspicuous and out of place than we already did.

Finally, as we listened to what they were saying, we pieced the scenario together. "Yeah, I wanted to see my kid after he's born," one of the guys said boastfully to another. "I want to see if he looks like me." The girl with him ran her fingers through his hair and said, "Well, let's hope he doesn't look like her."

These teenage boys had former "girlfriends" who were in the labor and delivery unit having *their* babies. While these girls were bearing the children of these boys, they—the fathers—arrived for the occasion with a new girlfriend on their arm.

Carey and I watched in amazement as they got beeped on their pagers, made phone calls, and roamed around the floor. We didn't consider ourselves to be sheltered or naive. Carey saw all kinds of situations in her work at the hospital, and as a police officer, I had seen just about every form of strange people and behavior imaginable, but we were both pretty shocked. What was even more unbelievable to us than their tangled relationships was that all of these kids were allowed to come and go from the labor and delivery rooms at will, while we were banned from seeing Nancy. As Nancy's friends and as prospective adoptive parents, we were given no rights at all.

My frustrations bubbled and churned inside me. My stomach was in knots.

Carey looked at me. "You're stewing," she said under her breath.

"Yeah, I'm stewing. I can't help it. There's nothing else to do. Just think about what's going on around here." Carey reached over and rubbed my shoulders, trying to relax me. "I'm going to call Nan Lahr," I told her. "She needs to know what's going on. Maybe she can get things back on track."

Nan Lahr took our call right away and listened patiently to my tale of frustration and anger. "Wait some more and don't make waves" was Nan's message. She reminded us that open-adoption situations were still very new and rare and that there were bound to be obstacles. She told us she'd find out as much as she could and keep us posted. I told her I didn't know how she could get ahold of us as we sat in "isolation" in the waiting room. I suggested she leave messages on our machine at home and we'd check it periodically.

"I know she's trying to help," Carey told me after we hung up the phone, "and I appreciate it. But I don't want to hear any more psychobabble; I'm sick to death of it. The minutes are ticking away, and we can't see Nancy. It's wrong, it's just wrong."

What Carey said was true. We didn't need to have the obvious interpreted for us, we needed to change what was happening and change it quickly. This was no dress rehearsal; this was a once-in-a-lifetime event. Nancy needed to see our love and support *now* as she faced the most difficult turning point in her life.

We reclaimed our chairs and sat side by side. Carey, always pragmatic, tried to look back over the sequence of events to see if there had been any indications that this was the way things were going to be handled. Carey reminded me that Nancy had expressed concern to us over the hospital social worker who had been assigned to her.

"Remember?" Carey prompted me. "Nancy told us she had met the hospital social workers, and that she had been assigned the one who she had hoped not to get." I tried to think back. "She said there was something about this woman that rubbed her the wrong way from the start," Carey told me. "I distinctly remember her telling us that she got a really uncomfortable feeling about this woman, as if the woman wasn't really there to help Nancy but more to make sure she followed the rules. Nancy even tried to switch to a different social worker, but she wasn't able to."

Suddenly it dawned on me that we could use the house phone to call Nancy's room. No one could censor her telephone calls. I suggested to Carey that we should call her, and Carey agreed that it was a good idea. We huddled around the cream-colored phone like Boy Scouts around a campfire.

Nancy answered after two rings. What a relief to hear her voice! Before I could tell her how good it was to be able to talk to her directly and how sorry we were that we couldn't be right there with her, she said *she* was relieved to hear from *us*. She said she was sorry about what had happened with the social worker. Despite the frustration of the situation I smiled. The unconditional goodness in Nancy's heart was completely natural and without ulterior motive, and that made her all the more incredible. It was typical of Nancy to think first about everyone else, even as she was ready to give birth to a baby.

I assured her that we were fine, completely fine, just worried about her, and that we were with her in spirit. Carey got on the phone and told her calmly and quietly that we loved her and would do whatever she needed us to do. Again Nancy said she was really upset by what had happened. She told Carey that she had been counting on us all being together for the baby's birth. She said she was going to make some phone calls from her bed to try to fix things.

Her determination touched us, and we were relieved to hear

that she wanted to be with us as much as we wanted to be with her. But we knew she needed things to remain as uncomplicated and stress-free as possible, and while we desperately wanted to be with her, we knew that the way things stood now, keeping our distance was the path of least resistance. We didn't want to give her anything more to worry about—labor was enough in and of itself.

"Nancy, you've got enough going on," Carey told her calmly. "Don't try to straighten things out. Dion and I will work on that. You've got a baby to deliver! Please don't worry about anything, just take good care of yourself and the baby. As soon as we can, we'll be with you. Okay?" She made Nancy promise not to worry about us but to focus instead on herself and her baby.

Nancy asked us to please call her back again in a little while and we happily promised we would. Even though it was brief, the phone call did a world of good for our spirits. We were surprised at how good she sounded given that she was in labor and was facing a momentous loss. Her poise and insight never ceased to astound us. The call confirmed that we were still very connected to Nancy, that we were all feeling close to one another despite our separation.

After we hung up, Carey and I went back to our seats of vigil. The coming hours turned out to be very uncomfortable and awkward for us. Apparently word had spread about our open-adoption plans with Nancy and our presence at the hospital. The hospital staff, for the most part, indelicately sidestepped us. If we happened to walk by the desk, the people behind it pretty much looked the other way. Most of the staff seemed careful to avoid catching our eye or answering any questions we might have.

Many made it clear by their purposeful silence and stony facial expressions that they viewed us as nothing more than predators. It was hard not to let their attitudes get to us. However much we rationalized their behavior as being ignorant, we still couldn't completely escape feeling hurt. To this day I look back and wonder how people who spent their days and careers in a "healing" environment could inflict such pain themselves.

We felt distinctly ostracized by them, although there were a few—a very few—kind members of the staff who bestowed smiles of understanding on us. Two nurses even asked us with genuine interest about the open-adoption program. However, these were the exception, not the rule, among the hospital personnel.

Our saving grace was Nancy's family. Without them we would have felt completely cut off from her as we sat, hour after hour, in the waiting room. Nancy's sister, Vickie, came out periodically to give us updates on her progress and genuine words of encouragement.

As the hours wore on, we met more of Nancy's family as they came and went. We met her stepfather, Don, and Nancy's boyfriend, Todd. Todd was quiet and reserved, but we could see that he was unconditionally devoted to Nancy. We were impressed that he was there to support her despite the fact that the baby she was giving birth to was not his. We met Nancy's father, who stopped by for a quick visit, and we had a chance to chat with two of her closest girlfriends, who stopped by to see her.

We especially enjoyed talking with Nancy's brother, Billy, and his fiancée. They really took the time to sit and talk with us and showed a sincere interest in what we were undertaking with Nancy. They asked us a lot of questions about ourselves and the adoption, and they thanked us for being there for Nancy. Billy explained to us that it gave his family a great sense of peace and comfort to know us and to know that this baby was going to be well loved and cared for by good, kind people. Moreover, he told us, the relief and comfort his family felt probably paled in comparison to the relief and comfort Nancy herself felt in knowing that her baby would be with us. He thanked us again, and we reminded him that what we were doing for Nancy was nothing compared with what she was doing for us.

Her family was gracious and open in their interactions with us. Still, in between their visits to the waiting room, we had no idea where things stood. For all we knew, the baby had been born. As the day wore on and turned into evening, we had the chance to meet almost the entire immediate family. One by one they found out that we were relegated to the waiting room, and they stopped by to introduce themselves and give us some moral support and encouragement. They treated us like part of the family as much as they could under the circumstances.

They all knew that we had established a close and open relationship with Nancy in the short time we had known her. Even so, Carey and I made a point of reassuring them that we were there to support Nancy and that if she changed her mind and decided to keep her baby, we were still there to support Nancy. In fact our words were superfluous. They trusted us implicitly. Carey and I were wearing our hearts on our sleeves, and Nancy's family treated us accordingly: with respect and gentleness. We quickly came to understand from where Nancy drew her incredible strength and insight.

Late in the afternoon a woman approached Carey and me in the waiting room. She was dressed in professional clothes with a hospital I.D. tag clipped to her blazer. She looked discouragingly "official." We cringed in anticipation of what was coming next. We didn't need any more disparagement. As she got closer, we braced ourselves for the worst. She verified who we were, and then introduced herself. She was one of the hospital social workers who had initially been in contact with Kate, Nancy's social worker from the agency.

She had heard what had happened earlier and said she had come to apologize for what her colleague at the hospital had said and done. She gave us the chance to tell her about the open-adoption plan we had with Nancy and listened patiently as we told her that we were there at Nancy's request. We told her that we were very upset by the narrow-minded actions of the social worker in question and the fact that no one else in the administration had bothered to come to talk to us. Above all else, we said, Nancy was hurt and angry and was being denied the support system she herself had planned on having in place. In our minds that was the greatest injustice of all.

According to her, her hands were tied. "The hospital doesn't have a protocol for this type of situation," she explained. We told her we were now painfully aware of that fact. Because this was an unprecedented situation, she said, the initial policy would have to stand: We couldn't visit Nancy until after the birth. However, she said—mistakenly thinking that this would be a consolation to us— we could see Nancy in the postpartum unit after the birth and watch the baby be cleaned, measured, and weighed.

She went on to assure us that the hospital would be looking into their policy for future open-adoption situations. If she could interpret the simplest of facial expressions, she could look at us and read our message loud and clear: That doesn't do us much good now, does it? Moreover, we wanted to say, if there was no existing protocol, why not handle things according to Nancy's wishes instead of slapping the equivalent of restraining orders on us all? But again, we didn't want to react in any way that would cause a backlash for Nancy. We thanked her courteously for her time and concern.

We watched through the windows of the waiting room as day turned into evening and the chilly darkness of an early-spring night crept in. People coming into the hospital now were bundled in heavy winter clothes. The workday was ending and now the waiting room seemed to fill with visitors for all the mothers-to-be.

We had the dreamlike sensation that what was happening around us made no sense and wasn't at all real. It felt almost as if we had imagined everything up to this point. We felt very disconnected from the baby who was about to be born. "I thought it would be so different from this," Carey told me sadly. "I don't feel any excitement. I just feel flat. As if this is leading nowhere. I always thought that the moments before parenthood would be filled with crazy excitement. I'm starting to wonder if this is going to happen at all."

Carey and I held hands much of the time and exchanged small

hugs of reassurance when we noticed each other's hope beginning to fade.

We waited, and we waited some more. We watched blankly as others around us got the exciting news that the baby they were waiting for had finally arrived. It seemed that everybody else's babies were being born but Nancy's and that everybody was sharing and rejoicing except us. We waited some more.

The day had already been a long one. As the ten-hour mark passed, we were still waiting and going on pure adrenaline and caffeine. Carey and I had had enough coffee to sink a ship. We were tired and hungry. Just as we were getting ready to wander down to the cafeteria, Marilou came to us and invited us to join her, her husband, and Vickie downstairs for dinner. Nancy still had a way to go before she delivered. Her boyfriend, Todd, was with her, and they needed some time to be alone together. We agreed that we should all go to the cafeteria and have a little break from our vigil.

The cafeteria was nearly empty, so it offered us some peace and privacy. Carey and I were happy to have a change of scene. It was a relief to at last be able to talk freely with Nancy's family. If we couldn't be with Nancy, at least we could be with her family.

Despite our overwhelming concern for Nancy, we were all incredibly hungry. Most of us hadn't eaten all day. Even the hospital food was smelling good to us by now. We each made our selection, filled our tray, paid for our food, and then sat down together at a large round table.

Dinner was relaxed, as though we had all known one another for years. Conversation flowed freely and comfortably as we ate. We weren't trying to size one another up, we weren't caught up in making plans, we weren't swapping stories, we were just *chatting*. It was a welcome relief for Carey and me.

We needed this distraction, and we needed the opportunity,

however brief, to be close to Nancy's family. Our belief at the time was that if this adoption was going to happen, we weren't going to see these people again. Nancy had requested that we exchange letters and photographs, but still nothing had been said by her about any of us ever seeing one another again, despite Carey's open-ended offer for Nancy to expand upon that request. As we understood it, this was a onetime opportunity.

Carey and I were trying to take in everything as we shared this meal with Nancy's family. We discreetly studied each person at the table with us, trying to memorize every detail of how he or she looked, sounded, and behaved. I watched out of the corner of my eye as Carey, the ultimate people watcher, absorbed everything that was happening around us. I knew she wouldn't miss anything, not a word, not a smile or glance. She would remember every facial feature or expression, every item and color of clothing, everything.

It was as if we had to piece together our child's history and ancestry into an indelible profile, all in a moment's time. We wanted to be able to tell our child in detail about this momentous day. We wanted him to know, always, that we not only acknowledged but respected his biological ancestry. We wanted to be able to give him as much information about himself and his birth family as we could. Someday we would tell him about our dinner in the cafeteria with his birth family. He would know that his gentle, soft-spoken step-grandfather wore cowboy boots. He would know that his grandmother was youthful and vibrant and that his aunt was completely devoted to his mother and to him too. We were stockpiling as many memories as we possibly could as quickly and as accurately as we could.

When we got back to the floor after dinner, we felt better. Being with Nancy's family had been inspiring for us. They were such good people, such giving people. They made us feel welcome and appreciated. We resumed our wait with renewed faith and patience. Late in the evening Vickie came out and told us Nancy's labor was progressing rapidly now. She went back to be with her sister.

After all that had happened that day, it felt as if an eternity had passed since Nancy's wake-up call to us. The imminent arrival of the baby didn't seem real now. Our reality was Nancy—hers the face we knew, the heart we loved, our friend in need. It was hard to get beyond that.

Our seats became too confining. We walked, we paced, we walked, we paced, back and forth through the waiting room, around the chairs that were arranged in clusters. Our repeating pattern threatened to wear a track in the carpet. The waiting room became too small to contain our anticipation. We went into the hallway and paced some more.

After twenty hours of labor the baby was born. Vickie emerged from Nancy's labor room and found us in the hallway. "Congratulations," she said, tears in her eyes. "You have a son. He's healthy, and he's beautiful." She gave us each a hug, and we asked her about how Nancy was doing. "She's fine," Vickie assured us, "except she's tired, and she's concerned about how the two of you are doing." Carey told Vickie to kiss Nancy for us and tell her we were absolutely fine and that we were so happy that both she and the baby were doing well.

Vickie went back into the room to be with Nancy. Out in the hallway Carey and I leaned against the stark white wall. We were in shock. Even with the long-awaited arrival of this child, nothing seemed real. Our minds were numb. We looked at each other blankly. "You have a son," Carey said to me in a quiet monotone, as if merely repeating what she had heard. "You have a son too," I responded. The day had been so long and so fraught with ups and downs that we had almost run out of emotion. We stayed in the hall, backs against the wall, overwhelmed and silent.

After about forty-five minutes Nancy was wheeled out of her room. She was pale and looked completely exhausted. A white hospital bedsheet was strapped around her middle, tying her to the back of the wheelchair to prevent her from falling out. The baby was cradled in her arms. As the nurse wheeled Nancy toward us, Nancy asked the nurse to stop by us. Having Nancy so near brought us out of our reverie.

We leaned down and kissed her forehead. Her lips seemed to tremble, and for a few moments she looked bewildered, almost frightened. She invited Carey to look more closely at the baby. As she spoke, she pulled the soft, pastel-striped cap from his head. He had a thick, full head of black hair and a perfect little newborn face. Nancy stroked his hair with her finger. She was clearly proud of him, and she wanted us to see that he was healthy and handsome. More than that, we could see that she loved this child. Being witness to Nancy's emotions as she held him was almost painful. "He's beautiful, Nance," Carey whispered. Suddenly we were overwhelmed with emotion—happiness *and* sadness—and I knew that I wasn't the only one fighting back the tears.

We followed behind Nancy as she was wheeled to the postpartum unit. While the nurses helped Nancy into her bed, we watched through the nursery window as the baby was measured and weighed and placed in a bassinet. He was absolutely beautiful, a perfect little boy. Here he was, at long last, after many years of heartache for us and months of intense emotion for Nancy. Nancy had named him Michael Anthony. He had entered this world at 12:47 A.M., March 31, 1992. He weighed six pounds, eight ounces, and was nineteen and a quarter inches long. He was, in the purest meaning of the word, a miracle.

CHAPTER

12

The hallways of the hospital were nearly empty. It was two A.M., no longer evening and not yet day. The lights of the corridors were dimmed for the long, dark somnolent hours of nighttime. After eighteen hours at the hospital Carey and I were ready to go home. We walked wearily along the dimly lit hallways. Everything felt muted and surreal . . . unrecognizable . . . not of our lives. It was as if we had walked into one building when we arrived the morning before and were leaving a completely different place now, without ever having gone anywhere.

Before leaving we had gone into Nancy's room to tell her good night. Marilou was sitting in a chair at Nancy's side when we walked in. Nancy was barely awake. We stood at the side of her bed and told her we were leaving for the night. "You did so well," Carey told her. "You came through with flying colors. You're amazing."

Nancy turned her head toward us. Her eyes were almost closed, her face was still ashen. "I could feel you with me," she said weakly. "I know it sounds strange. I don't know how, or why, but I could feel that you were there with me in the room. It was like I could feel you rubbing my shoulders, relaxing me. That's how I got through it. You guys were with me." Exhausted, she fell asleep as she finished her sentence. Carey and I looked at each other. Had she been able to sense our focus on her while we sat for hours in the waiting room? Despite her prolonged labor and childbirth, despite the fact that she was pale and drained, she was still stunning to look at. She radiated tranquillity and goodness. It was no wonder the baby was so beautiful. To look at Nancy was to look at an angel.

Carey and I walked slowly through the enormous hospital garage to our car. It was cold out, and very dark. Our footsteps echoed in the cavernous structure. I unlocked the car and we got in and started off on our way back home. We were both completely drained, physically and emotionally. Carey had reached her limit; she cried quietly the whole way home. I was very confused by all that had happened, and sank into a pensive silence as I drove.

By the time we walked in our front door, we were running on empty. Sam was waiting at the back door for us. Our good friend, Kit, had been over to let him out and feed him. He greeted us as if we had been gone for a month. He knew something was up, and followed me like a shadow as I got myself a glass of water in the kitchen. Aggie and Elizabeth came darting out of nowhere and then disappeared again.

Carey and I went upstairs. Our whole room was disheveled from our hasty exit after Nancy's call. We didn't care. The baby had been born. Nancy was safe and healthy; the baby was safe and healthy. That was as far as our thoughts went. We crawled into bed, pulled the covers up, and fell asleep in each other's arms.

I heard the click of Sam's nails against the hardwood floor. He lifted his giant paw and dropped it so that it landed on my arm. I opened my eyes and smiled at him. He was a creature of habit. He kept my routine going even when I didn't. I reached over and scratched his ears. He let out a deep, happy grumble. I followed him downstairs, sent him out the back door, and put on a big pot of strong coffee.

My thoughts went back to everything that had happened. It was like rifling backward and forward through a thick book of photographs. Snapshot images flashed haphazardly in my mind. I remembered Nancy's look of happiness combined with physical discomfort as we first walked into her hospital room . . . the look on the face of Nancy's doctor as he realized who we were . . . the pay phone where I had called our social worker after being told we had to leave Nancy's room. I saw the love and worry on Carey's face as we waited for Nancy to get through her painful labor. I saw her sister walking toward us, hugging us, telling us we had a son, and Nancy in the wheelchair, holding her newborn son . . . the perfect, tiny face and swaddled body of the baby.

Carey slept in that morning. She came down to the kitchen at nine-thirty, and gave me a hug. She looked groggy and very tired. I poured her a cup of coffee in her favorite mug. She sat down at the kitchen table and cradled her cup in her hands.

"This day is going to be even worse than yesterday," she said, looking down at the table. "It's going to be horrible, horrible . . . excruciating. Poor Nancy. That baby is so beautiful. I don't know how she's even going to think about the next step in this process. Her heart is going to be torn apart." She took a sip of her coffee and looked over at me. "I don't even want to think about it, but we have to. And poor Nancy has to be thinking about how she's going to say good-bye to that tiny little boy and survive it. He's a part of her. How can anyone be expected to say good-bye to a living, breathing part of themselves? How can it be done?"

I had no answer. I knew Carey was right. It wasn't going to be easy. I was worried about Nancy too.

Carey sat very quietly. I knew she needed the peace of silence. I sat across the kitchen table from her and scratched Sam's head while I drank my coffee. After a few minutes Carey got up and went to the phone. I listened as she called her office. I could tell that she was too tired to go into any kind of detail with anyone. She simply said that there was a lot going on and she would keep them posted.

When she was done, I phoned my office. To my surprise I was as reticent as Carey was. There was just too much happening to try to explain it to anyone else. I found myself promising, as Carey had, to keep everyone posted.

We decided we should phone selected family members and our closest friends to update them. We decided we had to stay current with someone, or we would ultimately face the daunting task of telling the whole story in retrospect. We gave them a thumbnail sketch of what had transpired the evening before and gave them each the same promise of future updates.

We were still operating in automatic-pilot mode, putting one foot in front of the next just to keep ourselves going. Somewhere out there in the real world, for everyone else but us it seemed, it was life as usual. Inside our little microcosm nothing was usual, nothing was familiar, nothing felt real. To keep up some kind of momentum, we focused on planning the day.

Our first priority was to see Nancy. After our experience the day before, however, we weren't sure whether we would be allowed to visit her. We also knew that she might need some time and space to herself. We didn't think it would be fair to her for us to phone her directly and put her on the spot. Carey called our social worker to get her input. She said she would call Nancy and act as an intermediary so that Nancy wouldn't feel pressured in any way. A few minutes later the phone rang, and she said Nancy was eager to see us.

That was all we needed to hear. We pulled ourselves together. We got showered and dressed and prepared for departure as quickly as we could. Just as we were getting ready to walk out the door, I stopped. Suddenly I felt empty-handed and awkward.

"Don't you think we should bring her something?" I asked Carey. "I mean, she just had a baby, and she's in the hospital. Don't you think we ought to bring something to her? A gift of some kind?" Carey thought for a moment and then agreed. The question then was what to bring her. It was a diplomatically diffi-cult decision to make. We didn't want to bring her anything inap-propriate, anything that anyone could misconstrue in any way. A personal gift for Nancy was out of the question, Carey deter-mined, because it could be interpreted by the skeptics at the hospital as being mercenary. A gift for the baby seemed not quite appropriate either. We debated giving her the Saint Nicholas me-dallion, but Carey still felt we should wait until later, until the dust had settled.

We settled on flowers. Roses. A dozen long-stem red roses. Not pink, not yellow, Carey decided, but red. Red because we loved Nancy. And, Carey added, absolutely no baby's breath in the bou-quet.

We left the house and headed for the hospital around noon. On our way through the city we stopped at our favorite florist. Carey waited in the car while I went inside and bought a dozen fragrant, long-stem red roses for Nancy. They were really exquisite, per-fectly formed flowers. They were arranged in a tall vase. I was pleased with our choice.

When I got back in the car, Carey turned to me. "I was sitting here thinking while you bought the flowers," she said.

"And?"

"And it occurred to me that I bought this car when we decided to quit the infertility routine. This car was my indulgence, my commitment to accepting my fate as a childless woman."

"And?"

"And here I am, sitting in this car on my way to the hospital to see the baby who might be my child. It's all very strange."

"It is," I agreed.

"And I've been thinking about the fact that Nancy has named him Michael Anthony. And the fact that David is our first choice for his name, and Michael is our second. I've been wondering what the right thing to do is . . . whether he should be called Michael or David if he becomes our son."

"And?"

"And I spent a few minutes going back and forth. First I thought he should be Michael. That's what Nancy named him, and that's one of the names we really like. He's Nancy's son, too, no matter what. So then I thought, he should be Michael Anthony. Then I thought, no, he should be David, because that's the name I've always wanted for my son should I ever have one. Michael. David. Which? Should he be Michael David? David Michael? Or David Evan, as you and I had planned?"

"And what did you decide?"

"If we bring this child home, if he becomes our son, then we'll call him David Evan," she said softly but with conviction.

I reached over and squeezed her hand. "Okay," I told her. "If he comes home to us, he'll be our David Evan."

When we arrived on the floor at the hospital, Carey and I marched up to the nurses' station. This time we didn't identify ourselves or explain anything. "We're here to see Nancy Miller" was as much as we told them. Ignorance is bliss. They told us to go right in to see her.

Nancy and her mother were in Nancy's room when we walked in. We hugged them both and gave Nancy the roses. She began to cry as she took them in her hands and thanked us. She turned and put the vase on the windowsill that was next to her bed. Carey gave her a tissue, and she dried her tears.

The baby was in a bassinet next to Nancy's bed. Marilou sat in the visitor's chair holding a camera. We could see that she must have been taking pictures of Nancy and the baby before we came in. The room was quiet. There was an overwhelming sense of pain, sadness, and discomfort in the room. Carey and I walked over and looked down at the baby. We could feel ourselves thinking the same thing: When we had walked into the room, we had walked into *something*. Carey and I looked at each other. Our faces registered the same thing: Something wasn't right.

Before we had time to talk to Marilou and Nancy, a woman walked into the room. She was carrying a large gift basket for Nancy. It turned out that she was one of Nancy's teachers from school. When she saw Carey and me in the room, and we were identified by Nancy, the woman looked less than pleased. Again, it seemed that to those on the outside looking in we weren't a legitimate part of what was happening. The cold, sinking feeling we had lived with yesterday began to creep its way in again. The woman handed the basket to Nancy and showed her what it contained. She pulled out the city newspaper that was printed the day the baby had been born. She left shortly afterward.

Nancy took control of the situation as soon as the woman left. She told us she was still committed to the adoption and still wanted to keep it semiprivate by having occasional phone calls, letters, and annual photographs. Carey and I told her we would handle it however she wanted to and needed to. "Your needs and the baby's needs are so important to us, Nancy," Carey reminded her. "I can't stress that enough. We're listening to you, waiting to see what you need from us. If it's time and space, you've got it. If it's something else, please just tell us." We reminded her again that we were there to support her, that she should always remember she came first with us.

Nancy reached over to the nightstand next to her bed. She opened the drawer and pulled out an envelope. She handed it to me and told us to read it. It was a letter she had written for her child. She requested that we please give the letter to him when he turned eighteen, or if not then, whenever we thought he was ready. As Carey and I stood together and read the handwritten letter, our eyes filled with tears. It was so open, and so honest, and filled with so much love that we felt as if our hearts were torn wide open by its contents.

Nancy watched us as we read the letter. She seemed to take solace in the immediacy of our reaction. It was as though she now knew for sure that we understood her pain and that we were in fact participating in it from where we stood. When we were finished with the letter, Nancy asked to have it back because, she said, she wanted to rewrite it on some nice stationery. She wanted her son to know that she had written it with love and respect for him.

The memory of the pain and impending loss that hung over those of us in the room will never fade. No one had to say a word about it. It was as if we were all thinking, talking and moving in slow motion. From the distance of time we had anticipated this birth as a time of the fullest joy and most festive celebration. Instead we were witnessing the demise of a mother, a grandmother, and a child. Our hearts were breaking: Nancy's, Marilou's, Carey's, and mine. Not one of us was spared.

The room was perfectly quiet. The baby broke the uncomfortable silence with a newborn cry. Marilou instantly jumped from her seat and picked him up. She turned to Carey. "Here, why don't you hold him?" She held the baby out toward Carey. "Here, go ahead." She seemed to be trying to take control of the situation. We could see that her eyes were red and that she had been crying. Carey took the baby in her arms. She cradled him and rocked him very gently. He stopped fussing immediately.

I stood close beside Carey and looked down at the baby. We had been told by our social worker that Nancy had explicitly said that she needed to see the three of us together—the baby, Carey, and myself—in order to bring closure to her decision. This was part of her plan. She needed to see her baby with us, together as a family. She had been able to imagine the scene after choosing us as her child's adoptive parents. Now she needed to literally see the family we formed together. She wanted that mental image to carry with her always.

As I stood with Carey, looking down at the baby, I wondered if this was really going to be enough. I looked sideways at Carey and knew from the expression on her face that she was really struggling. I knew in fact what Carey was thinking: *He's Nancy's baby.* The strength of the bond between Nancy and her child was so evident, so undeniable. We felt like visitors holding a friend's baby, not like parents holding their own child. There was a chasm in the flow of emotion that we had anticipated. Where was the immediate bond between us and this child? Months later Carey would tell me that at this moment she wanted to bring the baby over to Nancy, put him in her arms, and say, "He belongs with you, Nancy. Hold him, keep him. It's all right." It was what felt most right at the time.

To stand there—the three of us—felt nearly inconsequential, and very incomplete. I looked over at Nancy. She was mesmerized, watching the three of us closely. She smiled warmly at me when I looked at her. I saw the intensity of emotion that was in her heart as I looked in her eyes. She was working very hard at being in charge of her emotions. She was a very strong person, and she was tapping into her own strength while carefully orchestrating the way things were happening.

It was clear that she wanted to see that things were done the right way. The right way, in her mind, was to have the three of us together, calm and ready to work our way through life. Suddenly it hit me: The neat little image made up of Carey, the baby, and me was in no way enough, in no way complete or resolved.

I couldn't fathom walking out of that hospital with this baby in our arms and watching Nancy fade from our view, never to be seen again. I couldn't fathom our connection with her being so short and so intense and so passing. I couldn't imagine her never seeing, hearing, or touching her child again. In order for the picture to be complete, I thought, it had to include Nancy in some way. She was part of this family. The picture of our future had to include her somehow. If it didn't, it was going to feel like we had all experienced the death of a relative. There would be a permanent and very painful void, not just for Nancy but for this child, and for all of us.

And, I thought to myself, I'm usually the last person to understand things of this emotional magnitude. I knew without even asking Carey that she must be feeling and thinking the same thing. She had probably realized it long before I had, in her usual insightful way.

I looked back down at the baby. He was precious. Swaddled tightly in a flannel blanket, he looked like a cocoon with a sweet little face. Tufts of dark hair stuck out from under the soft cap he wore. He had the serenity only newborns can have. I thought about all the years he had ahead of him and how at this moment in time, as Carey cradled him, he was the six-pound center of the universe for all of us in the room.

I could see that Carey was caught between doing what was expected, what was appropriate, and what came naturally. She didn't cry, she didn't smile. She held him and studied him intently. She turned to me and asked me if I wanted to hold him. I had never held a baby before. I was very unsure of how it was supposed to be done. He looked so small and so fragile. But Carey put him right in my arms before I could react. I held him as best I knew how. Carey looked at me and smiled. "You can bend your arms, you know," she said. I got flustered and handed the baby back to Carey. "Why don't I go and get some coffee for us?" I offered. I left and headed for the cafeteria.

While I was in the cafeteria, Carey later told me, things in the room had continued to be strained. Marilou was continually wiping tears from her eyes. Nancy sat in bed, watching her mother, a look of growing impatience—directed toward her mother—on her face. David began to fuss, and Marilou told Carey to sit down with him and feed him his bottle. Carey, totally at ease with newborns, fed him.

When he was done, she held him and looked at him. As she gazed down at his tiny face, she spoke quietly to him. "What a handsome little boy you are . . . yes, you are. You're so special,

you know that? What a big boy you're going to grow up to be."
When she looked up, Nancy and Marilou were both crying. Carey
was taken by surprise, and her emotions, too, were caught off
guard. She began to cry as she laid David back down in the
bassinet.

Marilou was crying hard, grabbing tissues from the box on the
nightstand, wiping away her tears. "This is just so hard," she
sobbed. "He's so beautiful, just so beautiful. This is so hard. It's
just . . . so . . . hard."

"I'm so sorry," Carey answered, completely distraught.

Marilou continued to cry. "This is so hard, just so much harder
than we ever thought. He's such a beautiful baby." She cried
even harder.

Nancy was crying, too, quietly wiping her eyes and sniffing.
Carey looked over at Nancy, but Nancy was watching her mother
with an expression of annoyance. Carey didn't know what to do. It
seemed that there was something personal going on between
Nancy and her mother. Marilou seemed lost in her own feelings
for the moment. She continued to cry, repeating over and over,
"This is so hard, this is just so hard."

Carey watched Marilou. She was obviously overwhelmed with
emotional pain and fear, and at the same time her love for Nancy
and this baby was powerfully evident. Carey thought carefully and
quickly about what was happening. She watched as Marilou continued sobbing. Then it clicked. She remembered. Marilou had
given a child up for adoption years ago, when she was Nancy's
age. It all suddenly made complete sense. Marilou was reliving
the anguish she had gone through herself those many years ago.
She couldn't bear to see Nancy enduring the same kind of heartbreak, and she couldn't bear the thought of losing a grandchild
after having lost a child.

Nancy, still crying silently, looked over at her mother. Her expression changed from annoyance to sharp displeasure mixed with
outright anger. She was clearly very agitated. "I don't need this
right now," she said strongly. Marilou kept crying. Carey, over-

whelmed by the emotions of Nancy and her mother, fought to keep from falling apart herself. She was soon standing next to Nancy, sobbing. The baby was the only one who wasn't crying.

Finally Marilou realized that the three of them were sinking fast. She took a few deep breaths and turned to Nancy and Carey. "*Breathe*, girls!" she said with maternal love and authority, looking straight at Nancy and Carey and making upward sweeping motions with her hands. "Inhale! *Breathe!* Take deep breaths! Breathe!"

I walked in the door to Nancy's room, coffee in hand. The three of them were crying hard, grabbing for tissues. All those emotions each of us thought we could compartmentalize and minimize had exploded. The dam had burst. Pain, anguish, and confusion were everywhere. I looked to Carey, and before I could ask her what was wrong, she held her hand up as if to stop me and said, "This is really difficult, Dion. This isn't easy for anybody."

Nancy, still in tears, looked directly at Carey and me. "I'm so sorry! I'm so sorry, you guys, I'm so sorry about this," she sobbed. We told her, "It's okay, don't worry." Our words washed right over her, and she kept telling us she was sorry, so sorry . . . and we kept responding, "It's okay, Nancy . . . please, don't worry . . . everything's fine, everything's going to be okay."

We could see that right now nothing was being resolved by us being there. Our presence was only adding to the turmoil of Nancy and her mother. I told Carey I thought we should leave and she said she agreed. When I told Nancy that Carey and I were going to leave, she said she thought it was probably best that we did. She continued to apologize over and over again. "It's okay, Nancy," Carey tried to reassure her. "Don't worry, it's okay. We'll talk with you soon. . . . It's okay. . . ."

Carey held Nancy's hand and leaned down so that she could speak quietly to Nancy. Carey instinctively knew what lay ahead. "Someone is going to leave this hospital with a broken heart," she told Nancy. "Dion and I would survive that broken heart, because we have each other. But I'm not sure how you'd survive. So if you change your mind, it's okay; it's truly okay."

We kissed Nancy good-bye and told Marilou that we were going to leave. Marilou walked with us to the elevator. She had stopped crying, but she was still visibly upset. I took her hand. "Nancy is our first priority," I told her. "We will stand by her no matter what she decides. I mean that, Marilou. If she wants to keep her baby, we'll support her decision. She has to do what she feels is right. It's that simple."

Marilou's eyes filled with tears again. "You guys are really special." She hugged me. "I love you."

"Listen, Marilou. Please don't worry. The worst-case scenario in all this is that someone is going to take this little guy home and love him with all their heart. So there *is no* worst-case scenario for this baby. Okay?"

"Okay," Marilou answered with a hint of relief in her voice. "Thank you."

The elevator doors opened. We hugged Marilou quickly and stepped inside.

CHAPTER

13

We were back at our house within the hour. Our homecoming felt like a crash landing. Carey had been more than right that morning when she predicted that the day was going to be horrible. Our visit with Nancy had been saturated with pain and a sense of loss. Marilou was overcome with fear and pain. The memories of the child she had given up years ago had come back with irrefutable force. The thought of losing another child—her grandchild—was too much for her.

Nancy was being pulled in all directions. She knew what she needed to do to carry out her decision, yet underneath it all, her heart was breaking. The truth was we had all underestimated the emotions that would be at the center of this adoption. Every one of us could clearly feel the heartache that accompanied the thought of separating Nancy from her baby.

Despite the conviction with which Nancy had made her decision to give her baby to us, Carey and I both believed that she was going to change her mind and keep her baby. Marilou was clearly pushing Nancy in that direction. Nancy and her mother were extremely close to each other, and it would go strongly against Nancy's sense of loyalty to her mother to defy her wishes. Moreover she was struggling with her own attachment to her child. We believed that between her bond with her mother and her maternal instincts, she was in the midst of an emotional battle like no other.

If she chose to keep her baby, it would not have come as a surprise to us. In fact we had been so profoundly affected by the birth of the baby and the pain we had witnessed in Marilou and Nancy that we now felt Nancy *should* keep the baby. The extent to which Nancy would suffer in giving up her baby was clear to us. No one could have wished such suffering on another human being.

It was not that we didn't desperately want or love this baby as our own; we did. But something equally powerful was unfolding before our eyes: the power of a birth mother's love and attachment to her child. We had been prepared by our work with the Adoption Network and the adoption agency for these dynamics. But when it was happening with Nancy and her son—or our son— it suddenly became larger than life.

We knew we should begin to prepare ourselves for the possibility that the baby was not going to come home with us. It wasn't as hard as we might have once predicted. It had become the lesser of two evils. What was harder was knowing the pain Nancy would live with if she gave her baby up. Her inevitable pain was something we weren't sure *we* could live with.

Our thoughts and emotions went around and around in circles, becoming increasingly blurry and overlapping. Yes, we desperately wanted to become parents. But not at this kind of emotional cost to someone else. Moreover the baby was still the biggest unknown to us. We were attached to the idea of being parents; but the reality was that we were not yet attached to this tiny little individual. We had barely held him yet. Our exposure and connection to him was a drop in the bucket compared with Nancy's. We respected her relationship to her child. And although we never verbalized it to each other, we felt that if this adoption was not meant to happen, then maybe another one *was*. It was all so confusing and exhausting.

The phone was ringing as we came in our front door. I picked it up immediately, thinking it was going to be news of some sort about Nancy and the baby. Instead it was my police chief ordering me to come in to work. The coroner, I was told, was looking for the report on the fatality that had happened the night before the baby was born. The birth had pushed the horrible accident out of my thoughts. It wasn't something I wanted to remember now. Things were tense enough as it was; I didn't relish the thought of confronting another emotionally charged situation. Both Carey and I had enough to deal with as it was. Together it felt like we were barely holding up under the strain. The last thing I wanted to do was leave Carey by herself right now, let alone to reexamine the sad details of someone's death. Still, duty called, so I told the chief I would come in and take care of business.

The red message light on our answering machine was blinking. We played back the messages that had accumulated while we were visiting Nancy. There was a message from one of our neighbors telling us they had accepted a delivery for us. Carey ran across the street to pick it up. I watched out the window as she came back toward our house carrying a huge arrangement of blue and white flowers and balloons. As she headed down the sidewalk, I saw her stop and turn around. From behind her came some other neighbors waving their hands in excitement, signaling for her to wait for them. I watched as Carey talked with them, all the while holding the enormous flower arrangement. I could tell by the way she shifted her weight from one foot to the other and glanced over toward our house that she was impatient to move on.

When she got in our front door she let out a groan of irritation. "Look, this is what the delivery was," she said, holding up the flowers. "Then the neighbors accosted me on the way back."

"I watched through the window. What did they want?"

"What do you think they wanted? They saw these flowers and drew their own conclusions. They assumed we already had a baby boy here at home, and they wanted all the details." She was looking frantically around the living room as she spoke.

"What are you looking for?" I asked her.

"Someplace to hide these flowers. I don't want anyone else to see them. I can't deal with another situation like that. I can't explain it all to anyone else."

"Who are they from, anyway?"

She told me they were from some close friends of ours who lived in Connecticut. They were our age, but already had six children. They had been a source of sincere support and encouragement as we worked toward becoming parents ourselves. As the adoption had unfolded, we had been in close touch with them. They had been really excited for us and had waited anxiously for each update. Unfortunately the last update had been immediately following the baby's birth, before things had started looking more complicated.

"Obviously," Carey said, "they had no way of knowing the direction things took this morning." She showed me the card that was attached to a giant blue bow. "A baby boy! Congratulations!" it said in big blue letters. Carey cringed. "The flowers are beautiful, and I don't want them to go to waste, but . . ." She wandered into the dining room and put them on the table. "No one will see them here except us," she said.

I asked Carey if she would be all right by herself while I went to the station. I was worried that it would be difficult for her to be alone at this time, especially if there were any significant developments.

"I'll be fine," she assured me in her calmest voice. "You do what you have to do. I'll keep busy, and I'll let you know if anything happens."

Before I left for the station, we decided we should phone our social worker, Nan Lahr. She took our call right away. She had already heard from Nancy's social worker, Kate, and had an idea of what had happened. We described our impressions of what was going on. The anguish Nancy and Marilou were experiencing was obvious, we said, and we felt certain Nancy was going to keep the baby. She confirmed what we already knew: Marilou was pushing hard for Nancy to keep the baby. Nan Lahr told us that Kate was on the way to the hospital to see Nancy.

I drove to the police station and hurried inside to the squad room to file my report. To my relief the room was empty; no one to distract me with questions about the baby. I pulled out the report form and sat down at a typewriter. I began to type in the sequence of events and the times they had occurred. As soon as I began, the memories of that awful night came rushing back, and I had to stop and let my mind sift and sort through it before continuing with the report.

I remembered the man's lifeless body, and my talk with the man's wife . . . the hollow look of grief on her face. I looked down at my hands and thought about how I had rolled the man's body, only to hear the nauseating sound of crunched bone. Not twenty-four hours later, I realized, I had held a delicate bundle of fresh, new life and then witnessed an impending loss as Nancy prepared to say good-bye to her child.

My chief walked into the room as I sat typing. He and I had known each other for years. I had been open with him about our hopes to adopt a child and he had shared in our excitement when we were chosen by Nancy. He knew that things were under way, but because I had left no details when I phoned in, he didn't know exactly where things currently stood.

I sat in front of the typewriter, my fingers still resting on the keyboard, and told him that I was going to need to take some sick days, and I gave him a very brief and simplified explanation of what had happened. His response was cold and businesslike. He told me that I could use vacation time, but not sick leave, because it wasn't a member of my family who was in the hospital.

My every nerve was irritated and raw by now. His reaction was not the one I wanted to hear after everything that Carey and I had been through. Nancy was very much a part of our family, whether or not the baby became our son. To be told that it was inappropriate for me to take sick leave because it wasn't one of my family who was in the hospital was outrageous, and I told him so. Without reserve, in no uncertain terms, I told him that it was indeed my family—my son and his birth mother—who were in the hospital. Moreover, I told him, if I couldn't base my sick leave on their hospitalization, I could certainly base it on the fact that I was by now so exhausted and run down, and emotionally depleted, that I was on the brink of collapse. If that didn't merit a sick leave, I asked, then what did?

In eleven years on the force, I said, I had only used thirteen sick days. I prided myself on my attendance record and my job performance. It took a lot for me to call in sick. If ever I felt the need for time off for health reasons, this was it. At stake was not only my health but the health of Carey, Nancy, Marilou, and the baby. I stood up angrily and turned to him with defiance.

He took one look at my face and his expression changed from anger to real concern. When he spoke, his voice had a paternal compassion in it. He asked me, simply and forthrightly, "Dion, are you okay?"

I tried to answer him. I tried to tell him what had happened at the hospital that morning. Before I knew what was happening, my eyes filled with tears. I tried to regain my composure. Instead I lost it entirely. I started crying like a child, sobbing, unable to get enough air in my lungs to talk coherently. Without hesitation my chief stepped toward me and hugged me. "Don't worry about it," he said. "Consider yourself on official sick leave. Don't bother counting the days. Go home and take care of your wife and yourself. Do what you need to do for Nancy and that little baby. Those are the people who really need you. Forget about work."

He told me to give him all the information about the accident and said he would personally file the report for me so that I could go home. What could have been two to three hours of work for me ended up taking me less than an hour. He gave me his home telephone number and told me to call him anytime of the day or night if he could do anything at all to help us. Until then or until everything was settled, he said, he didn't want to hear from me. I thanked him for his support and sympathy, and left for home.

As I drove, I thought about what had happened in that squad room. I had been sitting at the typewriter, ready to confront my memories of a gruesome death and instead ended up confronting my own feelings. What was more amazing to me was that for the first time, someone outside of the situation appeared to truly grasp the magnitude of what we were going through. I was completely astounded as I thought about how my chief had had the tact, and the humility, to do a complete turnaround in his reaction to me and my situation.

It occurred to me that no one could possibly comprehend exactly what Carey and I were going through, or even more so what Nancy was going through. No one could understand the relationship that already existed between us and Nancy and the baby. There was no way someone on the outside could recognize what had evolved between us.

And now, as the weeks, months, and years have passed, I've realized that unless someone has been through a very similar situation, or has taken the time to get to know us, they are never going to be able to accurately see what we were all about. There are, however, those rare magnanimous people who can push aside all this and just give us the benefit of the doubt and the generosity of their spirit.

When I got home from the station, Carey was putting groceries away. The entire kitchen table was covered with brown grocery bags filled with food. "I went out to the store to pass the time. I wanted to go someplace where I could be anonymous," she said. "I didn't want to have to talk to anyone I knew." She put a carton of milk in the refrigerator. "I managed to get through the whole store without having to talk to anyone but the person at the register. The only bad part was the baby section. I flew past that aisle."

Carey filled the fruit bowl with bananas, apples, kiwis, and pears. "I took my time shopping," she told me. "It felt good to be away from things, to be able to just sort of zone out. The only problem is, we're going to have to eat like horses to finish all this food I bought." I laughed. These moments of lightness were becoming fewer and farther between. We were beginning to realize we had to leverage them for all they were worth.

Simultaneously Carey and I began to speak, then stopped. "You go ahead," Carey said.

"No, no, that's okay. It's nothing. You go ahead."

"I was just going to say, I wish we would hear something. I don't know what to think when we hear nothing. I wonder how Nancy's doing. I'm so worried about her. I have this uneasy feeling that she's really not doing very well right now."

From the moment they had met, Carey and Nancy had had an almost telepathic connection. Often, when Carey phoned Nancy, it turned out that Nancy had been just about to call Carey. And Carey seemed to know just when Nancy needed to talk, whether it was about boyfriend troubles or about how she happened to be feeling on a particular day.

In fact the three of us had had some strange, almost eerie connections. When we first met Nancy, she told us that she and her mother had had recurring dreams about Carey and myself. Upon meeting us, she said, we were exactly as they had both dreamed of us—from our mannerisms to the things we said, to our thoughts and ideas, to the sound of our voices. It was later that we came to realize that Nancy had been reading our autobiographical profile at the agency at the same hour on the same day that I had opened the mutual-fund account for the child we hoped someday to adopt.

The coincidences and connections we discovered were at times so extraordinary that we were hesitant to mention them to other people for fear of sounding a bit off our rockers. What mattered was that among ourselves we recognized these things to be serendipitous, and we appreciated them as indications that this was all meant to transpire.

"What were *you* going to say?" Carey asked me after she had expressed her worry about Nancy.

"Something along the same line, I guess. I was going to tell you that I wish we would hear something from somebody."

Carey's instincts about Nancy had turned out to be right repeatedly. So her concern right now unnerved me. Unfortunately things were out of our hands, and our only choice was to wait. Carey had checked the message machine when she came in, hoping for updates. There was nothing from Nancy or any of the social workers, just call after call from our friends and family. It was all we could do to keep ourselves from phoning Nancy in her hospital room; but we knew we had to give her some time and space.

The minutes crept by. We decided we ought to return some of the phone calls from our friends and family. Carey phoned her family first, then I phoned mine. We were up front with all of them. They deserved to know everything.

Later our social worker, Nan, phoned us again. Her voice was calm and steady. She told us that there was a lot happening, and it was important for us to listen closely and then let our emotions sift out.

Nancy's social worker, Kate, had gone to the hospital to talk with her. Kate reported that Nancy was struggling heroically to sort things out. She had asked Kate to tell us she was sorry that she hadn't been able to talk with us more that morning.

The doctors had diagnosed Nancy with severe postpartum depression. Marilou was, as she herself had told us that morning, having a very difficult time with the adoption. She wanted her daughter to keep the baby. Nancy was caught somewhere in the middle. Because of her postpartum depression, Nan Lahr told us, immediate surrender was inappropriate. Because of her confusion and her mother's feelings, Nancy had decided not to sign the permanent-surrender papers right away. Instead of signing them three days after the baby's birth, she had decided to postpone signing them for several weeks. She wanted reassurance from us, however, that we would still serve as the baby's foster parents.

We listened carefully to all that Nan was saying. It was a lot to digest, and it was hard to keep ourselves from trying to interpret each piece of information or ask for more.

"You need to consider, carefully, *very* carefully, whether or not you want to assume the risk involved in becoming foster parents," she told us. "You need to be realistic with yourselves and recognize that there is a very high emotional risk factor." Step by step she walked us through the various scenarios. She reminded us that if Nancy maintained her decision to place the baby with us, we would serve as foster parents until she signed the permanent surrender. If she changed her mind and decided to keep the baby, then the baby could be removed from our care immediately at any point in time, and we would have no recourse.

"Take some time to think about it. Talk about it with each other," she told us. "If either of you feels it would be too hard to care for him and then have to say good-bye, then you probably shouldn't do the fostering. This might turn out to be simple foster care—not foster-to-adopt." We told her we would call her back sometime that afternoon.

We sat down on the living room couch together to talk as Nancy had suggested. Our heads and hearts were swimming. There was so much to think about. Nancy's decision to postpone signing the permanent-surrender papers didn't surprise us in the least. Our emotions were so synchronized to Nancy's that we were actually relieved to hear that she had decided to give herself time to sort through her feelings and make her decision accordingly.

During our discussion the phone continued to ring regularly. We let the machine take it and picked up on any calls that were important to us. We spoke to a few friends and our mothers when their calls came in. We told them the latest news. Everyone seemed to have the same reaction: "What if she changes her mind and decides to keep the baby? What if you grow attached to him only to have to let go of him? What if everything backfires and you're left with nothing?" We tried to make them see it our way: Whatever the risk, we were going to do our best to be supportive of Nancy and this baby as we went through the twists and turns of this confusing, complicated journey.

Everything about our adoption had started out so beautifully, so easily. Nancy had come into our lives when we least expected it. There was a magic between us that was immediate and seemed predestined. We felt connected somehow. Our openness had dictated itself. It seemed impossible that this special relationship should come to an end so quickly. We couldn't imagine losing Nancy from our lives.

It alarmed us to hear that she was suffering from postpartum depression. Now, we said to each other, we knew Carey had been right: Nancy was indeed having an extremely hard time.

"Nancy's postpartum depression really has me worrying about her," Carey said. "Nancy is going through enough without having to do this kind of battle too."

I agreed with her. We hadn't picked up on it when we saw her; we had just taken her reticence for exhaustion. The diagnosis sounded serious to us, and we were very worried about her. We wanted only the best for her.

"I understand what the social workers are trying to do," Carey said with a sigh. I could hear her exhaustion in her voice. "I know they always have to remind us of the possible downside of each scenario. But let's just step back a minute. We could go back and forth forever on this decision. Protect ourselves or help Nancy— that's what it boils down to. Let's just step back and stop agonizing over this."

She lay down on the couch and tucked a pillow under her head. Carey's fatigue kept her voice low and quiet. "First of all, we agreed that we were going to enter adoption as we would a pregnancy. We agreed that in deciding to pursue adoption, we had to be ready and willing to face anything that happens along the way. And as far as that goes, every pregnancy carries the risk of loss as well. So we can't let that determine our course of action." She took a deep breath and then continued.

"But more important than that, Nancy is fighting too many battles as it is. Let's not give her something more to struggle with. We promised her we would foster the baby. We morally obligated ourselves to her, and there's not one good reason to refuse to meet our obligation. If the adoption falls through, it will fall through whether or not we foster this baby. We'll have to deal with it either way. Think of it this way too: If it doesn't fall through, and someone else does the fostering, won't we feel sad and sorry that we missed out on that time with the baby, and that we missed providing that security and comfort to Nancy? The bottom line is this: Nancy needs us, and let's face it, this baby needs us, even if it's only in a fostering capacity. They're both practically family to us. Let's not let the two of them down."

"Okay," I said, nodding. "Then our decision is made. We made a promise to Nancy that we would serve as foster parents for the baby. It's a promise we'll keep."

CHAPTER

14

Somehow we got through the rest of that day. We talked with Nan Lahr and gave her our verbal agreement to do the fostering of the baby. She passed our message along to Nancy. It helped us to think that Nancy now knew we were going to stand by our commitment to her. We hoped it would give her at least a little relief, and we hoped she would see that our loyalty to her and our love for her were unconditional.

We went to bed that night totally wiped out, both physically and psychologically, having no idea what the next day would bring. When we woke up, it was to a gray sky; it seemed to predict the worst. We moved slowly in our continued exhaustion. The first order of business for the day was to clear ourselves of any outside obligations. Carey phoned her office and told her staff not to expect her in until they heard otherwise.

I phoned Nan Lahr to check in for any news she might have. She advised us strongly that we not go to the hospital again.

"Things haven't settled down yet," she told us. "It's probably best if you stay clear of Nancy for the time being." She was a bit vague about what was happening, and we were too tired to push for details that weren't forthcoming. The phone call was short and to the point.

We took what she said to mean that Marilou's efforts to persuade Nancy to keep the baby were probably taking effect. That in and of itself didn't really bother us. What bothered us was that we were so closed out of what Nancy was doing and feeling. We felt lost and helpless, and we had no idea how things were going to turn out. We disliked the fact that we were unable to be of any support to Nancy when she was in real need. Our hearts ached for her. We felt as if our wheels were spinning.

We had no idea when the next "development" would take place, or when we would hear anything. Carey went to work in the kitchen methodically straightening the already neat cabinets. When that was done, she moved on to baking. The smell of chocolate chip cookies and brewing cappuccino wafted out to me where I lay resting on the living room couch.

The hours passed slowly. I stayed on the couch, too tired and drained to do anything else. In the early afternoon I decided I should go in to work for a short time to finish up some paperwork. While I was there, Carey's uncontrolled productivity continued. She began doing laundry at a great rate. She stormed around the house, finding anything that needed laundering. In addition to all our dirty clothes, every towel, curtain, and throw rug was dragged to its fate in the washing machine.

At three o'clock in the afternoon the phone rang. By now Carey and I were highly sensitized to the ring of the phone. It was the only link we had to Nancy. When the phone rang, it was like a fire alarm going off. Carey picked it up on the first ring, knowing it could be the deciding call.

"Carey, hi, it's Nan Lahr."

Carey tried to remain calm. "Nan, hi. What's going on?"

"Well, a lot's happening really. I'm calling to tell you that Nancy has been released from the hospital."

"You're kidding. Nancy's left the hospital already?" Carey was stunned.

"No, I'm not kidding. She left a short time ago. Before she left, she signed temporary custody of the baby over to the agency," she answered.

It seemed impossible that all of this had happened without us knowing about it. The close communication we had nurtured and enjoyed with Nancy was gone. Suddenly we were the last to know. The bureaucracy was creeping back in, and with it came an increasing feeling of isolation and estrangement from Nancy.

Carey was shell-shocked. Before Nan Lahr could continue talking, Carey stopped her. "Is Nancy all right?" she asked.

"I'd say she's as good as can be expected."

"What happens now?" Carey asked.

"Nancy wants to make sure that you two, as his foster parents, will go down to the hospital and visit the baby until he's released. She said she doesn't want him to feel alone."

"Of course we'll visit him. When should we go?"

"Within the next few hours would be ideal."

"Okay, that's what we'll do. I'll phone Dion. He's at work."

Carey called me and said she was extremely upset by the news of Nancy's departure from the hospital and her signing of the temporary surrender. "I have this image of Nancy signing her name on a sheet of paper, slowly spelling out the letters of her name, knowing that as she writes, she's only moments away from giving her child over to someone else. It just breaks my heart." It was more than Carey could stand. She was crying as she repeated the conversation she had had with Nan Lahr. I tried to calm her down, but she was devastated by the fact that Nancy had already partially severed her ties with her son. Carey felt Nancy's pain as if it were her own. I told Carey I would head home immediately.

While she was waiting for me to get home, Carey phoned my mother. She needed to talk to someone. In tears she told her that

Nancy had signed the temporary surrender. My mother, thinking this was what we had been hoping for, gleefully responded, "That's wonderful news!"

"No, it's not! It's not wonderful at all!" Carey tried to explain the reality of the situation, that Nancy was having her heart torn out and so were we. My mother had a hard time seeing the tragedy of the situation, as would most people who were not in the middle of it.

Carey tried to reach her own mother on the phone. Thinking she could talk this through with her, and that she would understand her feelings, Carey reiterated what had happened. Her mother had an almost identical reaction to my mother's. Again, Carey was completely distraught. Naively we didn't see that from the outside it looked as if this adoption was going as it should. Anyone on the outside looking in simply couldn't see the emotional devastation that was running rampant with each step of perceived "progress."

When I walked through the front door, Carey was sitting in the large easy chair in the living room, tears running down her face. "I can't believe it," she sobbed. "People think this is a good thing that has happened. How can they think that? Nancy's heart is broken. She said good-bye to her son today. That's not good, that's horrible. I can't even imagine how she's functioning right now."

I went to where she sat and hugged her. "I know," I told her. "It's about as sad as anything can be. I know exactly what you mean. But remember, hon, that they don't know Nancy. To them it probably looks like our dream is coming true. They don't see the downside." My words had no effect on her. "Let's go to the hospital now so that we can at least visit the baby," I told her. "We need to do that much for Nancy and the baby."

Carey agreed. We wasted no time. We pulled on our coats and jumped in the car. As we drove we talked. We couldn't believe Nancy had already left the hospital. To know that she was no longer there gave us an empty, helpless feeling. Although we knew it wasn't so, it was as if she had packed up and disappeared from our lives. It felt as if she were just gone, with no indication of when or where she would next surface or how she was going to survive her grief. We suddenly felt very cut off from her.

Nancy's wish for her son not to be left alone in the hospital broke our hearts all over again. And like Nancy, the idea of the newborn baby being without family nearby left us cold.

"Thinking of him lying in the nursery there, with no one to call his own, is unbearable," Carey said sadly. "I just hope the nurses are holding him and comforting him. I'm not his biological mother and it's making me feel sick to think of him there by himself, without anyone who is *just his* to hold and love him. We need to get there and be with him." We drove as quickly as the law allowed. The heavy clouds of winter seemed to droop all the way down to the road. Things looked and felt very bleak.

I pictured us in Nancy's hospital room and her beautiful face as she watched us hold the baby. Now, I thought, that room was empty, the bed freshly made up so that the next new mother could recuperate. Or maybe the next mother was already there, and another set of happy, doting family members filled the room.

We didn't know where to picture Nancy now. The reality was we had no idea where she had gone. Despite the friction we had noticed between her and her mother, we assumed Nancy had gone home with Marilou. But we didn't even know exactly where that was, although we had the telephone number and a vague idea of the location of their home. "I'm sure she's at the house, taking a hot shower, losing it big-time," Carey said. "I'm sure she's wondering who's with her baby, and whether or not he's registering her absence."

We got to the hospital at lightning speed. The memories of how we had been treated while Nancy delivered were still fresh. Neither of us knew quite how we would be treated this time. We walked in with determination, prepared for the worst. There was a nurse sitting behind the circular nurses' station in the postpartum unit. She was looking over a clipboard of paperwork.

We introduced ourselves to her as the foster parents of "Baby Miller," and told her we had instructions to visit him in that capacity.

The nurse looked at us and said, "No, you're here to take the baby home." Carey and I turned to each other. Surely she was confusing us with someone else.

"No," I said slowly, trying to make her understand. "We're the baby's foster parents and we're here to visit him."

"I understand that you're the foster parents. But you're here to take him home," she said calmly. "Didn't your social worker get ahold of you?"

"We talked to her about forty-five minutes ago," I answered, "and she told us to come down to visit him."

"Oh," she said with a sense of dawning realization. "A lot has happened since then. I'll fill you in." She told us the baby was to be released and that we as his foster parents were to take him home. "Before you do," she said as an addendum, "we require that you watch a parenting video."

Carey and I looked blankly at each other, thinking of the baby nursery we had set up. We had gotten all the big things in place, but there were a zillion small things we hadn't added. We didn't have bottles or formula, or even diapers because, up to the night before, we didn't know whether to buy boy or girl diapers. And thinking this was just an in-hospital visit, we certainly hadn't brought anything with us to transport him.

It was hard to think things through rationally. I told the nurse we weren't ready to take the baby home, that we didn't have the things we needed to care for him. She wasn't the least bit ruffled by our frantic deliberations. "Don't worry," she told us, "your foster-care social worker, Lori, is on the way. She can help you sort through everything. In the meantime go in there." She pointed to an adjoining room. "There are gowns and soap in there. Wash your hands and put on a gown so that you can go into the nursery."

Carey and I looked through the glass window that separated the nurses' station from the nursery. We spotted Nancy's baby immediately. He was in a bassinet in the first row, close to the window, swaddled tightly and sleeping soundly.

Carey and I walked into the scrub station. "This will be perfect," Carey whispered to me as we lathered our hands at the sink. "I can't wait to get my hands on him and just hold him. I just want to hold him and talk to him without someone looking at me like I'm doing something wrong."

Carey's maternal instinct had kicked in. It was like someone had flicked a switch. Here was a baby in need, and we were the ones who had been chosen to help him. For the first time she felt a rush of maternal bonding with Nancy's baby, and at peace with letting go of her defenses. There was no other option. Carey looked at me and smiled. "He needs us, Dion. *He needs us.*" And that was all Carey needed. She was going to mother him now for all she was worth.

We finished washing our hands and pulled on yellow gowns to cover our clothes. Carey was meticulous about following the nurse's instructions, but she was very anxious to be with the baby. We went back to the nurse and told her we were scrubbed and ready. "Okay, follow me," she said as she stood up and signaled for us to go around to the other side of the desk and follow her. We looked at each other in confusion. The baby was in the nursery behind us and she was pointing us in the opposite direction.

"Where are we going?" Carey asked suspiciously. I pitied the woman if she gave Carey the wrong answer. She was going to be with this baby, and heaven help anyone who stood in her way.

"We're going to take you and the baby down to an unoccupied room so that you can visit privately," she reassured Carey. Another nurse pushed open the nursery door and wheeled a bassinet through the door. We breathed a sigh of relief when we saw that it was indeed "our" baby. We waited for the second nurse to come around with the bassinet to where we were. Carey positioned herself alongside the bassinet, and we followed the two nurses.

We walked down the hall slowly, as if we were in a church

processional. Carey was completely absorbed in staring at the baby. Her face glowed with love and satisfaction as she walked next to him. I knew she wanted nothing more than to reach into the bassinet and take him in her waiting arms. She was using every ounce of self-control she had to resist the temptation.

The nurses slowed down and went into a room on the right-hand side of the hall. We followed them into the room. Once inside, Carey looked up from the bassinet. She grabbed my arm frantically.

"What's the matter?" I asked. As soon as I opened my mouth, I realized exactly what was wrong.

"This is Nancy's room," she answered.

The nurses looked at us. It took them a moment to understand what she meant. "Oh! Would you rather go someplace else? To another room? We can find another empty room for you."

Carey stopped them. "No, no." She shook her head and then looked around the room we had just left the day before—the room where so many difficult emotions had crashed into one another. We stood on the opposite side from where Nancy had been in the double room. I looked at Carey and I could see the wheels turning. I knew the memories were flying through her mind. I also knew we were both thinking the same thing: *As long as we stay on this side of the room, it feels okay, it even feels right.*

"This is just fine," she said calmly. "Let's stay right here."

Carey turned to the bassinet, reached in, and picked up the baby. As she did, she looked up at the nurse who had wheeled him in and appeared to recognize her. "You were on duty when we visited Nancy earlier, weren't you? Were you here when Nancy was discharged?" Carey asked her.

"Yes, I was," she answered.

"How was she?" Carey asked. She held the baby up against her and swayed automatically to soothe him.

"Not good," the nurse said with sincerity. "She was very sad, she was heartbroken, about saying good-bye to her baby. She signed the papers and then said good-bye to him. He started to cry as soon as she kissed him good-bye. It was really very rough on her."

Carey's eyes filled with tears. It was an excruciatingly painful image that the nurse had described. We knew for sure now—and had known instinctively before—that Nancy was in trouble. Our hearts were crushed, yet we were supposed to be excited about bringing the baby home. It all felt backward and jumbled and cruel.

On top of our consuming worry about Nancy we now needed to focus on the baby and his well-being. This little boy was waiting for his parents, whoever they were, to take him and love him and nurture him. He needed pure, undistracted devotion, and he deserved to be loved unconditionally regardless of whether he was going to become our son or remain Nancy's son.

We wanted desperately to help Nancy directly. We felt helpless. We wanted a baby, but we now believed that Nancy probably needed to keep him and raise him herself for her own sake as well as his. The best we could do was to uphold our promise to her to be kind and loving foster parents.

The nurses reminded us there was a policy that we had to watch a parenting video before we would be allowed to take the baby home into our foster care. I could see that Carey was furious over this added "requirement." It felt more like an insult to our integrity. Carey had had her fill of being told what to do and what not to do as far as Nancy and this baby were concerned. She was walking a fine line between putting up with the red tape and rebelling against it.

Still, she bit her tongue. She didn't want to create any waves that could make things any worse than they already were. I could see her anger in the way she focused even more intently on the baby. She sat in a chair and rocked him gently, her cheek pressed against the side of his head, her eyes almost closed. Her attention never deviated from him. She didn't see one frame of the video.

Lori, our foster-care social worker, walked into the room just as the video was ending. We were relieved to see her, since we were still confused about why we were taking the baby home with us and into our foster care that afternoon. According to Nan Lahr, we said, we were merely supposed to visit the baby. Why the changes?

"Well," she said, "Nancy was very clear that she didn't want him to have to stay alone in the hospital. She said she didn't want him to feel lost or to have to spend any time without a family to love him. Since she was released today, she requested that you be allowed to bring him home today."

"Of course we'll take him home. In a heartbeat we'll take him home," I told Lori. "That goes without question. We'll just stop on the way home and buy diapers and formula. But we don't have a car seat to put him in for the ride home. I suppose I could run out now and buy one while Carey waits here with the baby." I was trying to piece it all together. It was getting late in the day, and I didn't know where I would go to buy a car seat. It was state law that no one could transport an infant without a car seat, and the hospital wouldn't discharge an infant without proof that the child would be in one.

"Not to worry," Lori assured me. "I've brought a lot of things with me." She had a huge paper shopping bag with her. From it she pulled item after item of baby linens and clothing, many of them brand-new and still in their original wrappings or boxes. "And I have an infant car seat for you out in my car. We can transfer it to your car when you're ready to leave."

I was relieved and more than a little embarrassed that she and the agency had gone to the trouble and expense to assemble everything we needed. Reaching for my wallet, I asked her how much we owed the agency. She told us they were contributions from the Christ Child Society for Infants in Need. Carey and I looked at each other. We were speechless, totally humbled by the gesture. Lori continued to pull things out of the bag. "Are you sure? This is so much." I fumbled for words.

"I'm positive," she said. "That's what the society does."

I had never imagined my child to be a child in need or that I would ever be forced to accept "handouts." But here we were, and we had no choice. My pride had to take second place to this baby's well-being. I looked at the pile of things Lori had brought and then at the small speck of a child in Carey's arms. It all fit together. We couldn't do any of this alone. Something bigger was at work here. It had been at work for us all along. Something had brought Nancy into our lives. We had been given the chance to have a child and we were being given the details necessary to bring him home right now. Instead of feeling embarrassed, I thought, I should be grateful.

Lori, Carey, and I sat down together to get everything organized. There was a gentle knock on the door. The door was pushed open, and nurses started parading in and out of the room, each bringing us another item or supplies. They brought a heavy knit cap and enough formula to get us through several days. One nurse came into the room with so many ten-packs of diapers in her arms that they were falling onto the floor as she walked. Another nurse carried in as many pacifiers as she could hold in her hands.

The nurses pulled together some plastic bags, and we stuffed them with all the supplies they had gathered for us. Their cooperation and thoughtfulness contrasted starkly with how we had been treated by others as we waited for Nancy to have the baby. Suddenly we weren't the bad guys anymore. We were worthy of this baby, and worthy of compassion. These nurses were like angels of mercy. Their concern and support were sincere. Carey and I desperately needed that kind of help at that point as we struggled to be strong and do the right thing.

Finally a nurse walked in with a white handknit sweater and cap in her hands. They were beautiful, soft, and clean, with a delicate, intricate pattern woven into them. She brought them over to Carey and showed them to her. She explained that a mother had left them at the hospital because she had had a boy and her family didn't think white was masculine enough. "We've been waiting for the right baby to give these to," the nurse told us. Using one hand, Carey took the sweater and cap from the nurse and looked at it. I saw her eyes fill with tears as she fingered the small white buttons that looked like pearls. She thanked the nurse profusely.

Lori told us it was time to sign the foster agreement. In our haste to pull together the necessities, Carey and I had forgotten about the legalities. We already knew the stipulations, responsibilities, and risks. Nan Lahr had gone over everything with us in preparation for this very moment. We had no doubts or hesitations even now.

I went over the papers with Lori while Carey changed the baby into his new clothes and then sat in the rocking chair and rocked him. She was lost in her love for this baby, and lost in the contentment of being a mother at long last. She only came up for air when I carried the papers over to her and showed her where we needed her signature. The stress of all the preceding days had vanished from her face. Peace and contentment had washed over her with her new purpose in life: to care for this small, fresh life.

It took about half an hour to complete all the foster-care forms. Before the paperwork was complete, we were asked to name the child. Neither of us knew that we were going to be asked to name him as part of the fostering agreement. We didn't expect to have to make that decision until—if—he came home to us as our adopted child. But because we were doing foster-to-adopt, Lori told us, we should give the baby the name of our choice.

Carey and I looked at each other. We were both thinking of our conversation in the car outside the florist. There were a few heavy moments of silence.

"He'll be David Evan," Carey said steadily, with unmistakable purposefulness.

It took two nurses, Lori, and myself to load all the supplies onto a hospital cart. Carey had David dressed warmly for the ride home.

She stood near the door, anxious for us to be on our way. I told Lori we were ready to head home, and she said she'd help us to the hospital entrance, then go to the garage with me so that she could help me get the car seat strapped into our car.

"Let me just tell you something important before you leave," the nurse in charge told us. "Very few babies leave the hospital this soon after they're born. By law they have to have a PKU blood test, which requires they be at least forty-eight hours old. If you take him home now," she continued, "you'll need to bring him back for testing."

I didn't want to leave the hospital with David only to have to come back again. After all we had been through there, it was time to leave the hospital and the memories behind. We needed a clean break from this place. I knew Carey was thinking the same thing.

"Can't we have a private doctor do the test?" I asked Lori.

"Of course . . ." She hesitated. "But I don't know how many doctors will accept Medicaid."

"Well, they all accept cash," I told her.

As we got ready to leave the room, Carey stood by the door to the room, cradling David in her arms. The nurse pushed the bassinet over to her. "You can't carry him out of the hospital," she told Carey. "You have to wheel him in the bassinet."

For a moment I thought Carey was going to explode. We had endured so much unfair judgment, so many restrictions and bureaucratic red tape, that this final limitation, thrown in at the last minute, could easily have been the proverbial straw that broke the camel's back. There was no way Carey would willingly put that baby down now that he was her responsibility, dependent on her love. A flash of fury passed over Carey's face. I cringed in anticipation. When Carey decided to fight back, she usually came out the winner.

Carey stared back at the nurse. She took a deep breath. "All right," she said very calmly as she gently laid David down in the bassinet. The nurse reached to push the bassinet. "Just a minute," Carey told her. "*I* think he's *hot*." She reached into the bassinet and pulled off the knit cap that all babies were supposed to wear on the unit. I smiled. I knew what she was doing. That was her act of defiance, her mother's prerogative. Carey, the mom, was in charge now.

Carey waited with David and the nurse at the main entrance to the hospital. I followed Lori to her car and transferred the infant car seat to the backseat of our car and went to retrieve Carey and David. We strapped David into his car seat, tucked a blanket over him, thanked Lori, and left the hospital. We didn't go back.

CHAPTER

15

As we drove out of the parking lot and headed toward the highway, a metamorphosis took place. The importance of the tiny being who lay peacefully in the infant car seat enveloped us. The realization struck that this small wonder was no longer invisibly and conveniently nurtured and protected inside of Nancy. His safety and well-being were no longer attended to by nature. He was out in the real world, completely helpless and completely our responsibility. Circumstances demanded that our priorities be re-arranged instantaneously. At the top of the list in big, bold letters was David Evan.

I was in shock the whole ride home. Carey sat in the backseat next to David. I tilted the rearview mirror downward so that I could see them both with a glance. Carey's face was turned toward David's, her vision fixed on his small round face, her gaze broken only by the blinking of her eyes. David gripped Carey's index finger tightly with his fist. To me it looked as if he were holding on for dear life, not daring to let go of anyone again.

Snow fell through the darkness, swirling toward the glass of the windshield at a dizzying speed. The windshield wipers pushed it aside only in time for the glass to be covered again. The sound of the wipers was as hypnotic as a metronome. I was exhausted, functioning on a very automatic level. I found myself rotating through a pattern of watching the road and looking in the rearview mirror, back and forth, back and forth, synchronized to the sound of the wipers.

"Is he all right?" I whispered to Carey. It was frustrating to be separated, even by just a car seat, from them both. I wanted to be able to see David's face closely, watch his expression, and know that he was okay.

"He's fine," Carey told me. "He's sleeping. The motion of the car is soothing him." Carey's voice was calm and steady. I knew that it was her presence more than anything else that was soothing him. Already her maternal instincts had kicked in. She was in total control. I was so proud of her strength and composure. I knew David was going to be fine, because he was in Carey's hands.

As we neared our neighborhood, the snow began to fall harder. It seemed too late in the season for this kind of snow. Lost in time, I tried to think of the date. How could I forget? David had been born the day before, March 31st, just after midnight. So that meant today was April 1st. Wasn't it past the snow season? Wasn't it almost spring? April 1st. It hit me: April Fool's. It seemed appropriate. It was in keeping with the way things had been *not* going according to plan.

I looked in the mirror again. Carey looked so peaceful, so focused. A wave of fear went through me. Carey was going at this with blind, unconditional devotion. She was giving every ounce of her heart and soul to this baby now. To me that meant she was extremely vulnerable, completely open to being hurt as she invested herself in being David's foster mother. Carey's commitment to this child was powerful, spiritual. In her mind, in her emotional commitment to him, she was going to be his mother, not his foster mother. She would hold nothing back.

What if something changed? What would happen if David were taken from us? We still believed Nancy might very well decide to keep her baby. We knew it was a strong possibility, and we knew we would be in total support of her if that were to be her decision. I was afraid Carey was setting herself up for a terrible fall.

"Carey?" I said quietly.

"Yes?"

"Let's do this one day at a time. Let's take care of him, good care of him . . . but let's be careful. Our hearts are at risk here."

There was a long pause. I knew from the silence that I had said the wrong thing. I waited for her response. "No," she said finally. "I can't do it that way, Dion. I have to do it my way. He's my son, whether I'm going to raise him for two days, two weeks, two years, or forever. He's my responsibility. He's my child, whether or not it's temporary. He's the one at risk, Dion. He's the one who stands to lose everything if we don't commit ourselves completely to him. I'm not going to break his heart or Nancy's just to protect my own."

We turned onto our road. David hadn't made a noise the whole way home. It was as if he knew that he could relax, that he was with people who loved him. I pulled the car into the garage. Carey asked me to close the garage door behind us. It was dinnertime and we knew that our neighbors would all be returning home from work and settling into their evenings. Carey wanted to slip into our house with David without being noticed. We didn't want to go through any more explanations or any more interrogations.

Carey took David, still in his car seat, into the house. I went ahead of them to turn the lights on and push the heat up. Sam was at the door to meet us. He smelled my hands carefully, and then smelled his way to David in Carey's arms. He was glued to Carey's side, nose up in the air. He knew something big was happening.

Carey unbuckled David and took a layer of blanket off him.

Gently she lifted him out of the seat and then sat down in the big easy chair next to the fireplace. David didn't stir. His eyes stayed closed, an expression of utter serenity on his miniature face. Sam wandered up and sniffed lightly around David without touching him. "It's okay, Sam," Carey whispered. "He's just a baby, just a little tiny baby. It's okay." David still didn't stir.

I sat on the couch, opposite Carey and David. I couldn't relax. I needed to do something. Carey looked up at the clock on the mantel and saw me fidgeting.

"What?" I asked her. "Do you want me to do something? Get you anything?"

"I don't know," she answered. "I'm thinking. I'm trying to get with the program here. I wonder if I need to change his diaper . . . or feed him. . . . It must be time for me to do *something* for him."

"Well, I've always heard people say, 'Let sleeping babies lie.' "

"He does look pretty content."

"I've got an idea. As long as he's this asleep, maybe I'll take some pictures. What do you think?"

"I think it's a great idea."

Part of me was afraid to take pictures, everything was still so uncertain. David's homecoming was extremely bittersweet, and I was worried that if things took a turn, we would end up having created sad memories instead of happy ones. I got out the video camera and filmed Carey and David together, close-ups of their two gentle faces, Carey oh-so-quietly introducing David Evan.

The telephone rang. I ran to get it so that it wouldn't wake David. It was Lori. She was calling to make sure we had gotten home safely. I assured her that we had and told her David was still sleeping. She gave me her home telephone number and told me we could call anytime we needed her. She said she'd be checking in with us the next morning. I thanked her and hung up the phone.

As soon as I hung up, the telephone rang again. It was Nancy. Relief surged through me. I was so glad to hear her voice. We had

Picture of Dion and Carey used in profile.

Nancy and Todd.

David, safe and loved,
between his mom and dad.

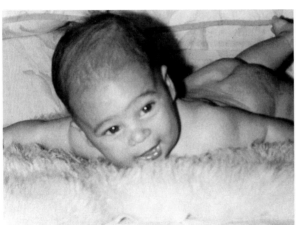

A picture that shouts, "I'll
get back at you one day!"

Getting ready for bed.

NancyMom's first weekend visit.

At St. Paul's Church after the
baptism, June 1992.

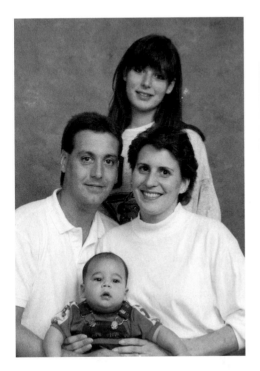

First family portrait, July 1992.

David finalizing his own adoption,
December 1992.

At his first birthday party, David eating his cake with a little help from NancyMom.

David happy about life.

On patrol with Dad.

Grandpa Don and Grammy Lou.

Party at Nancy's home with Dion holding Corey.

Christmas portrait of Grammy Lou's grandchildren. From the left: Jake, Ashley, Corey, and David.

Christmas tree ornament testing lab, 1994.

Preschool photo in 1995, age three.

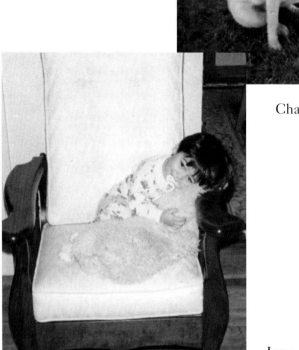

Charlie and Sam—the other kids.

Jams, Lamby, and
bee-bee (pacifier).

The best partner a father could have.

Sidewalk sledding, winter of '95.

David's first time on a pony, 1995.

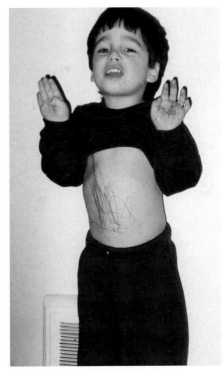

Body art.

Dad's car, also known as David's giant toy box.

Walt Disney would be proud, as we celebrate birthday four.

planned to call her after we got David settled in. I was grateful that she had called us, and so soon.

As she spoke, I could hear that she was exhausted and in a lot of physical pain and emotional anguish. There was a tremble in her voice; I knew she had been crying. Just listening to her sweet, sad voice sent another wave of pain through me. In the past forty-eight hours she had been through more pain and loss than anyone should have to go through in a lifetime. She told me she was home and that she was calling to make sure we had gotten the baby and that he was okay.

I told her Nan Lahr had called us late in the afternoon and that we had rushed to the hospital as soon as we had been told of her release. Everything had gone smoothly, and we had arrived home from the hospital just a short time ago. I told her we had been planning to call her as soon as we got settled in. She sounded very relieved that we had reacted so quickly her request.

As I spoke, I signaled to Carey, asking her if she wanted to talk with Nancy. Carey nodded her head yes and pointed to the baby. "You hold him," she mouthed.

I told her Carey was holding the baby and was rocking him in her arms as he slept but that she wanted to talk to her. Nancy was pleased when I told her this. She needed to know that he was being loved and cherished the way he would have been if he were with Nancy and Marilou, and she needed Carey's reassurance.

Carey stood up with David and put him in my arms. She took the portable phone and motioned to me to stay in the living room. She went and sat at the top of the basement stairs, out of earshot of me and the baby. I knew she was doing that so that Nancy wouldn't have to hear him if he started fussing. Carey was very concerned about Nancy, especially after hearing that she was suffering through postpartum depression. She seemed to know how to buffer the pain for Nancy.

Carey and Nancy talked for a few minutes When she hung up, Carey came into the living room and sat down in the chair again.

She covered her face with her hands for a moment, then reached out for me to hand her David.

"What's wrong?" I asked her as I put David into her arms. "Is Nancy all right? Did something happen while you were talking to her? What did you two talk about?"

"We talked about Nancy and how she's doing, and David and how he's doing. I didn't call him David, though. Did you?"

"No, I didn't. It seemed like it would be too much to tell her right now that we're calling him David. I guess I called him 'the baby' when we talked."

Carey said that when she picked up the phone to talk, Nancy said "Hi, Mom!" Carey said she had returned the salutation, verbatim, automatically. "It's like we're both his mother," she told me. "We're both 'Mom.' Neither one of us is more 'Mom' than the other."

I listened mesmerized while Carey told me in detail about her conversation with Nancy. She said that Nancy was definitely grieving. "She told me that leaving the hospital was really hard for her. She said she could hear him crying in the nursery as they wheeled her down the hall to the elevator. She said it was as if he knew she was leaving, as if that's why he was crying." Carey's eyes filled with tears. "She told me she could hear him crying even after the elevator doors closed."

Carey stood up and walked slowly around the room, gently swaying David in her arms. "She's so amazing," she continued. "She's so tired and upset. She was really weepy, and very sad. But still she kept asking how we're doing, if we're okay. She just amazes me."

"What did you tell her?"

"I told her we're fine, that we're worrying about her and thinking about her, but that we're okay and the baby is fine. I could tell she was glad to hear that you were holding him while we talked. It's so important to her that he have a father. I was glad, too, that you were holding him. She needs to know that you're there for him as well."

We were quiet for a few moments, then Carey spoke again, slowly. I knew she was fighting back her tears. "Nancy told me she kept him in her room with her last night. She told me it was her special time to be with him. She said she fed him and held him all night." She stopped. "She said it was a constant cycle of trying to get him to eat, then burping him, changing him, swaddling him. . . . She said he kept her up all night. Then she said something really incredible. She said she knew after that one night that she had made the right decision. She said she knows she's too young to be a mother."

Tears rolled down Carey's cheeks as she repeated what Nancy had said to her. "She told me that her mother said they could bring the baby home and keep him, that it was fine to do that. But she told Nancy that he would be her responsibility. Nancy said she knew she couldn't do that, she couldn't go to school and take care of a baby too."

I brought a box of tissues over to Carey. She took one and dried her face. I rubbed her shoulders. "I think that what she was trying to say . . . ," Carey said very slowly and quietly, "what she was trying to do . . . was to reassure me that it's all going to happen . . . that we're going to adopt him. I think she was trying to say that we're already his parents."

CHAPTER

16

We sat quietly for a few minutes trying to digest everything that Nancy had said on the telephone. It was a lot to think about, and it hit Carey especially hard. She was devastated when she heard Nancy describe the pain she had endured in leaving David. She had to consciously pull herself together and keep functioning.

She decided it was time to go upstairs and put sheets on the crib, which had been sitting in wait for months now. She asked me to take David so that she could get his room ready.

I paced nervously with David in my arms. Carey has always had enough maternal instinct in her to bottle and sell it. My paternal instinct was totally dormant at the time. As Carey disappeared upstairs, I held David and walked in a repetitious circle through the living room, the kitchen, the dining room, and back to the kitchen. He was quiet, and I hoped I could keep him that way.

I turned off all but one small lamp in the living room. In the dark I could see the outside clearly through the big bay living-room window. It was still snowing steadily. A solid white ground cover made it look unusually light outside. It made me think of Christmas, and as I stood in the window, I found myself thinking, *"Silent night, holy night, all is calm, all is bright. . . ."* Above me I could hear Carey's footsteps as she walked into David's nursery.

The falling snow was silhouetted against the glow of the street-light. I was mesmerized as I watched the the constant blur of snow in the air. A car crept down the street. It was getting icy out. I looked at the houses across the street. Their windows, glowing from the inside light, made the neighborhood look like the front of a Christmas card. A movement in one of the windows caught my eye. I looked closely. There were two people standing in the window, their faces looking back out in my direction. I looked at the next house over and saw another face looking out a window.

Another movement outside caught my eye. There were two of our neighbors walking toward our house. They saw me in the window and waved at me excitedly. It suddenly dawned on me that the faces and people I was seeing had seen me first. They had spotted me in the window holding David. The word, it seemed, was out.

I went to the bottom of the stairs and called softly up to Carey. "We have company!"

"What do you mean?" she asked, coming quickly down the stairs.

The doorbell rang. "The neighbors," I told her. We looked at each other, trying to decide how to handle this surprise visit. We became instantly protective of David, and of Nancy too. Everything was still so new to us, we didn't feel ready yet to share it all. We knew that this fostering period was filled with risk; he could be removed from our guardianship at any time. It didn't seem like a good idea to complicate it by having all sorts of people coming and going and looking for explanations at every juncture.

On the other hand these neighbors were friends of ours and knew that we had been hoping to adopt a child. We had been very open with our friends, so those who were among our circle were aware to some extent of what was going on.

"Okay," Carey said. "Give me David, and you go ahead and answer the door. But I don't think we should have anyone in the house for too long. He needs to rest. He needs a calm, quiet house. I want to get him settled in."

As I opened the door, two more neighbors came up our walk. I welcomed them in. Before I could ask, they told me that they had seen me in our living-room window holding David and had seen the light on upstairs in the nursery and had put two and two together. They came over to see if we needed anything and to lend us moral support, they said. And of course they were interested in any details we might be willing to share with them. They were genuinely happy and excited for us.

I gave them a quick synopsis of what had transpired, while Carey held David in her arms for them to see. They all surprised us with their compassion and kindness. No one overstepped any bounds, no one overstayed their welcome. Two of the women even helped Carey to finish setting up the nursery. Everyone left within a half an hour, and we had the house to ourselves again.

We ordered pizza to be delivered. Despite our exhaustion we couldn't sit still. We ate standing up, walking, carrying David. Carey held David in one arm and busied herself organizing the kitchen with the other. She cleared a spot for all the formula the nurses had given us and tried to devise a system for sterilizing bottles and nipples.

We phoned our mothers to tell them that David was home with us. I heard Carey greet her mother on the other end of the phone. "Hi, Mom! Guess who's in my arms right now?" Our families were thrilled. When they heard that David was in our care now and that he was in fact "David," they assumed everything was fine and dandy. They still didn't comprehend all the anguish that had preceded and accompanied his homecoming. We tried to keep the conversations short, but it was hard. There were so many questions to be answered. We were relieved when none of our family tried to push an immediate visit on us. What we needed most was time to think and time to adjust.

I found a notebook in my desk and we began our fostering log. We were expected to keep a detailed journal of David's "activities." Carey told me how to label the pages, and she chose a spot to keep the book on the kitchen counter so that we wouldn't lose it in our new-parent confusion.

At nine P.M. Carey changed David into his sleeper, and took him up to the nursery. She sat with him in the rocking chair and gave him a "good-night bottle." Sam and I roamed the house, not knowing what to do with ourselves. I walked by the nursery and peeked in. Carey was rocking gently with David in the crook of her left arm. On the wall behind them the night-light shone. It was all that lit the room. It cast a perfect halo of light around the two of them. When I saw them, all I could think of was the Madonna and Child. They looked so serene, so perfectly content. Carey was tired, and worried about Nancy, but caring for David brought out a tranquillity in her that was captivating. My heart melted as I watched them. I never imagined that a baby could have such power.

Carey rocked David long after he had fallen asleep in her arms. Now that he was with us, it was really difficult to make a conscious decision to be apart from him, even for a short time. But he was ready to rest, and so was she. She stood up slowly and tiptoed to the crib. I watched as she gently lowered David over the rail. She had rolled up two bath towels and laid them parallel to each other on the mattress. She put David down on his side between them. The towels kept him propped in that position. Carey seemed to know everything about taking care of children.

With David safely tucked in, Carey and I headed for bed ourselves. I could have slept soundly all the way until morning. Carey, on the other hand, sat bolt upright in the bed at two-fifteen in the morning. "Why isn't he awake?" she said in a burst of panic. "He should have woken up by now to eat. Something must be wrong." She threw back the covers and jumped out of bed.

She hit the floor running. I barely came to, and fell right back to sleep. Carey came back to bed quickly. David was sleeping soundly in his new crib. He simply hadn't gotten hungry enough to wake up yet.

The next morning was clear and sunny. The snow had stopped. I woke up to find that Carey was already up with David, giving him a bottle in the living room. She had dutifully recorded every diaper change, every ounce of formula consumed, and every burp to date in the log book.

When David was done with his bottle and had burped enough to please Carey, she just sat with him in her arms. We hadn't yet gotten all the assorted baby accessories we would need. There was no downstairs bassinet or cradle to put him in. None of that bothered Carey. She probably would have chosen to hold him in her arms even if we had every baby item ever made. Carey had already fallen in love with David, and as long as he was in her arms, they were both completely satisfied with life.

I poured myself a cup of coffee and joined Carey in the living room. Next to Carey I felt like a fish out of water. Parenthood came so easily and so gracefully to her. For me it was quite the opposite. I couldn't tell my right hand from my left when it came to holding a baby, and I had certainly never changed a diaper. I was paralyzed by my own lack of experience and confidence.

Carey looked up at me and smiled. "He has a doctor's appointment this afternoon," she told me. "He has to have that PKU test. You'll come with me, right?" I nodded. I would be happy to do the chauffeuring and the transporting. That was about my speed.

Carey had researched and interviewed pediatricians the moment she found out we had been chosen by a birth mother. Easy accessibility was one of her criteria. Her reasoning paid off. Always thinking ahead, Carey had allowed double the real time to get packed up and over to the office for this first trip. Somehow we managed to get David changed into a clean diaper and some winter baby gear, strapped and buckled into the car seat, and the car seat strapped into the car. By the time we fumbled our way into the front door of the office building with the overstuffed "diaper" bag (an old canvas tote was our improvised diaper bag), the infant seat, and a very bundled-up David, we were right on time.

We traipsed through the lobby and over to the elevators. I carried the diaper bag, the seat, and Carey's purse; Carey was in charge of David. The elevator door opened and we stepped into an elevator full of people. Next to Carey stood a man with his young son. The man looked approvingly at David and asked Carey with interest how old he was. Carey told him that David was two days old. Next to Carey a woman gasped. "And you're that skinny?" she shrieked. "That's a sin!" I looked at Carey for her reaction. She smiled with false courtesy at the woman and said nothing.

The waiting room at the doctor's office was crowded. Kids were everywhere. I hadn't been in a pediatrician's office since I was a kid. It was chaos. We found two adjoining seats and settled in for the wait. The noisy confusion was a total distraction for me. I watched as children in every shape and size raced or crawled back and forth across the room. Carey sat next to me with a look on her face like she was in paradise. For her it was gratifying to at long last be sitting in a pediatrician's waiting room holding a baby. She was in her element.

David cried uncontrollably when the doctor stuck his heel for the PKU test. The nurse had suggested that maybe Carey wouldn't want to stay with him as he was being tested. "You don't want him to associate you with the pain of the needle," she told Carey. On the contrary, that made Carey determined to stay with him. Carey stood right next to David, holding one of his tiny hands in hers. She felt helpless as she watched David cry. She couldn't bear to see him in pain. But she was his mother, and she was there to comfort him. As soon as the doctor was finished, she scooped David up off the table and held him close to her. He stopped crying immediately.

Nan Lahr phoned us at home that afternoon. She told us that we needed to limit our contact with Nancy. She said Nancy's postpartum depression was a serious condition and that she was to be given time and space to come out of it and make her final decision about the adoption. Our open communication with her, she said, could later be considered coercion by the courts. We were to adhere to the foster-care guidelines and nothing more.

Carey and I were shocked. We had assumed that we were past the irritations of outside interference in our relationship with Nancy. To have another set of restrictions imposed on us felt like a huge blow and a major setback. We weren't sure how to react. On the one hand we felt we should be able to act on our feelings. If we wanted to talk to Nancy, we thought, we should be able to. On the other hand we wanted to be fair to her. If indeed, by some stretch of the imagination, our dialogue with her could influence her in any way that might be detrimental to her, then we absolutely would refrain from contacting her.

We talked together about this new development at length. With a fire roaring in the fireplace and David snoozing upstairs in his crib, we lay on the living room floor in utter exhaustion. We discussed and discussed and discussed all the ups and downs and pros and cons of the situation. Our openness with Nancy was something we couldn't place a value on. Nancy meant the world to us, and we wanted what was best for her.

"We have to do what's best for Nancy," Carey said. "The question is, what's best? And then there's David. What's best for him? If they start restricting our communication with Nancy now, how is it going to manifest in the long term? Is this going to send us off in the wrong direction? Is this going to jam the lines of communication so much that they're never clear again? I don't know," she said solemnly. "It feels like a gag order. It feels like it goes against freedom of expression, for that matter."

I agreed with her. "But," I told her, "the people who are imposing these limits are professionals. This is their line of work. Maybe they really know something we don't about what's best for Nancy right now. I'm afraid to make a mistake that would cause her any kind of harm."

We went around and around in circles trying to decide what was the right thing to do given what Nan Lahr had just told us. At last we decided that we would let Nancy initiate communication. If she wanted to talk with us and contacted us on her own, then we would talk freely and openly with her as we always had. Short of that we would comply with our social worker's recommendations.

Nancy called us later that night. I answered the phone and knew right away that something was wrong. Nancy sounded empty, hollow, as if a piece of her had vanished. Her depression was right at the surface; there was no disguising it.

She told me almost right away that she had been hoping and expecting to hear from us that day. "I thought you guys would have called me," she said without hesitation. My heart sank.

I told her about our phone call from Nan Lahr and her strong recommendation that we stop all contact with her. Nancy was furious. "Damn the social workers!" she said in her characteristic forthright manner. "I need to be able to talk to you guys when I want to and need to. . . . I need to know that the baby is okay, and that you guys are okay. That's the only thing that's helping me get through this right now, the fact that I can talk to you directly and know what's going on with you and him. And other than you guys and Mom and Todd, there's no one I can talk to who really understands what I'm going through. Without having you guys to talk to, I'm not sure I can handle this." She stopped for a moment. "Besides all that, I really love you and Carey."

As always her complete and forthright honesty blew me out of the water. "Damn the social workers!" I agreed. I told her that we loved her, too, and were thinking of her constantly. I reminded her that we, too, needed to know how she was doing, so the openness was vital on both sides.

Carey knew from my reactions and what I said that it was Nancy on the phone. She signaled to me that she was going to try to move David to another room so that if he got fussy, Nancy wouldn't hear him over the phone. As she picked him up and carried him toward the upstairs, he let out a beautiful newborn squeak that chimed through the air and into the telephone line.

I paused, not knowing what to do. Certainly, I thought, Nancy had heard him. I was right. In reaction she was silent for what seemed like forever. I knew I couldn't ignore the problem. I asked her if hearing him was difficult for her. "Yeah," she told me very quietly. "It pretty much tears my heart out. But it's also good, because I know he's in the best hands, being taken good care of . . . better care than I could give him right now. And I know he's getting plenty of love. And I know I can call you any time I need to just to remind myself of all that."

I told her she could count on that for as long as David was in our home. I assured her that he was doing really well and that Carey was doing really well with him. Nancy began to cry quietly. She was really hurting. So much emotion was crammed inside her heart and soul that she wasn't able to sort through it all. The postpartum depression was making everything worse, making her burden much heavier than it already was. I told her that anytime she needed to talk, we were there for her. "I know you are," she said. "That's why I love you guys so much. And that's why I know he's where he belongs."

I asked her how it felt to be home now after all that had happened. Nancy was never anything less than honest. She responded by telling me that nothing could fill the emptiness she was feeling now. All she could bring herself to do was to lie curled up on the couch with a pillow against her belly. The physical and emotional emptiness she described was so profound that I knew it was as if a part of her had died. She was confronting an irreconcilable loss. We talked about David together. I assured her that he was safe and well cared for. Carey, I assured her, would happily lay down her life for that baby.

After Nancy and I finished our phone call, Carey and I resumed our discussion. Carey had me reiterate the conversation with Nancy practically verbatim. By the time I was done, Carey was reconfirming her commitment to openness with Nancy. She was worried about Nancy, worried that she wasn't going to be able to weather this ferocious storm. "Nancy said it herself," Carey told me. "She can't handle this unless she's able to communicate with us. We owe that to her, no matter what any court might say. It's our *responsibility* to help Nancy. I have to follow my heart, and my heart says forget what they say. Nancy is making the ultimate human sacrifice, and she needs to be able to talk about it and she needs to know that she and her baby are both loved by us."

Everything Carey said was true. We made a pact to maintain openness for as long and as far as Nancy chose.

CHAPTER

17

Legally, fostering meant we were little more than glorified baby-sitters for David. We were expected to record and account for every detail of his existence. In addition we had to have visits from our foster-care social worker, Lori, every five days so that she could document David's care and environment. For round-the-clock care along with record-keeping, the state of Ohio paid us the grand total of ten dollars per day. Clearly anyone involved in fostering isn't in it for the money.

The pages of our spiral-bound notebook filled quickly. The legal parameters and disciplines of fostering made no allusions to emotions. That part was left entirely up to us. The rules and demands of fostering clashed with our approach to having David with us. For Carey especially it presented a contradiction. It meant mixing her natural instincts and feelings for David with a dose of objective managerial discipline. Mothering came so naturally that it just flowed out of her. She got very frustrated with the stop-and-go protocol of having to record diaper changes, nap schedules, feedings, and other daily details. She was living for the time when she could just be with David, feed him and hold him, and put him to bed without having to stop to make a log entry for everything or answer to anybody.

For me the fact that we were in a "foster-care" position meant—bottom line—that we were still facing the possibility of losing David. He was still a ward of the state. Both the state and Nancy legally had a more binding relationship with him than we did. Although I had agreed with Carey that we were going to parent him with complete and unconditional commitment, I couldn't help but sense the risk we were undertaking.

I was worried that Carey was going to have her heart broken. We had waited so many years for the chance to be parents, and now that chance was here, but riddled with risk. Carey was already deeply attached to David. She had immediately put everything else aside and was completely devoted to fulfilling David's every need. She was willing to expose her heart completely for David.

Somehow Carey was able to move past the intense emotional turmoil we had all been struggling with the past few days and get to the heart of the matter. There wasn't a doubt in her mind that things were unfolding as they should and that David was where he was meant to be. I thought that I, too, was willing to make that commitment, but I could feel myself holding back. In retrospect I know that I maintained a barrier around my heart for those first few uncertain weeks. As a result I was a few steps behind Carey when it came to parenting David at the outset.

Carey did all the hands-on care of David. At the very least I knew I should be as busy as Carey was. By default I made it my role to become head housekeeper. When I wasn't on duty at work, I was at home scrubbing bathrooms and doing dishes and laundry. Carey was graciously reticent about my obvious denial of emotion. She recognized what was happening and gave me the space to work things out at my own pace.

A couple of days after David arrived home, I was cleaning the house. As I was vacuuming, Carey asked me, "Do you want to feed him?" I retorted, "Do you want to vacuum?" and I kept my hand on the vacuum cleaner. Later that day I was still in a cleaning frenzy. Carey asked me politely, "Would you like to change him?" I responded pointedly, "Do you want to scrub the toilets?" Carey took my cue, left me alone, and went and changed him.

A few minutes later I put down the scrub brush and took my rubber gloves off. I went to Carey and told her the truth, quietly and clearly. I told her I was overwhelmed, and truly afraid of what lay ahead. Beyond that I felt sadly inadequate to the new role I was undertaking. "Actually," I told her outright, "I guess you could say I'm terrified."

Carey told me to sit down on the couch next to her, and she looked at me with gentleness and patient love. "I'm really struggling, Carey," I confessed. "Emotionally and intellectually I'm struggling. Here I am, a seasoned police officer, and I've seen every possible gruesome and difficult situation imaginable, and yet I'm afraid of six and a half pounds of baby boy." Carey reached over and rubbed my back gently. I knew she was telling me that everything was okay.

"I'll make you a compromise," I suggested. "If you just give me time to adjust, time to get used to all this, and time to get past my fear of us having our hearts torn out, I'll take care of everything else. You take care of little David, and I'll take care of everything else. I'll do the housecleaning, the shopping, anything that needs doing, and you will have the sole responsibility of David."

I knew Carey would agree, because she was never one to push me. She had long ago learned that pushing me was a sure way to avoid the desired outcome. I wanted to be like Carey was, but I had to get there on my own terms. I keenly felt my lack of parenting skills, and as I thought about how inadequate I was feeling, I began to question the adoption process itself. As I reviewed what we had been through, I realized that the home study prepared us to deal with adoption-related and technical issues, from being sensitized to the emotional elements of the process to having a written fire-escape plan. But there had been nothing more than a fifteen-minute video about parenting a newborn, shown to us at the hospital. No other physical parenting skills were taught in any way, shape, or form. My only resource was to watch Carey and David, and try to move beyond my intimidation.

I actually envied Carey for her calm composure in the face of such gigantic uncertainty. Her determination was obvious. She tackled the administrative demands of "fostering" against an almost palpable backdrop of constant maternal love for David. It was remarkable to watch the two of them—somehow they just seemed to fit with each other. If David was fussy, all it took to calm him was Carey's touch. When Carey was tense, all it took to relax her was to cradle David in her arms. They seemed to exist in a world of their own.

Still, I felt something changing inside of me, but it was a mystery to me. That evening I was having actual waves of muscle twitches. I had no idea what to attribute them to, but I had a strong suspicion that they were the physical manifestation of my emotional confusion and anxiety. As Carey changed David into his night clothes upstairs in the nursery, I lay exhausted on the living-room couch. I had put on a videotape of a *Star Trek* episode that I had missed. It turned out to be the episode where Lieutenant Worf died (though only temporarily). As I lay on the couch, my muscles twitched spasmodically and relentlessly. Still it felt good just to lie in the darkness, mindlessly focused on something other than our own personal melodrama.

I watched as Worf went into his descent to death, and as he passed away, I felt my eyes fill with tears. To my complete surprise the tears began to fall down my cheeks. Within moments I was crying uncontrollably but quietly. I was dumbfounded. It was like my heart and my body were in cahoots, unbeknownst to my mind. Frankly I was unnerved by my emotional outburst. I was relieved that it had been in private.

I closed my eyes to try to pull myself together and found myself thinking about all the death situations I had encountered in my years on the force. They had never affected me this way. Then, to my amazement, a wave of emotion came over me as I relived the scene of Nancy saying good-bye to her son. The sadness that came over me was huge and heavy. I felt like a rubberband, stretched to the limit before it snaps.

Something was changing in me. I noticed, unwillingly, that my emotions were floating closer and closer to the surface. It was a little scary for me, and something I wouldn't want to admit to anyone. But it turned out that I couldn't disguise it. Over the next couple of days I found that when I was telling my friends and family the story of how we brought David home from the hospital, when I got to the part about his clothes and blankets coming from the Christ Child Society, I would become very teary-eyed.

My self-appointed role in our household had always been to protect Carey as best I could from any kind of pain. My newfound role as a father was superimposed upon my long-standing role as a protector. It felt very foreign to me. What I didn't see was that the two roles were beginning to bump into and challenge each other.

This shift in my personality concerned me so much that I called my mother and mentioned it to her, hoping she could offer advice. "I guess you really are human after all," she said lovingly. She meant this as a compliment, as she had always seen me as being in complete control of every facet of my life, emotions included.

"I don't like the way this feels," I told her. "I can't seem to get a grip on myself these days."

"Welcome to the human race," she said gently. "Listen, Dion, don't worry about it. Embrace it. Go with it. It's okay to feel this way. It's okay to *feel*."

I went back to work after three days. For me work was a respite from the intensity of home. My squad car was my personal sanctuary. I had started a brief diary the day we got the call from our social worker that we had been chosen by a birth mother. Now I wrote in the diary with a vengeance. Every day I would write a little more, looking back at what had happened and looking at what was happening then. I was keeping this diary for David, I thought, but I now realize that it allowed me an outlet for all my confused and pent-up emotions. I could write on paper what I was too controlled to say out loud to anyone. I was feeling guilty about burdening Carey, and I felt selfish about being so consumed with my unspoken feelings. I could release my guilt and anxieties on paper.

Carey stayed home with David. We told only a few select people at work that David had been born and was at our home with us. It would have been too much to have to explain it all to anyone but those we were closest to, particularly if David ended up going back to Nancy.

Carey had shared our infertility ups and downs with some of her closest staff members. They had lived through the months and months of frustration right along with her. They had taken so many calls for her during the long cycles of daily medical protocols that they knew the names and voices of Carey's doctors and nurses almost as well as she did. Carey kept those few people posted on what was happening on our home front. Everyone else at her work and in "the outside world" thought she was out on a medical leave. She didn't want to have her private business out on the table, and she definitely didn't want to have to rehash everything repeatedly if things fell through.

So Carey became something of a hermit, both by choice and by default. As Carey put it, she went underground. The pediatrician had urged her to keep David somewhat sequestered, since it was the thick of flu season. He advised her to avoid crowded places with him and to limit visitors. Carey followed his instructions to a tee. She wasn't going to go against anything that was for the benefit of David.

Carey and David hunkered down inside our house to take care of matters at hand. From one day to the next Carey went from a full-time career woman to a full-time mother. She went from juggling payroll and accounts receivable to juggling dirty diapers and bottles of formula. She became a round-the-clock, every-two-hour-feedings mom.

My work buffered me from the grueling demands of constant parenting. I had only told a handful of people that we were adopting. Because of the newness of the concept of open adoption, I really didn't want to deal with the curiosity of outsiders peering into something I was having a difficult time comprehending and defining myself. At work I could fall into the normalcy of the routine I had been practicing for fifteen years. My uniform and my badge were really like a shield for me. I could be who I had always been, and I was the one in control.

David's first real visitors were our close friends Nick and Debbie. They had been with us every step of the way, from our first thoughts about adopting to our call to them from the hospital when David was born. They had the insight to know that because David had been released so early from the hospital, we were almost completely unequipped to clothe and care for this precious newborn. They showed up the day after we brought David home. Our doorbell rang and there they stood on our doorstep, Nick holding a huge "care package."

As the official housekeeper and doorman I let Nick and Debbie in while Carey held David in the living room. Before I would let them in to see David, I told them they had to wash their hands with antibacterial soap. They agreed with smiles on their faces. They knew me well enough to know what was going on. This was just my way of having a role in this new parenting thing, a role that didn't demand that I expose my feelings. I was the King of Hygiene, making sure that anyone who came near my child was fit to do so.

Nick and Debbie, hands dutifully scrubbed, sat on our living-room floor with the box between them and pulled out sleepers, little cotton undershirts, blankets, baby bath towels, baby bath soap—the box seemed to have no bottom to it. Carey sat in a chair holding David.

When we reached the bottom of the box, Carey stood up and, still holding David in one arm, hugged each of them. "This is really nice, you two," she told them, "but I don't know if he's going to be staying with us permanently." She wanted them to understand clearly that we were still skating on some thin ice as far as the adoption went.

"Carey, relax," Debbie said gently. "They're for the baby, not for you. They're for David, *wherever* he goes."

And that was enough for Carey. That was how she viewed the situation, so Nick and Debbie's insight put them on the inside, right next to her. She hugged them again and thanked them for understanding. From that moment on Nick and Debbie have been an essential and fundamental part of David's life.

Each day Carey and David fell more deeply in love with each other, and were more and more inseparable. The whole rhythm of our life changed. We spoke in hushed tones much of the time to avoid rousing David. We were so busy learning the ins and outs of parenthood that we rarely if ever sat down to a meal together, and if we did, we ate in the living room while watching over David as he lay sleeping on the couch.

As Carey nurtured and cared for David, I observed her from my self-imposed distance. I watched as she fed David his tiny bottles of formula and burped him patiently. I watched as she gave him warm, gentle sponge baths, then dressed him in soft, clean clothes. In the evening I would tiptoe to the nursery door, which Carey left open just a crack while she rocked David and gave him his last bottle before bed. I would watch quietly as they rocked rhythmically, Carey's pink bathrobe draped gracefully to the floor. She had an almost contagious calm about her as she took care of David. She was consumed with mothering him. Still, I stayed a step or two away. It was all so new to me and still so full of risk.

By the second week even Carey found herself with some adjustments to make. I came home from work one day to find her uncharacteristically frustrated. "This is crazy," she told me. "I'm a planner, a manager. I manage a business office, and I'm used to things going the way I've planned. But babies are different! It doesn't work that way with motherhood! _David's_ in charge of _me_, and I'm trying to follow _his_ plans." I could understand what she was saying. I had underestimated how much control a tiny baby could have over two grown-ups' lives. Carey was trying her best to accommodate David's schedule as he set it, but it wasn't working the way she wanted it to.

At the end of the second week Carey called "a board meeting," which in our house means a serious talk where we present pressing issues to each other. So one evening after David was tucked safely into his crib, we sat together at the dining-room table. This was probably the first time we had really sat down together face-to-face since David had come home.

Carey outlined the problems and resolutions. As she saw it, the problems were twofold. One, we were used to planning our lives out months in advance, and now we were having difficulty planning out an hour. Solution: We would have a board meeting every morning to establish our goals for that day. Two, David's lack of schedule. Solution: Carey was going to get him on her schedule.

Not only did Carey put David on a schedule, but she put herself on a schedule, emphasizing good eating and sleeping habits. Then she put me on one, too, with some new limitations. I wasn't allowed to burn myself out by taking on too many things at once, as was my usual modus operandi. In addition she requested that I limit my overtime work. I had volunteered to do overtime in an effort to offset the cost of the adoption. But Carey reminded me that as a dual-income couple we had managed to squirrel away a nice nest egg. The total estimated cost of the agency adoption was quoted to us as around seven thousand dollars. "We can pay up front, in cash, for everything," Carey told me in her managerial mode, "and still have more than enough left. I'd rather you save your time and energy for David and me." I acquiesced.

True to her determined self, she had David on an established schedule by the time he was four weeks old. With an occasional exception, everything ran according to schedule. Before David was eight weeks old, he was sleeping a minimum of eight hours a night.

David, as it turned out, thrived on routine. We soon discovered that even as an infant he was very strong-willed. When it was just about the appointed time to eat, he would fuss ever so slightly, as if to warn Carey that she'd better not be a minute late with his bottle. Carey would produce the bottle, and if it wasn't exactly the right temperature, he'd let her know that too. If he wasn't swaddled in his blanket exactly the way he liked it, he would do his little fussy act until Carey corrected the problem. But as soon as everything within the routine was right according to Master David, together he and Carey would sit in total contentment. The security of a routine suited them both perfectly.

At seven o'clock on the dot each evening he had what Carey called his fussy time. Carey very quickly figured out that he was just unwinding, or as she liked to say, he was "just releasing his system overload" so that he could calm down for the night. It didn't fluster Carey in the least. In fact the fussier he was, the calmer she was.

Each night during his fussy time she would walk through the house with David cradled in her arms, whispering to him. "It's okay, little man," she would say. "Everything's fine. Don't worry about a thing. Mommy's going to hold you and walk you until you feel better." She would walk with him, stopping from time to time to point out items of interest in the house or to hold him up to the living-room mirror so that he could see his own reflection. She walked with him and talked softly to him until he quieted down, while I made myself scarce but useful, washing dishes or lining up the evening's bottles.

After he was calm and quiet, she would take him upstairs and give him his bath. She would lay a bath towel in the bottom of our tub and start running the warm water. Ever so gently she would lay David on the towel in the tub, his head and shoulder cradled in one of her hands, while she gently bathed him with the other hand. She kept the water running lightly "for atmosphere." David loved his baths, and always emerged totally calm and smelling like the first day of spring. Then it was into a sleeper and time for his good-night bottle.

The only other problem Carey was having with David was getting him to sip more than a few ounces at a time. He kept her in a state of constant feeding. I saw my opportunity to shine. "I may not know much about parenting," I told Carey one particularly frustrating evening, "but you have to admit that I know something about eating." I made him a full bottle, sat in the rocker with him, and told him I had filled the bottle with good, big-boy junk food from McDonald's, and I told him this was to be a male-bonding food fest. He looked up at me as he sucked and never took his eyes off me until the last drop was gone from the bottle. Carey was astounded, and knew I was proud of myself. She made a big deal out of my parenting accomplishment, and I accepted her compliments like a peacock with feathers in full fan.

Carey purposely kept visitors at bay at the outset. Even our families had to wait until she felt David was settled enough. She was very protective of him. David's next visitors were Carey's sister, Jennie, with her two young children, Emily and Paul. They came over about a week or so after David came home. By then Carey was beginning to feel ready for company. The lack of sleep that came from the demands of night feedings was catching up with her, and she was still adjusting to being at home instead of at work. It was definitely time for a family visit.

We hadn't told Emily and Paul about David before he was born for fear they would feel hurt and disappointed if the adoption failed to happen. When Paul, who was then six years old, found out about David, he was ecstatic to hear that he had a cousin, and moreover he was thrilled to have another boy in the family. As Carey changed David's diaper, Paul looked over the edge of the changing table, and showed obvious relief when he saw the proof that David was in fact a boy. Emily, a very mature eight-year-old, quickly assumed the role of sous-mother, and tried to help Carey every chance she got.

As the hours and days unfolded, we frequently wondered how Nancy was doing. Because the social workers had advised us so adamantly that we were not to contact Nancy, we were still a little hesitant to initiate contact with her despite the fact that she had told us to ignore the social workers' advice. We were still very concerned about doing what was best for Nancy during this painful time. We knew from what the social workers told us that she was still struggling with her emotions as well as with her clinical postpartum depression. Any reticence on her part, we knew, was a result of this.

When she finally did call, she confirmed that she was still having a very hard time. She was feeling lost and empty. By the time we hung up, Nancy was feeling at least a little bit better. She had been able to openly express her sadness and at the same time find reassurance from us that her baby was fine.

When we spoke with Nancy, we always listened patiently and with much interest to what she had to say. She seemed comfortable talking to us about everything from boyfriend troubles to how David was doing and how we ourselves were doing. If there was any advice or insight we had that we felt might help her, we shared it with her. Much of the time, though, just serving as a sounding board for her thoughts was all she really needed. For us, talking to Nancy helped us to feel that the bigger picture was still working in its mysterious, mystical way.

Most of the time Nancy would phone in the evening. Usually I would end up talking with her because, given the choice, I felt more competent to talk with Nancy than to watch over David. Carey would tend to David while Nancy and I carried on our conversations. Without realizing it, Nancy and I were finding a special source of strength in each other. We were both struggling with the uncertainty of what had happened and where things were going, and both of us were thrown off balance by the extreme emotions we were going through from our respective vantage points.

As Nancy and I found a bond through our long phone conversations, I began to feel very protective of her and her feelings. One evening, during one of our talks, Nancy told me, "I hope you don't mind me saying this, but you're like a father to me. I feel like you're always there to protect me." Nancy's candid expression of her feelings also showed me how cathartic such openness could be.

I told her I didn't mind at all. In fact, I said, this gave me a source of strength in confronting the emotions I was feeling. Knowing she looked to me for that kind of guidance allowed me to fall back into the role of protector, and to someone other than a newborn baby. It put me in touch with those protective "father feelings" and gave me a middle ground from which to build a bridge to my somewhat suppressed feelings about being a father to this tiny little person called David. If I could serve as a father figure to Nancy, I thought, then just maybe I could learn how to be a father to this tiny newborn.

Carey also talked with Nancy. Carey could clearly see the confusion she was feeling. Here she was, an eighteen-year-old girl who had just lived through nine months in which her attention was focused on caring for her unborn child. Now not only did she not have that focus but she had to deal with the profound loss she felt. She was trying to get back on her feet, but it was a tall order for someone who had just gone through such a range of physical and emotional changes.

Nancy had stayed in school until very close to her due date, and she did plan to go back to school soon after having the baby. Beyond that she felt uncertain about her future. She was worried about going back to school, since most girls who got pregnant kept their babies without question. Before taking her leave from school to have David, she had been looked upon by her school peers as doing the less noble thing, when in fact she had gone far and beyond doing what was right or noble. She had faced several cruel situations with her peers, who out of ignorance would make comments to her such as, "I can't believe you would just give your baby away."

We were always very saddened when Nancy alluded to what she had endured at school as her pregnancy progressed. We were thankful that she was comfortable in confiding to us the cruelty she had faced, and we were able to share in her pain and provide her some sincere support as she dealt with these issues. To us Nancy was mature and courageous far beyond her years. She was someone to be looked up to, not harrassed or ridiculed, for her brave and difficult decision. And always we were amazed that despite this peer pressure she never seemed to waiver even slightly in her commitment to her decision.

After all the cruelty she had faced before leaving school, going back was something she wasn't looking forward to, especially on top of her debilitating postpartum depression. Nancy found support from her wonderful family and from her boyfriend, Todd, who was doing his best to help her through this difficult time. Todd was like a security blanket for Nancy, protecting her and shielding her as best he could from the taunts of her peers.

Marilou supported her daughter's healing more than she realized when she told Nancy that she was so proud of what Nancy and we had accomplished. She told her to stand up for her decision because it had been a good and noble one. She told her that she ought to be proud not just to return to school but to take pictures of David with her to show to her friends and teachers, as well as the profile of Carey and me.

As her postpartum depression began to lift, Nancy became very open again. Carey and I would spend leisurely evening hours talking with Nancy on the phone. We were pleased that she was willing to keep that openness despite the warnings the social workers had given us about putting ourselves in a position that might be considered coercion.

Nancy told us how she was working hard to get through this difficult time. She was trying to socialize as best she could, and get back into the swing of things with her friends. One day when we talked, she told us about how she and a group of her childhood friends had gotten together at one of their houses to have a small party. No one had mentioned the baby, she said, and without having to be concerned for her pregnancy she drank a beer. The evening, she said, had allowed her "to almost feel like a teenager again." I was impressed by how astute she was in seeing how her experience had set her apart from her friends in so many ways. I wondered how much of her youth had been sacrificed when she chose to follow a course of action that was adult in every manner of speaking. At the same time I realized that, ironically, her remaining youth would have been sacrificed had she chosen to mother her child. Nancy had done her very best with what some might have called a no-win situation.

Todd, she told us, was really helping her to get back on her feet. She told us how he had taken her to the mall to pick out a scrapbook so that she had a place to store her mementos of David. She told us how Todd had taken her for a drive through the Metroparks to let her see the budding flowers of spring. When Nancy talked with Carey, she often talked about her relationship with Todd. There were the occasional rocky spots of any relationship, but she and Todd seemed committed to staying together.

Her feelings toward and focus on Todd seemed to give her some much-needed change from all she had just been through physically and emotionally. Their relationship served as a vehicle to carry her forward. It gave her a future to work toward. She told Carey that she and Todd planned to get married and that she was looking forward to when the two of them could begin their family together. Despite their ups and downs, their devotion to each other seemed never to wane. He had stood by her through the pregnancy and delivery, and now through the adoption, even though David was not his biological child.

We could tell from our talks with Nancy that she was still in a lot of deep emotional pain, probably deeper than we will ever truly know. But in her style of strength and conviction, Nancy was also ready to get on with life. She told Carey that she was in fact looking forward to "hanging out" with her close friends, despite the reception she knew she would get from some of the other kids.

When Nancy did go back to school, she met with disappointment. People asked her where her baby was and expressed disapproval when they heard the answer. Between some ups and downs with Todd, and the friction from classmates at school, Nancy was having a hard time finding any kind of balance in her life.

When the social workers had advised us against talking with Nancy, they told us in no uncertain terms that we were absolutely not to talk to Nancy about the topic of permanent surrender. In fact they didn't need to tell us this, because we found it natural not to. We knew it was Nancy's decision to make, at her own pace, on her own time. Our love and concern for her were far too great to broach that topic.

We were much more interested in tracking her personal progress and trying to do what we could to help her. We knew everything else would take care of itself in the end, whatever the outcome. Our hearts held great trust in fate and in God, and we knew that David would end up where he belonged. In fact, when we spoke with Nancy on the phone, we rarely talked much about David. Despite the fact that we had told Nancy we were calling him David (something that didn't surprise her, since Carey had told her in an initial conversation that David was her favorite name for a boy), Nancy would always ask "How's he doing?" and as soon as we answered, that was about as far as she carried the topic. We knew that by not referring to him by name, Nancy was delicately distancing herself. Even in the way she phrased her question she implied that David was no longer her baby but ours.

We began to feel a strain, not in our relationship with Nancy but in our relationship with certain friends and family members. They made no bones about voicing their concerns. No matter how often we reassured them that we were comfortable with the situation, they implied that Nancy was posing a threat to us and might very well try to take David away from us. At first we were dismayed by their ignorance and explained repeatedly that we were enjoying a positive, sincere relationship with Nancy that centered around our mutual love for David. As time went on, though, we got tired of defending ourselves and Nancy. We finally had to conclude that until they saw how well things went farther down the road, the doubting Thomases were better left alone. We didn't need any more to deal with than was already in front of us.

In our conversations with Nancy there was never any discussion about future visits with one another, and this was something that Carey and I did think about. We knew that if David stayed in our lives, we wanted Nancy to stay in our lives, too, in any capacity she chose. We never discussed specific plans as far as birthdays or holidays, but with her incredible maternal instincts, Carey knew that somehow, someday, Nancy would come into our lives again.

After a couple of weeks at home with David, nearly in complete sequestration, Carey was ready for a reprieve. She broke it to me that she was going to need to get out of the house from time to time and leave David at home with me. I was too proud to say that I continued to feel inadequate in the baby department, and I loved Carey too much to stand in her way if that's what she needed.

One afternoon Carey announced that she was going to go out for an hour. This was really the first time she had left the house by herself since David had come home. She charged off to the grocery store, list in hand, ready to grab what we needed and get back home. Two neighbors had seen Carey leave and came over to offer their assistance, knowing me as they did. I happily invited them in, but assured them that I had things running smoothly. They sat politely near me, as if ready to rescue me should the scene turn "ugly." David, obviously appreciating an audience, graciously filled his diaper to overflowing with "rooty-toots," as Carey said. I was terribly embarrassed as I tried to clean up the mess while these seasoned moms sat on the sidelines waiting for me to let them help.

Despite the hours I had spent carefully observing Carey's techniques, I was fumbling badly. Things were out of control at the moment Carey walked back into the house. She found me with David laid on a towel on the living-room floor, his diaper off, and diaper wipes and ointment spread all around. There I sat holding David's tiny little legs up in the air, wiping furiously at the mess I had discovered in his diaper and on his bottom. When Carey came through the door, I looked up aghast. I knew I was doing everything wrong. When I looked back down at David, I was horrified. He was continuing the job he had apparently only just begun. There was mess everywhere. I grabbed at wipes and tried to catch it midflow, but it was overwhelming. I felt myself blush.

I looked up and saw Carey suppressing a smile. The two neighbors giggled softly. "Here, Dion," Carey said as she put down the grocery sacks she had carried in, "you take a break. I'll finish up. Just let me wash my hands first." She took over and got David cleaned up and diapered in the time it took me to carry the bags out to the kitchen. It was a humbling experience for me, yet when all was said and done, I began to realize that I could in fact tackle taking care of this baby. In Carey's eyes it was a turning point. She was thrilled that I had finally broken through my hesitations and initiated myself into the hands-on parenting of David.

As April wore on, the weather began to lift a little. One of Carey's friends had given her a nice, gently used stroller. With the temptation of a warm day Kit had come over and taken the stroller outside to scrub it in preparation for its maiden voyage with David on board. When it was clean and dry, Kit and Carey dressed David in his Sunday go-to-meeting clothes, and put him in the stroller. The three of them took a leisurely walk around the block in an effort to get him some fresh air and alleviate some of Carey's cabin fever.

David seemed to enjoy the change of scenery as much as Carey did, and was quiet and content. Carey relished the change of venue, too, as well as Kit's upbeat company. Midway down the road a neighbor of ours walked over to Carey and asked with curiosity, "Who's this?" Carey stroked David's cheek and answered with a surge of pride, "This is Dion's and my baby."

She paused, not knowing whether to add the warning "Don't get too excited—right now we're just doing foster care." Instead she told him briefly that we were planning to adopt David. The neighbor looked surprised and seemed to be momentarily at a loss for words. "I didn't know you guys were trying to adopt!" he exclaimed. Carey told him we had been hoping for quite some time and that David was the little miracle that our prayers had brought us.

That walk around the block and the encounter with our neighbor was very significant for Carey. She told me all about it when I came home that evening. Just a few months ago we had been ready to pack up and leave the neighborhood we loved so much simply because it was too painful for us to watch all the other parents strolling with their babies down our sidewalk, let alone for us to see the beautiful children the people around us were blessed with. Now, after we had nearly given up all hope, we were the ones pushing the stroller while others stopped us to admire our beautiful child.

I decided to try the stroller contraption myself. The way I saw it, it allowed me to do something as a parent instead of just watching, and it was something I felt I could handle fairly well. One afternoon I loaded David into the stroller and took Sam outside to join us on our walk. I learned, after one failed attempt, never to leash Sam to the stroller. Thinking I was being very organized, I tried tying Sam's leash to the side handlebar of the stroller. All went well until Sam caught wind of a cat and took chase. With each gallop the stroller would bump Sam's hindquarters, and in terror he would run a little faster, wildly pulling the stroller along with him. What a sight we must have made, with me racing behind, trying to keep up with the runaway dog-and-stroller, while trying not to trip and fall in the effort. I'm not sure whose panic was worse, but I'm sure I had a close brush with cardiac arrest that afternoon.

My revised technique was to have Sam heel to the left of the stroller. Sam caught on quickly and became David's and my strolling companion. We must have logged a few hundred miles together. At last I had found a helpful niche in taking care of David as a newborn.

We often ran into neighbors on our walks, and in the beginning, much as Carey had, I would introduce David as the child we were planning to adopt. The oohs and ahs always made me feel so proud, not just of David but of Nancy and Carey and how we were all handling the situation. The fact that both Carey and I were now out and about in our neighborhood, staying and belonging instead of packing up and leaving, was a clear flash of reality. It was as though the fresh air helped to reawaken us to the fact that our story might very well have a happy ending after all.

CHAPTER

18

The permanent surrender loomed ahead of all of us. Carey and I really didn't talk about it with each other, let alone with Nancy. There really wasn't much to discuss. It was either going to happen or it wasn't. To talk about it felt almost sacrilegious. Moreover we felt it was perfectly natural for Nancy to take her time making her decision, and we knew she needed time to let her depression lift.

In our phone conversations the most Nancy said was that she was going to be the one to tell us when the surrender was signed, not the social workers. She was adamant about this, saying that she was the one giving up the child, not the social workers. It was so in keeping with Nancy to take personal responsibility even in the face of such a horrendously painful decision. It also spoke of her attachment to her child, despite her decision not to raise him herself.

We had a fairly clear picture of what Nancy faced in signing the final surrender. This process had been discussed with us at length by the social workers in our home-study group. It wasn't pleasant; in fact, they told us, it was very brutal on the birth mother. In signing over the baby to someone else's custody, the birth mother was read every line of the supporting document, emphasizing in gruesome detail the fact that in signing she would be severing forever every legal right she had to her biological child.

Like everything else in the adoption process, only the legalities were addressed. It was left up to the birth mother to handle the lifetime of emotional repercussions from relinquishing her child. We could only begin to imagine what it must must feel like to face a decision of that magnitude. The only comparison we could make was to imagine giving David back to Nancy and never hearing from them again, and having no legal right ever to contact them again. We couldn't fathom making an appointment to sign papers establishing such an arrangement, let alone keeping the appointment and putting pen to paper on the dotted line. How could we expect Nancy, who had carried David inside her for nine months, to do exactly that? It was a horrible thought.

So as we waited for some final decision, our wait was fraught with the thought of Nancy's continued emotional demise. When we talked on the phone with her, it was about everything but the surrender. She really was trying to get on with her life. She was incredibly stoic and focused. Still, there were undertones of depression and confusion. We knew that the surrender must be on Nancy's mind constantly. We felt for her with all our hearts. The pain involved in even the best of adoption situations was growing ever clearer to us.

One evening in the middle of a phone conversation with Nancy, she very matter-of-factly told me that she had made an appointment to sign the permanent-surrender papers. She told me the date and time, as if it was nothing more than an appointment at the dentist for a root canal, an unpleasant but necessary task that had to be taken care of. As she spoke, I simply made a checkmark on the calendar in the kitchen to signify the date. And just like a planned root-canal procedure, an air of impending pain lingered from that moment on. It was not a question of *if* it was going to hurt but of exactly *how much.*

Nancy's appointment to sign the permanent surrender fell on the evening of April 16th. Not having her driver's license yet, Nancy had to wait for a time when her mother could drive her to the agency for the signing. The day of Nancy's appointment Carey and I could barely speak about it to each other. There was unbelievable tension and sadness in the air. Neither one of us would have been surprised or blamed Nancy if she couldn't bring herself to sign the papers. We both knew that Nancy could be at the table, pen in hand, and still change her mind. And, we thought, who could possibly blame a mother who chose not to confront life's deepest imaginable pain: the loss of a child?

And yet we had grown to love David too. It would have been much harder for us to let go now than if the adoption had been halted right at the time of David's birth. The day of the surrender appointment Carey moved in slow motion through her morning ritual. As she held David and gave him his bottle, she was blinking back tears. "I think I know what Nancy's going through right now," she said, sniffling. "We're both facing the same thing. One of us is going to have to give up our rights to this child. One of us will become a forever mother to this baby, while one of us surrenders our motherhood. What one of us loses, the other gains. It's only a question of which one of us gives him up to the other. It's like I told Nancy in the hospital after she had him: *Someone* is going to suffer a broken heart. The only guarantee, the only thing I can be glad about, is knowing that David's welfare is not at stake. He will be loved and cared for no matter what. Thank God for that."

I worked the three-to-eleven shift that night. As I drove around in my patrol car, my thoughts and prayers for Nancy were almost constant. I stopped frequently to phone Carey to see if she had heard anything from Nancy. Each time I talked to her, the conversation would begin with one of us saying "Our poor Nancy." We believed she had resolved to sign the papers, so the question in our minds wasn't so much if she would sign but what kind of shape she would be in afterward. We couldn't imagine what signing this surrender would do to Nancy and her mother. Their hurt, we knew, would be unbearable. As I drove, the refrain from a song played over and over in my mind. It was one that had been popular during my teenage years, sung by Dan Fogelberg, and I hadn't heard it in ages: "Her heart was so fragile, and heavy to hold . . ."

The night passed without word from Nancy. Out of respect and love for her we didn't phone. She had said she would be the one to tell us when the papers were signed, and that was promise enough for us. We would wait to hear from her. She would tell us where things stood.

When the phone rang the next morning, we thought it would be Nancy. Instead it was Nan Lahr, our social worker. She told us that Nancy had indeed signed the papers, but not without incredible anguish. The meeting had been extremely difficult for Nancy and her mother, and many tears were cried by both. We knew that this must be true, that Nancy and her mother must have been incapacitated by their grief, otherwise Nancy herself would have been the one calling us as she had planned.

She told us that there had been a moment when Nancy very nearly changed her mind about signing after being told in more detail of the legalities of the surrender. In explaining the terms of the surrender the social worker told Nancy that she was signing custody of David over to the agency, who would then place him in an adoptive home. There were no specific guarantees about David being placed with us, the parents whom Nancy had chosen for David.

In fact it was stipulated that it was up to the agency to decide with whom David would be permanently placed, and they retained the right to deem us unfit to be his parents if—heaven forbid—they found just cause to do so. Nancy was horrified to learn this, she told us; she had assumed that her wish to place David with us would be upheld unconditionally. They had strongly reassured Nancy that they were committed to placing him with us and that unless extraordinary circumstances occurred, that was what would happen. Only after much reassurance would Nancy sign the papers. She was terrified by the thought that there was even the slightest, most minuscule chance that David might fall into the system and get lost. She wanted David to be with us, and if he was not going to be, then she wanted him to stay with her. The permanent surrender guaranteed neither, and no one had forewarned her of this.

By the time we finished talking with the social worker, Carey was ready to explode. She was furious at the way Nancy had discovered the terms and conditions of the surrender only at the end of her already painful journey. We knew the social workers had done their best to serve and protect us all and that they had everyone's best interests at heart. Still it seemed inconceivable that Nancy had not been told the specifics of what she would be asked to sign.

As soon as we hung up, Carey let loose. "This is inexcusable," she said angrily. "This system is horrendous. It's done nothing but create problems for Nancy and us the whole way, and it's done nothing to serve or protect David." She sat down on the living-room couch and took a deep breath. "What's happened up to this point has all been miscommunication, and in the end I suppose that can be written off. But this was information that was never made clear to Nancy until the moment of greatest pain and vulnerability. How could the system be so cruel? How could they take her that far down the path without preparing her for what she could encounter? Poor Nancy. I don't blame her at all for having been ready to forget the whole thing. It's as if they were saying, 'Just hand everything over to us and we'll take it from here. Don't worry, don't look back, and don't count on things going the way you requested.' "

Carey was very protective of Nancy, and her anger was more for what added pain and fear Nancy had been put through than anything else. She wasn't worried that David would be taken from us, we were sure he wouldn't be. Carey was worried that Nancy's heart had received its final blow.

When Nancy finally phoned us later that afternoon, we were relieved to hear from her. She apologized for not calling us the night before, telling us it was just too hard for her. We told her we understood fully and that we hadn't called her because we knew she probably needed time to herself.

Carey went on to tell her that we had heard about the confusion and that we were more than a little upset that somehow in the course of events she had not been prepared for the exact process and documents she would be dealing with. Nancy confirmed that she had "almost lost it" when she was told that she was relinquishing David to the agency and not to us. Moreover she told us that the wording used in the documents was so brutal that in signing it a birth mother was made to feel like she was admitting that "yes, there is something wrong with me and I can't raise this child." We could hear, even then, the pain and fear in her voice. We knew she needed some love and support and encouragement. Her spirits had sunk about as low as they could go.

She spoke quietly and sadly, her voice a little shaky. She told us of her fear that David might not end up with us, and if not with us, then who knew where? As she spoke, we could also tell that this felt to her like the end of the line. It was the end of all she had been working toward, the end of her relationship with her tiny child, the end of things with us. Things were out of her hands. Any control she had over how things would go had come to an end. And what an ending—it must have felt to her as if a cruel trick was played on her at the last minute, when her options were so few and her vulnerability so great.

There had never been any question in our minds that Nancy loved David with all her heart. As our conversations with her had become more in-depth and personal, we clearly sensed that Nancy loved David dearly for who he was, her child. We also sensed that she deeply regretted that circumstances were such that she couldn't keep him. She was very open about her commitment to

Todd and their hope to marry someday, and she was excruciatingly sad and regretful that things hadn't happened slightly differently, in a different order and under better circumstances.

We told her that everything was going to work out and that we really loved her and would be there for her no matter what. We wished we could make her understand that it wasn't the end of the line, that we weren't going to take David and disappear from her life. At this point, if there was anything that was certain, it was that we couldn't and wouldn't just let Nancy and David go their separate ways forever. We knew Nancy was going to be a part of our lives on some level, because anything else would have felt too cruel, and just not right.

So Carey told Nancy, "Look, they've done it their way up to now. We've abided by the rules and nuances of the system. Over and over we've followed their rules, and look where it's almost taken us. We love you, and we love David, and we want only the best for all of us. Let's make an agreement to do this thing our way from now on. Let's make our own rules and follow our own hearts." Nancy's quiet agreement was plenty for us. We knew she was depleted and needed only this reassurance from us to help her to keep going.

It seems the right things always come to mind at the right time. Suddenly I knew it was time to ask Nancy a question Carey and I had been thinking about. We had discussed having a birth announcement printed for David's arrival. We had talked with a friend of ours who ran a print shop. I had picked out a simple format like our wedding announcement—ivory with raised black script. Carey had thought about how to word it and had come up with some good ideas.

The one thing we had really focused on was how we were going to include Nancy in the announcement. We knew she needed to be a part of it, as she was a very real and important part of ours and David's lives. We had thought long and hard about how to word things. We didn't want people to think we were coparenting with Nancy. We just wanted people to know that Nancy was still a loving member of our family. Finally I had come up with an idea, and now the time seemed right to ask Nancy herself if she would approve.

"What would you feel about us printing at the bottom of David's birth announcement, 'We request your prayers for our birth mother, Nancy'?"

Quietly, in a voice choked with emotion, Nancy answered, "That would be beautiful."

While I wasn't the greatest caregiver an infant could ask for, one thing I could do well was fight to protect my family. This was where I focused my energies now. I assured Nancy that she didn't have to worry about the loophole that existed in the permanent surrender, that I was going to make sure that David either stayed with us or went back to her, period, the end. I told her I was making arrangements with my attorney and friends to fight a legal battle on her behalf should something happen to Carey and me prior to the finalization of the adoption papers or should any kind of complication arise preventing the finalization.

In an effort to protect Nancy, I took my understanding of the legal system to new extremes. I had wills drawn up specifically naming Nick and Debbie, his godparents, as guardians for David. I made sure that all our assets would be available to them to fight a mean legal battle to return custody of David back to Nancy if it came to that. If that didn't work, I figured, by the time the legal battles had been fought and lost, David would be a teenager anyway and capable of expressing his own wants. When I told Nancy of my extensive contingency plans, designed to keep us together under any possible scenario, she simply and sincerely said, "I know that you will always take care of me. Thank you."

The legal process of adoption began after Nancy signed the permanent-placement papers. On April 23rd we were to meet with our social workers at Lake County Catholic Service Bureau for the formal presentation of the adoption papers. For us it was more or less a formality, as we were David's foster parents. However, the agency is required to present all information about the child's health and family history, foster care, and so forth. As requested by the agency, we arranged to leave David at home with a sitter, something that took some convincing for Carey. Our neighbor's eighteen-year-old daughter, a frequent visitor to our household, came to stay with him. With her knowledge of David and her mother right across the street, she met Carey's standards of a suitable sitter. She arrived on the dot, and after Carey had briefed her on everything she needed to know about taking care of David for the evening, we prepared to return to the building where we had made our first face-to-face successful step toward finding a child of our own, now to finalize the placement of our new son.

For Carey this was one of the few times she had gotten out of the house to do anything other than take a quick walk or go to the grocery store since David had come home. She went upstairs to put on some "real clothes," only to find that in her frenzied days of caring for David she had lost so much weight that her pants hung loosely on her. She looked at herself in the mirror and laughed. "What's so funny?" I asked her.

"This is typical. Everything has been the opposite of the norm from the word *go*. Look at me. I finally have a baby, and I'm the opposite of being pregnant or postpartum. I'm skinny and I have circles under my eyes. Certainly not the picture of radiant maternal beauty."

I hugged her. "To me you are. And to David too."

We arrived at the agency and walked through the familiar hallways. As we turned a corner, we nearly bumped into George, who along with his wife had been part of our home-study group. We were surprised to see one another. It turned out that George worked in the building and was on his way home. It was our turn to explain our presence in the building. George looked at us expectantly and I knew that what we had to say was going to hurt. We had been in his shoes, too, hearing that other people had been chosen to adopt. It wasn't easy news to take if your heart was aching to have a child to love and hold.

I told him, almost apologetically, that we were on our way to sign our papers for the adoption of our son. He couldn't disguise his sadness and envy, but congratulated us sincerely. "I don't know if I'm going to tell Julie," he told us. "I know how hard it will be for her." We understood, we said, as we had all been through it. We wished him and Julie well and went on to our meeting, freshly reminded of how extraordinarily lucky we were to have Nancy and David in our lives.

The formal presentation went quickly and easily. Our openness with Nancy and our fostering of David had allowed us to be privy to almost all the information they presented us with. We met with our social worker as well as with Nancy's social worker, Kate. The most enlightening thing we learned in this presentation came from Kate, who had interviewed David's birth father. In describing her meeting with him, she said she considered him to be quite intelligent, and remorseful about the entire situation. And while he wanted no part of the openness, he did consent to providing a complete medical history and genealogy of his family. For this we will be forever grateful. Its importance cannot be overestimated.

Our presentation package included all of David's hospital birth records, copies of his hospital crib identification card and hospital bracelet (Nancy had chosen to keep the originals as precious mementos of her son), pediatrician notes, and the social and medical histories of David's birth parents. Everything we were presented with ended up in the cloth-bound scrapbook Carey had started the day Nancy and David entered our lives.

As we were getting ready to leave, the social workers raised a red flag. They asked us if we had talked with Nancy, because they were worried about her. When we asked them why, they told us that they were concerned because usually birth mothers continued with postadoption counseling, but Nancy had refused further counseling. We were unaware of this, we told them, and left the meeting very concerned for her well-being.

In all the meeting took an hour. We were on our way to finalization, which by law could not occur until six months after permanent surrender. Very few things could interrupt the adoption process at this time. Nothing short of abuse, morals charges, fraud, deception or coercion, death, or failure to comply with state requirements could prevent us from becoming a family. We were happy to be done with it, happy to be past one more technicality, and happy to go home to our waiting son. As we drove, Carey looked back over the papers we had been given. "Hmm," she muttered under her breath.

"Hmm what?" I asked.

"Here's something I actually didn't know."

"What's that?"

"It says here that Nancy is allergic to caterpillars."

"Allergic to caterpillars? Is that medically significant?" I chuckled.

"I don't know," Carey answered much more seriously than I asked. "But all we have to do to find out is call Nancy."

Soon after we got home, we decided that we should report back to Nancy that the papers were signed on our end too. In addition Carey's curiosity got the better of her. She phoned Nancy, and what might have been a heavyhearted conversation turned out to be a lighthearted talk between friends as Carey asked the burning question: How can someone be allergic to caterpillars, and how does someone find this out? The ensuing conversation was filled with laughter as Nancy explained that when she was a little girl, she let a caterpillar walk on her arm and small red bumps had appeared. Carey was in stitches and said, "Well, if David ever encounters a caterpillar, I'll know what to expect."

On a more serious note we told her that the social workers were concerned about her because she had refused counseling. Nancy's answer was straightforward: "Anytime I feel blue, all I have to do is call you guys and I feel better." She told us that she was sure that people who didn't have the openness in adoption probably needed the counseling, but that she got all the help she needed from *us*.

CHAPTER

19

A new chapter opened in our lives. Our fostering was over. David was no longer our foster child. He was our son. It sounded momentous, a gigantic leap forward. In contrast it felt almost anti-climactic, hardly different at all. Where we had already been functioning as if we were a legal family, things had changed only on paper. During the first few days Carey remarked several times about how strikingly less dramatic the change felt than we had predicted. She truly had given herself over to David completely from the moment we arrived at the hospital as his foster parents.

It was only in retrospect that I realized that for me it was indeed a turning point. After those permanent-placement papers were signed, my emotions began to open; my defenses were whittled away. I should have seen the red flag go up after our chance meeting in the hallway with George. My heart had gone out to him instantly. I had known that we had finally landed—at least technically—in a safe haven, with our arms around our son, while he and his wife were still floating in uncertainty and dwindling hope. I felt terrible for him. That was new for me, something I had been trained to avoid. I didn't realize at the time that my sensitivity to his pain was part of the pain Nancy, Carey, and I had been struggling with.

Word leaked out that our permanent-placement papers were signed. Inevitably each family member we told would tell us, "Congratulations! That's great!" as we informed them of the permanent surrender. We thanked them for their support, and in doing so tried to explain that our "gain" was at the emotional expense of David's birth mother. It was hard not to feel frustration when our friends failed to realize that Nancy's pain affected us, too, and that our happiness at becoming parents was tempered by that pain.

When we told Nick and Debbie that the permanent papers had been signed, we knew we had chosen the right people to be David's godparents. Nick's immediate and solemn reaction was, "How's Nancy?" Only after we had updated him on Nancy's well-being did he and Debbie ask us how we were feeling with this new gift of parenthood. I knew they understood the whole picture, and I was grateful that he and Debbie were such an integral part of our lives.

As part of our finalization we were required by the state to have follow-up visits by our social workers. Our agency, Lake County Catholic Service Bureau, allowed its clients to fulfill this requirement by attending the meetings of their Friends of Children group. These once-a-month, two-hour meetings were held at the location where we had first met Nancy.

Again we were amazed to find how everything seemed to come full circle. Going through this part of the finalization process within the very walls of the building where we had made our connection with Nancy helped us to see that. The meetings themselves were a great experience. Held in a large room upstairs, they were attended by foster parents, adoptive parents, and their children. Because the meetings served as a supervised visit, the adoptive and foster parents were expected to bring their children with them.

We derived a great deal of moral support from the other meeting members, as well as a lot of practical parenting and adoption advice. I listened to the other parents talking about the daily challenges of childrearing, such as feeding, sleep routines, doctor's visits, and so forth. As I listened to stories of colicky babies, sleepless nights, and goofed-up schedules, I realized with a surge of pride that I was really proud of my son! He was, I realized, a really terrific baby. I was also reminded of what a great mother and wife Carey was as I thought about how beautifully she had handled her newfound motherhood and everything else that went along with it. The three of us made a wonderful family, I thought, and simultaneously I realized that I was now seeing myself as both a husband and a father.

Each meeting was inevitably a happy three-ring circus, with everyone working toward one common goal. For our first meeting David was too young to attend, being less than a month old. Carey, who was by now exhausted from her new role as mother of a newborn, stayed home with David. I attended by myself, and was surprised and happy to find that our friends from our home-study group, Bob and Lori, were there too. They were well into the finalization of the adoption of their son and were thrilled to hear that we were on our way to becoming parents too.

As a first-time attendee I was asked to introduce myself to the group and give some background about why I was there. I introduced myself and began to explain our experience, from our first meeting with Nancy up through David's birth and our conversations after the birth. Almost immediately I could sense a certain uneasiness in the room, and I observed several women's mouths literally drop open.

Today I know that what was normal for us was a bombshell to the others in the room, as almost all of them were involved in traditional adoptions. The only real support I got was from Bob and Lori, who had adopted their child in an open adoption as well.

However, even their situation was different from ours, as the openness of their relationship with their birth mother blossomed at a much slower and more reserved pace than ours. They were very supportive of us, though, and truly embraced our experience as they learned about it in detail.

Following the first meeting one of the social workers took me aside to talk with me privately. She told me our experience was so unique that a lot of people were feeling uncomfortable. To this day I remember the look on her face as I told her, "I will bring forth the issue of open adoption not just to this group but to our state and country as well." She laughed and told me, "You'll be taking on a big task." Little did she know the degree of my resolve.

Seeing Bob and Lori at the meeting triggered a reconnection between us and them. Lori phoned Carey a couple of days after the first meeting and chatted animatedly with her about the FOC meetings, and how things were going in general. Carey was never one to complain, but by then she was beginning to suffer "newborn burnout," as she called it. She was burning the candle at both ends, and was feeling the effects of her change of pace. She was glad to have the chance to talk to another new mom, especially someone who could relate on a personal level to what we had been through in the previous weeks with Nancy and David.

At one point in their conversation Carey, in a tired stupor, wasn't quite following what Lori was saying. Lori realized that she had lost Carey and slowed down. "It's okay, Carey," Lori told her with compassion, "*it gets better.*" Those were just the words of encouragement Carey needed to keep her going through those long "newborn" months. To this day Carey looks back on Lori's words of support as one of the most precious and often-used gifts she was given as a new mother.

Carey was excited at the prospect of attending the meetings, too, and in May, when David was two months old, she and David joined me at their first Friends of Children meeting. We were still operating in new-parenthood mode. Carey hadn't even had time to go out and buy a real diaper bag, so she made her appearance holding David and a flowered gym bag bulging with too many bottles and too many diapers. She was just happy to get out of the house and have the chance to socialize and gather information from the attendees and social workers. She held David on her lap the whole meeting, in her element, absorbing everything that was happening around her.

We quickly found out that other than Bob and Lori we were in fact the first really open adoption to be part of the FOC group. In some regards it was a disadvantage for us. We had no precedent to look to, for example. We *were* the precedent. No one, other than Bob and Lori, could offer us insights about openness issues. We were going where no one had really gone before. As time went by, we found we needed to learn about and discuss issues that began to confront us, such as outsiders' perceptions, family concerns, and how to balance the ongoing relationship we had—or hoped to have—with David's birth family.

Even the social workers seemed to have a difficult time handling openness in the Friends of Children meetings. While they were in support of it, they were somewhat hesitant to point to us as a standard of any sort. They would sometimes add disclaimers when referring to our situation, suggesting that others shouldn't compare their adoptions to ours. While Carey and I wanted to serve as a resource to others who were considering or were involved in open adoptions, we, too, understood that not all open adoptions would look like ours. In fact our adoption process was ongoing, so we were still nowhere near defining what, in the end, *open* would mean to us.

In May the social workers running the FOC meetings requested that Carey and I make a presentation for the group about open adoption. We were happy to comply. I gave a fairly detailed synopsis of our experience, along with some of our insights into the advantages that could come with open adoption. Carey, holding David, fielded questions. We soon learned what the most common question was, and it always came first: "How do you establish who David's real mother is?" Without hesitation Carey answered that "being a mother has more to do with giving love than giving birth." As a mother caring for this precious child, she said, she could clearly understand the loss Nancy had suffered as a birth mother.

When we were done with our presentation, and the meeting was over, it was obvious that there were more questions being asked than answered. A few people still couldn't grasp this concept, and some people avoided us. We weren't surprised, though. We knew not everyone would "get it" as quickly as we had been forced to.

Spring was in the air. We could feel the tension beginning to lift as the days grew sunnier and warmer. Carey, David, and I were a family now. It was time to get settled into some kind of normalcy. As the days and weeks went by, our lives seemed to pull together, and with each passing day we could feel ourselves bonding.

Mother's Day arrived. It was Carey's first, and I picked out a nice card for her and bought her a bouquet of spring flowers. Knowing it would be a day of intense and mixed emotions for Nancy, Carey had chosen a special Mother's Day card for her. She had signed it and addressed it; then as the day approached, Carey didn't feel right about sending it to her. She was keenly aware that Nancy was focused on getting back to school and that she was working hard on getting back to being just herself, just Nancy Miller. She was trying to move forward. "She's probably still so sensitive and so overwhelmed," Carey told me. "The card might stir up those difficult feelings even more. Let's just call her and talk to her."

David gave Carey the best Mother's Day gift she could have asked for: That night, he slept through the night from eight o'clock in the evening to well past six o'clock in the morning. He had become a good sleeper on the schedule Carey had imposed, but this was definitely a banner sleepathon for David. From that point on Carey began to catch up on her rest. As Carey began to feel more rested, I grew more comfortable with parenthood, and actually began to be of some help to her in taking care of David. I offered to give him his last bottle of the day each evening so that Carey could go to bed earlier. I found that I looked forward to this quiet, private time with David. I would sit with him in the rocking chair as Carey did and look into his beautiful green eyes. He would look right back into mine, and we would maintain this transfixed stare until his little eyelids grew so heavy that he fell asleep in my arms.

At last we were free to let our guard down. The friends we had kept at a distance came to visit us frequently now; the unspoken hiatus had come to an end. What had been an awkward and often painful situation was now turning into a cautiously joyous one. Our friends were no longer confused about how to approach us, although many of them still couldn't grasp the enormity of what we had been through.

We could feel our hearts slowly healing, and our parenthood vulnerabilities beginning to fade away. Only a few months ago Carey had been in such emotional pain that she not only avoided other people's babies but she avoided going to baby showers at any cost. Just a short time ago she couldn't even bring herself to walk into the baby department when she went shopping for a baby gift. She would always pick out a neutral, non-baby-specific gift, such as a picture frame.

Those days were gone. David had filled the emptiness inside her and resolved her pain. Now Carey's friends threw a baby shower for her. She was absolutely exuberant as she prepared herself and David to attend the party in their honor. She had never imagined that she would be the mother for whom a shower was given. This was her time to shine. She dressed David in her favorite outfit for him, and together they drove down to Nick and Debbie's house in Akron, where they spent the day being lavished upon by her friends.

She and David came back that afternoon tired and content, the car loaded down with gifts. Knowing she was an avid antiquer, one of Carey's friends had bought her a vintage baby-formula pitcher. We had to laugh later when Carey's mother looked at it and told us how very useful it would be. "It's vintage, Mother," Carey said, "it's just for show." "Vintage?" her mother said in shock. "I used one of those to make your formula when you were a baby."

Carey and I began to find a kind of equilibrium again in our daily life. We began to visit with our friends again, although we found we gravitated to a new style of entertaining. Where we had enjoyed "fine dining" at Cleveland's best restaurants before, we now took to ordering pizzas and having people in to visit. We went from theater tickets to video rentals. We learned, after many years, where the Pause button was on our VCR. Our close friends adjusted to our changes right along with us. Even our childless friends welcomed David with open hearts and arms.

While Carey and I felt our life blossoming and moving in new directions, Nancy continued to go through some intense ups and downs. She had returned to school and was having a hard time feeling comfortable there. The whole experience of having David and placing him with us put Nancy far beyond most of her peers in terms of maturity. She found it difficult at times to relate to her schoolmates. The school year was coming to an end, and while her classmates were heralding the coming of summer and were in a festive party mood, Nancy was still trying to work through her own issues.

We talked with Nancy on the phone at least a couple of times a week. She spoke to us candidly and let us know what was going on in her life. She was making a valiant attempt to get back into the swing of things, so to speak. She was spending time with her friends and was going to parties again, something she hadn't done while she was pregnant. She also found a part-time job at a cookie store at the mall near her house. She enjoyed this job a great deal, and many of her friends made it a point to stop by to see her during her work hours.

One day, without warning, David's birth father went to see Nancy at work. The two of them had spoken on occasion but had not maintained any regular communication. Nancy had been open-minded and forgiving enough not to cut off communication with him entirely, but she had grown increasingly resentful of him for washing his hands of the situation. While her life had been put on hold and she had suffered the anguish of relinquishing her baby, he had gone on with his own life as if nothing had changed.

When he appeared at her workplace, Nancy, always poised, pulled out a picture of David and gave it to him. Later, in the fall, he came back to find her at her job and gave her money for a Christmas present for David. Surprisingly even these encounters seemed to provide some healing for Nancy's wounded spirit.

For a stretch of time Nancy seemed to be pulling herself together and feeling stronger, until one night she called and told me, "Dion, I feel so hollow inside." When I heard her say this, my heart just about broke. I could hear the sadness in her voice, and her simple statement cut right through me. "We need to go farther in this relationship," I told her. I decided I had to cut to the heart of the matter. "Let me ask you something, Nancy," I said. "Who is David to you?"

Nancy was quiet for a moment. When she spoke, she was crying. "He's my son," she said.

"Exactly," I responded softly. "Isn't it a nice thing to finally say out loud?"

Nancy's emotions overflowed at that point. There was so much bottled up inside of her, and it was finally finding an outlet. "I didn't want to say those words because it almost seemed like I shouldn't, like it would be wrong of me to say."

I told her it was far from wrong, that it was a fact, and it was right. I told her she should never hesitate to say those words and that hopefully in the future we could all say those words without thinking twice. I told her someday I hoped she would feel comfortable saying, "These are the people who adopted my son, and I love them very much." Nancy listened carefully to all that I said and began to realize that now it was up to all of us; we had moved beyond what the laws and social workers could dictate.

I offered an analogy to Nancy with the hope that it would make her truly understand what I was saying. "Your mom and dad are divorced, but they still acknowledge and care for each other, right?" She agreed. "Your stepfather isn't your birth father, but you love him very much, right?" She agreed. "And David is your son, and you love him very much. What's wrong with you loving him and acknowledging that he's your son? There really are no rules about who we're allowed to love." Somehow my reasoning made sense to Nancy, and she ended the conversation by telling me, "You guys always make me feel so much better! I love you so much."

When I got off the phone with Nancy, I told Carey in detail about the conversation. Carey, too, was terribly dismayed to hear that Nancy was so sad. We knew we needed to do something to help her, since she had so obviously reached out to us for help. As Carey and I talked together, we realized that the bottom line was that for Nancy there had been no true "closure."

The permanent surrender had been a devastating and terrible finale to her act of courage. She needed something better, she deserved something better. What she needed, we realized, was to have her surrender of David to us be recognized for what it was, a completely pure act of love and selflessness. Together we stumbled upon an idea that became a brainstorm. We wanted to have David baptized, and we wanted to include Nancy in that ceremony by asking her to give David to us in the eyes of God, as part of an otherwise traditional baptismal ceremony.

I called Nancy back that same night and told her about our idea. I explained that we were planning to have David baptized and that we wanted her to be a part of the ceremony. She listened to our idea, and after I finished, there was a long pause from her end of the line. In a voice breaking with emotion, she answered, "I would love to, it would be perfect."

Carey and I were really excited about the prospect of including Nancy in the baptism. We felt strongly that by allowing her to hand David to us in the eyes of God, rather than by the laws of the state of Ohio, we would all be brought together in a special bond. The idea just felt right to us, and while we didn't know how we were going to piece it together, we knew we were going to see it through.

The next day I called our church to try to get the ball rolling. Although Carey and I had attended the church since we were children, a new generation of clergy had arrived, and we weren't on familiar terms with them. My call connected me with Father Fuller, a priest we didn't know. I asked him for some time to discuss an important matter. He told me that he wasn't busy at the moment and it would be fine for us to talk then.

I asked him point-blank if we could arrange to have a private baptism for our son. He responded in a kind voice, but told me that the church didn't allow private baptisms. The church's practice, he said, was to bring children into the church before the whole congregation.

I realized then that I had put the cart before the horse; he had no idea why I was making such an unusual request. I backtracked, and gave him an overview of what had happened in our adoption process. I was somewhat surprised to find out that he had really no understanding of open adoption. It was a new concept to him, as it was to many people. When I explained it to him briefly, he reacted extremely favorably, telling me that he thought it was a wonderful idea.

"It is," I told him. "If it's handled correctly, with love, it can work out beautifully for everyone involved. The thing is, we want to include David's birth mother in our ceremony so that she can present David to us in the eyes of God in addition to him being initiated into the church. But after everything this young lady has been through, I think it would be cruel to expect her to do something so courageous and so emotional in front of a church full of strangers. That would be asking too much of her."

He listened to me patiently and kindly, and when I was done, he reiterated that this was a wonderful thing that we had accomplished. He suggested that he come to meet with us at our house in order to discuss our idea in more detail. Elated, I agreed, and we set a date and time for a meeting later that week.

Several days later, on a weekday afternoon, Father Fuller rang our doorbell. When I opened the door and we stood face-to-face, we recognized each other not from church but from childhood. We had grown up in the same neighborhood, and while we were a few years apart in age, we clearly remembered each other from our youth. The familiarity felt like a good sign, and I instantly had the feeling that things were going to work out.

Carey had prepared a large pitcher of iced tea, which we took to the back porch. We sat in the warmth of the late afternoon, David in Carey's lap, and explained to Father Fuller in great detail what had transpired in David's adoption. I was really excited to be telling him about Nancy, David, and ourselves, and excited to be pursuing an idea we felt so strongly about. At last the situation was back in our control, being shaped by us and not by outside authorities. I was determined nothing could hold me back. We had been through enough. Now the adoption was going to proceed the way Carey and I thought it should be done, morally and spiritually.

He listened with undisguised fascination to our story, repeating over and over, "Amazing, amazing." When we were done detailing the story for him, he agreed that the ceremony could and should be held privately out of deference to our feelings and respect for Nancy. As soon as he said that, Carey and I breathed audible sighs of relief and thanked him.

But we knew it wouldn't be *that* easy. "You're probably going to run into a problem," Father Fuller told us. "There *is* no such service offered, and the prayer books contain nothing in them specific to adoption or adopted children. There's only the traditional baptism ceremony in which the child is presented by his or her godparents for initiation into the church." He said this not with a sense of discouragement but matter-of-factly.

I was really confused by what he was telling us. It seemed incredible to me that there was no religious service in which the church would acknowledge adoption in any way. In fact I found to my surprise that my feelings were almost hurt. I wanted the best for my son, who happened to be adopted. Not finding anything to fit the bill was a blow to my ego as his father. I thought back to the Bible stories I had learned as a child, and remembered that in the most literal sense of the word, Jesus and Moses were both not only adopted but openly adopted. How could the church not recognize that adoption was an everyday event, a special and historically documented way of creating a family?

We could see that Father Fuller was thinking carefully about something. "I have a suggestion," he said, turning to me. "You've obviously thought about this, and you both feel really strongly about it. That's what's most important. Here's my suggestion: Dion, why don't you write the service yourself? That way it's what you want it to be. And we can also go back and look in the older prayer books to see if we can find something appropriate to adoption."

It was an incredible idea, and I stopped to think about it for a minute. It sounded like the perfect solution. The problem was I didn't feel capable of writing anything that could be presented in church, before a priest, a small congregation, and before God. I wasn't a writer, and I didn't believe I had the religious or intellectual knowledge necessary to write something so profound. But I was so committed to our concept, to helping us all come together and leave the hurt behind, that if this were the only way it was going to happen, then I wasn't going to back down.

I told him I would give it my best shot, because Carey and I wanted to see this thing happen. Father Fuller recognized our unrelenting resolve. He agreed to arrange the service the way we wanted it, on the date that we had chosen.

Carey and I were ecstatic. He was so gracious and so open-minded, and was obviously in support of our endeavor. At last, we felt, things were headed in a direction that would be healthy and right for us all. We thanked him for his time and set a date to meet with him at the church in several days. He asked that I bring my ideas about what I was going to say so that we could review them and plan the service.

I spent the rest of that evening preoccupied with thinking about what I was going to write. My mind was drawing a blank. I knew the essence of what I needed and wanted to say, but putting it into words that would be received by an audience felt like an insurmountable task for me. I kept going around in circles, and nothing I thought of seemed to hit the nail on the head.

Carey, recognizing that I was stewing over my assignment, gave me wide berth and gentle encouragement. "It'll come to you," she told me, "I can guarantee it. I've never seen you unable to say what's on your mind, and this is definitely on your mind. It'll all come clear to you. Just loosen up a little bit and let the thoughts flow into your head." But I was stumped. I didn't know how to put my thoughts into words, my words into a speech, and I certainly didn't know what I was going to call this whole thing, since it was such a break from tradition.

Then, without warning, everything came together. Nancy called. She wanted to know how our meeting had gone, and we told her that it was very positive, that it was going to happen the way we wanted it to. She told me she was very excited about the service, and in fact she sounded more bubbly and happy than I had ever heard her. It was inspirational just to hear her voice, so filled with love and trust and optimism. She told me she was thrilled about having the chance to see us all again. She asked if it would be all right if she invited her whole family and her close friends to the service so that they could witness her passing her child to us in the eyes of God.

I listened carefully to what she said, and as she spoke, she gave me the perfect idea. She wanted to pass David to us in the eyes of God . . . to pass David to us. . . . Then it came to me. This was a "Baptism of Passage." I told her she could invite whomever she wanted, and I told her I loved her. We hung up, and I sat down at the dining-room table with my pen and paper. In ten minutes I had written my part.

We met again with Father Fuller at the church several days later. We sat in his private office, which had been a teen room when I was a youth attending the church, and worked on our service. We went over the date and time, and Father Fuller outlined to us what he thought the service should consist of and how it should flow. He got out some old prayer books and we each looked through them for anything that pertained to adoption, any psalms or prayers that were significant for an adoption situation. We came up with nothing.

Again I was amazed, and told Father Fuller so. "How can there be nothing about adoption," I asked him earnestly, "when two of the most important people in the Bible were adopted?" He looked at me, puzzled. "Jesus and Moses were both adopted in open adoptions," I told him. He thought for a moment and said, "My gosh, you're right!"

Father Fuller asked me to read what I had written. I pulled out my notes and began to read. It was the first time I had read my words out loud. As I read, I became very emotional, and finally choked on my words. My reaction surprised even me. I couldn't seem to get ahold of myself, and I found myself actually crying. Father Fuller, sensitive to my feelings, handed me a tissue and asked me if I would prefer that he read it in church if it would be too difficult for me.

Without hesitation I answered him, "No. Thank you, but this is my son, and I owe it to him to read this about him and to him." I added, though, that if I were emotionally overwrought during the reading, I would simply pass the text to him and he could finish it for me. There was no way I was going to bow out of standing before God myself, in appreciation and love for my son and Nancy. They both deserved that from me. This Baptism of Passage was crucial for all of us. We each had our own closure to make, and our own beginnings to embark upon. We were going to do it together, as a family, and we were going to do it in church, with God as our witness.

CHAPTER

20

Carey and I were extremely excited by the upcoming baptism, which was to be on June 21st. We spoke to Nancy on the phone over the next few days, and she maintained her own enthusiasm about it too. Everything felt so good, so promising, so as-it-should-be, for the first time since we had embarked on our journey. Carey began planning the reception for after the baptism and found beautiful invitations to send our invited guests. She hand-addressed them and put them in the mail two weeks prior to the baptism. We wanted to make sure people could save the date for this special event.

Carey and I knew that it was going to be an extremely emotional event for Nancy. She hadn't seen us or David since we had been together at the hospital. While she had been working hard to resolve everything, and while this ceremony was designed to help us all do just that, we knew it wasn't going to be quite that simple. We knew it would be too much for her to do so for the first time in a church setting in front of friends and family, many of whom on our side, she didn't know.

We suggested to her that we meet with one another sometime before the baptism, to reunite ourselves privately, with no one else watching. Nancy was delighted by our suggestion. She agreed that it was a wonderful idea, and said she thought Marilou would agree to it also. Carey and I were thrilled that Nancy was so receptive to the idea. It felt as if we hadn't seen each other in ages, and so much had transpired in the interim. Before now the time had never felt quite right for us to see one another again, face-to-face. The occasion of the baptism cut through any awkwardness and gave us a valid, positive reason to come together. At last there was an undeniable reason we should all be together: to dedicate our son's life into God's hands.

We invited Nancy and Marilou out to our house, but Marilou declined that plan. We offered to go to their house to visit. Again Marilou subtly refused the suggestion. It wasn't long before we realized that she was still not at all comfortable with what was happening. We could sense that she still felt threatened and uncertain about where we were all headed. She suggested that we meet at a family restaurant that was at a halfway point between our locations. We wanted to be sure that she was as comfortable as she could be with the situation. This restaurant idea, we could see, afforded her a "safe spot," a neutral ground on which to come together again. We agreed to her request.

The only mutually convenient day to meet turned out to be the day before the baptism. We arranged to meet one another for lunch around noon.

Carey got us out our door right on time, as always, and we arrived a few minutes early at the restaurant. We waited anxiously inside the foyer, David in his carry seat on the floor, Carey standing right next to him, me at the window in the door, scouting for Marilou and Nancy. It dawned on us that we had never seen Nancy when she wasn't either pregnant or postpartum. We were also very aware that the last time we had seen her, it was a time of great pain and sorrow. This meeting promised to be a happy one, a joyful reunion. Most important, no one else was involved; it was just us. There would be no one to tell us what was right or wrong, and what we could or couldn't do. We had at last found some freedom to begin making our family into the kind we wanted it to be: one that included Nancy and her family as well.

Marilou and Nancy turned the corner to the restaurant walkway. Their emotions were written all over their faces. Marilou looked very worried, very upset. Nancy, on the other hand, was radiant. She positively glowed. Her face was gleaming, and she wore a smile that would turn any head. She was dressed like a teenager on the brink of adulthood, and she looked trim, fit, and healthy. She was, in a word, beautiful.

As they approached, Nancy saw us through the door and picked up her pace. The door flew open, and she was suddenly inside, grabbing us in a group hug, carefully stepping around little David, who watched the scene from his seat on the floor. Carey picked up almost-three-month-old David in his seat and held him so that Nancy could see him clearly. Nancy stepped back and looked at us, taking in the picture we formed as a family. Her smile never wavered.

We turned and walked into the restaurant. Marilou was nervous and crying. I put my arm tightly around her shoulder and walked with her to the table. As we walked, Carey held David up high so that Nancy and Marilou could see him from head to toe. Nancy was in awe. "He's so beautiful!" she told Carey and me. Marilou looked at him, too, and with the tears falling even harder, repeated what Nancy had just said. "He's beautiful! So beautiful!"

Our table was ready, and we sat down. We all began at once talking about David, trying hard to keep the conversation normal and comfortable. Carey asked Nancy if she wanted to hold David, and she scooped him into her arms with obvious love and tenderness. Marilou wanted her turn, too, and held him closely. "He's so big!" Marilou said in amazement, with Nancy voicing her strong agreement. We continued to chat about David's schedule and habits, and the mechanics of running the household and caring for him. All the while David was passed lovingly from one set of hands to the next, with Marilou and Nancy frequently remarking about how big and beautiful he was.

Marilou participated in the idle chatter, but I could easily see that she was still very nervous and not at all relaxed. Our food came, and we all ate and continued our lighthearted conversation. Carey, Nancy, and I were happy to be together again. We were practically floating above our seats at the table. Marilou, on the other hand, continued to be quiet and somewhat distanced. Finally after forty-five minutes I just had to address Marilou's discomfort. I couldn't bear to see her in such turmoil. I asked her what was wrong.

No one can ever accuse Marilou of beating around the bush. She's about as forthright as they come. Without hesitation she told us that she was still very ill at ease with the openness of the adoption and was very concerned about what the effects were going to be on her whole family. She was very protective of her family, and this mysterious new relationship, she felt, might pose an emotional threat to them. She told us that the permanent surrender had felt like a death to her and her family. They had experienced an overwhelming sense of loss after the papers were signed. The children in the family were especially hurt and confused; Nancy's little brother and niece had never even seen David.

I understood her concerns, I really did. I told her a story about my nine-year-old neighbor, Julia. "Two years ago, when Julia moved in," I said, "she was a very shy, loving little girl, who was the product of a bad divorce situation. Julia and I quickly developed a close friendship, and one day she asked me if I would be her part-time dad. I happily agreed. Then," I told Marilou, "when Julia found out that we were adopting a baby, she came to me and with great concern said, 'I guess you won't be my part-time dad anymore, because you'll be a full-time daddy.' I immediately told her, 'No, I'm your part-time dad in my heart, and I'll always be your part-time dad. So what you have to figure out is what you want to be to this baby.' Several days passed and I hadn't really given much more thought to the incident, until Julia saw me outside and jumped into my arms, giving me a big hug and a kiss. 'I figured it out,' she told me. 'Figured what out?' I asked. 'I figured out what I want to be to the baby. I want to be his part-time big sister, and you can still be my part-time dad in your heart.' I hugged Julia and told her I happily accepted her offer, and I told her, 'We can all adopt this baby.' "

Marilou had stopped crying long enough to listen to my story. I could see that she was thinking carefully about what I was saying. In completing the story I told her that what this nine-year-old had taught me was that once we figure out what we want to be in a relationship, we can go forward in a healthy way.

With that, Marilou seemed to see the light. She slammed her hand down on the table and said with spirit, "I want to be Grammy Lou, damn it!"

I smiled at her and covered her hand with mine. "That's great!" I told her, "and that's exactly who you'll be, damn it!"

And from that point on the defenses were down, the awkwardness diminished, and we were all happy to move forward. We talked and talked together, and our quick lunch date turned into a two-and-a-half-hour joyful reunion. The mood was relaxed, and there was constant chatter. Carey was thrilled to be able to fill Nancy and Marilou in on the plans for the baptism. She talked with Nancy and Marilou about the special heirloom baptismal gown from her family that David was going to wear. "It won't snap closed around this chubby little neck!" Carey told them, caressing David's chin. We all laughed. Then Carey told Nancy and Marilou how she had laid him on the living room floor to try the gown on him, and he had rolled over for the first time. "When David made that momentous roll," Carey said, "Dion insisted it was because our little manly man was trying to wriggle out of wearing 'a dress,' as Dion calls the gown." Marilou and Nancy had a good chuckle over that one.

Midway through the lunch I realized we were going to be using that table for quite some time, so I excused myself and gave the waitress a twenty-dollar bill. I told her I hoped this would cover the tips she would lose by us monopolizing her table. She was a very sweet woman, and I felt compelled to tell her briefly what was going on. Her eyes filled with tears and she said, "Honey, you sit there all day if that's what you want." This gentle waitress was so affected by our story that every time she walked by our table, I could see her reaching for a tissue.

Before our visit ended, I gave Nancy a copy of what I had written for the baptism. I told her to take it home and read it, and to let her family read it too. I knew it would be very emotional for her, and I thought it was only fair that she have a chance to preview it before hearing me read it in the church, surrounded by other people. She thanked me for it and tucked it inside her purse.

Carey had brought some things for Nancy too. She had put together a small gift bag of things she thought Nancy might like to have. In the package were a stack of the birth announcements, an invitation to the baptism, and the Saint Nicholas medallion, which we had bought to give her the first time we met her. Carey had also picked out a gold cross on a necklace for Nancy and had wrapped it and tucked it into the package. Nancy was thrilled to receive everything and told us she was going to put one of the birth announcements in her scrapbook and give some to her relatives and close friends.

When we were done with our lunch, I went to the cash register to pay the bill. The waitress gave me a big hug and told me she had never witnessed anything so special. With tears in her eyes she smiled and said, "And it happened at Bob Evans!"

We said good-bye to Nancy and Grammy Lou, hugging each other tightly and with real feeling. We went our separate ways, knowing we would see each other again the next day at church.

As we drove home, Carey and I spoke about our meeting with Marilou and Nancy. We were both really pleased with how it had gone. "I was worried about Marilou at the beginning," Carey said. "Nancy looked so happy and Marilou looked so upset. I wasn't sure how to interpret her discomfort. I was afraid the lunch was going to be a disasater." I told her I, too, had been surprised by how upset Marilou had been initially.

"You did a great job at helping her to relax," Carey told me. "She seemed to truly get past it. Then it all seemed so perfect," Carey said. "I thought it was so cute that Nancy and Marilou couldn't stop saying how *beautiful* and *big* David is. It made me feel so proud."

I agreed with Carey. "And I think Nancy really appreciated the things you brought for her," I told her. "She seemed to genuinely appreciate the significance of everything you put into the package."

"I hope so," Carey said. "I don't ever want to make her uncomfortable, or feel like we're pushing her. I know that things take time. We have to be patient and let everything evolve as naturally as possible."

When we got home, we still had a lot of last-minute things to pull together in preparation for the baptism the next day. David, exhausted from the celebrity-quality attention he received at the luncheon, went straight to his crib for a much-needed nap, and Carey and I made phone calls and tied up loose ends.

Nancy phoned me in tears that night. Worried, I asked her what was wrong. She told me she had just read the script for the baptism. "No one has ever said anything so nice about me . . . thank you." I told her that Carey and I loved her and that we would see her the next day for the baptism. After I hung up, I thought about how my words had affected Nancy. There was real healing power, I realized, in merely being able to tell her how we felt about her and her courageous act of love. I knew the baptism was going to help all of us to begin healing the tremendous wounds we had been dealt. The healing had begun; we were on our way home.

June 21, 1992, dawned. It was a warm but overcast day. Carey and I woke up and looked forward to what the day held ahead for us with a certain nervous anticipation. What lay ahead, we hoped and believed, was a chance for healing and moving forward. For us it was the next step in making everything about our adoption right. But no one else had met Nancy at this point. Even our closest family members knew her only by her name and our description of her.

We headed for the church in the late morning. We needed to be there early so that the church registry could be signed by us and so that we could get David dressed. We also needed time to get things set up for the reception, which was going to take place in the great hall of the church.

We hoped the hall, which was furnished with groupings of comfortable chairs, couches, and tables, would provide a relaxing and calm atmosphere for our guests to mingle following the service. Carey and her mother had prepared heaping platters of sandwiches and gallons of punch, and had ordered a large cake and dozens of cookies. Carey's family joined us early to help set up.

We soon began to wonder where Nancy was; we had expected that she, too, would arrive on the early side. She and her mother walked into the hall just a few short minutes before the service was to begin. They had gotten lost on the long, confusing drive from the other side of the city.

Nancy looked calm and elegant in a pressed white blouse and black skirt. She hugged Carey and me in greeting, and as I hugged her, I noticed she was wearing the cross Carey had given her the day before. Even though we had seen her barely twenty-four hours ago, we all felt a rush of happiness at being together again. As we finished saying hello to one another, Carey's mother came over and stood by us. This was the first time she had seen Nancy. We introduced the two of them, and Carey's mother broke into tears and hugged Nancy tightly. Carey and I looked at each other gratefully; we knew things were going to be just fine.

I introduced Marilou and Nancy to Father Fuller, and he gave them a warm welcome. I had mentioned to Father Fuller that Nancy's mother was a divorced Catholic and so had not been able to participate in communion at her church since her divorce. Upon greeting Nancy and her mother, Father Fuller invited them into his office for a quick private meeting. Inside his office he told them he felt strongly that everyone involved in the baptism should feel comfortable and welcomed, and a part of the spiritual event we were celebrating.

Knowing how much anguish Marilou had suffered by not being able to accept communion for so long, Father Fuller openly invited and encouraged Nancy's family to participate in the sacraments. He reminded them that in the Episcopal Church, the only requirement for accepting communion is to be a baptized Christian. He told them he thought that taking communion would help their healing process.

His suggestions met with a very grateful and positive response from Nancy's family. Father Fuller quickly decided to adapt the service to include Nancy's family in the "passage" by inviting them to accept communion as one family. As Nancy and her mother left Father Fuller's office, I could see the relief on their faces.

Carey and I had a brief chance to greet and talk with Nancy's family before the service began. I spoke with Nancy's sister, Vickie, and tried to tell her about the lunch we had enjoyed the day before with Marilou and Nancy. I began to try to tell her about the revelations we had shared and how we had come to a mutual understanding of what our relationship was and where it was going. Vickie interrupted me midsentence and said graciously, "You don't have to say another word. I'm Aunt Vickie and my daughter is Cousin Ashley."

Nick and Debbie came to wait with us for the service to start. It was the first time they and Nancy had met, although they probably felt they knew one another after all they had heard from Carey and me. Nancy knew that in Nick and Debbie she had another source of strength, compassion, and support. She knew that as David's godparents, and as the wonderful people they were, they were our strongest allies. They were part of our inner circle, and they respected what we had accomplished together. There was a preexisting bond between all of us, so this first-time meeting was almost a moot point. Unhesitatingly Nick and Debbie and Nancy hugged one another.

Just before we entered the sanctuary, Nancy and I stopped to speak with one of the other priests, Father Ralph, the church's youth minister. He introduced himself and told us he had come to witness the service, because he believed that what we were doing held great importance, more than we might realize. He told us that what we were doing, what we had experienced, provided an alternative for others. In his counseling, he said, he helped many other people who were faced with unplanned pregnancies. The options, he said, had always seemed to be too few and too drastic: keeping the child, aborting the pregnancy, or placing the child in a traditional adoption. What we were exemplifying, he said, was a fourth and very humane alternative.

In a very quiet but very strong voice Nancy replied, "I believe my purpose in my life from God was to give Dion and Carey this baby." Father Fuller and I were both clearly awestruck and humbled by her spiritual conviction and her obvious love and respect for human life. She never ceased to amaze me.

The guests began to arrive. I was chief greeter for the occasion, and stood at the front of the sanctuary, welcoming people as they walked in. What had been planned as a small, intimate ceremony had grown to include eighty people who were among our close friends and family members. When we started our guest list, we found ourselves continually extending it. What we were really doing was reaching out, trying to include people who hadn't been able to participate in the adoption because of our fear back then of letting too many people become part of an emotionally risky situation. We felt that by having them be a part of the baptism, they would be better able to grasp everything we had been through, and what David and Nancy meant to us. It gave me goose bumps to see our friends and family gathering in honor of this very special occasion.

Quite a few people came close to me and asked me, "Which one is Nancy?" They asked, I knew, not out of a lurid curiosity but as a sign of respect. I responded by telling them that she was sitting in the front pew with us.

The ceremony went beautifully. Father Fuller introduced me, and I went to the pulpit and addressed our guests. I began by reading part of a letter I had written to Bishop Anthony Pilla, the priest whose office directed us to Lake County Catholic Service Bureau, where we had met Nancy. "As a police officer," I said, "I am always reminded of human failure and tragedy. However, I believe it is more important to embrace human success out of failure, such as this unplanned pregnancy. Achieving that kind of success depends on people who are caring and loving, such as you and your staff. If you ever wonder if the ministry is working, all you need is to look into my child's eyes, and into the hearts of the people who made this not a tragedy but a miracle of loving life."

I then read what I had written for the service, the Baptism of Passage. I read it this time without choking. Being in the moment, in the midst of the actual event, gave me an inner peace and strength. Still, I could hear people sniffling, and I avoided eye contact with Nancy, Carey, and Marilou, because I knew I could easily fall apart if I saw the emotion that was undoubtedly showing on their faces.

This is what I read:

> *The specialness of this baptism shouldn't be overlooked. The specialness is first and foremost dedicating this child's life into God's hands and welcoming him into Christ's Holy Catholic Church through this house of prayer. This christening, however, represents more than a baptism, it represents a passage of human love in its purest form.*

Let me try to explain this passage: You are witness to an ultimate act of unselfish love and courage, that being from a very special person, Nancy, David's birth mother; and from Nancy's family. In detail Nancy signed permanent custody of David to Carey and me. This legal document left Nancy feeling very hollow inside. Therefore we asked her to pass this child to us in the eyes of God, through this special Baptism of Passage. This passage is very much like parents giving their child away in marriage, so that that child can establish a new family and life while still embracing the person who gave him life.

Therefore David will never have to wonder if he was abandoned or loved, nor will he have to live in secrecy or shame, or the cruelty of erasing his heritage. These answers will always be very clear to David.

So in addition to witnessing David's baptism, you are witnessing an adoption of extraordinary love. Each and every person in this church—our friends, family, and clergy—deserves to be a part of this adoption. This adoption is more than David to Carey and me. Rather it is an experience we can all embrace and participate in, for I believe Jesus would have wanted us to adopt everyone in our lives the way David has been accepted with open hearts, minds, and arms by all of you.

In closing I would like to leave you with a question and a statement. The question occurred between Carey and me when we became frustrated and overwhelmed in David's first two weeks of life, a stress I understand many new parents feel. We ended up asking each other, "Is this the very best we could offer our child, in fact is this the very best we can offer each other?" The answer was no, we could and are doing better. Being aware that some of our family and friends have personal strife in their lives and relationships, I believe this simple question may provide an answer and a solution. The statement came from a dear friend, whose wisdom continually astounds me. He said, "Give your child the best gift you can—lose any anger, hurt, or hate from your heart, and you will enjoy life's highest heights, and give this child the life he deserves."

We then performed the actual passage, which consisted of all the families and godparents being summoned to the altar by Father Fuller. Nancy held David. She wore a look of peace and determination, and although her eyes were dry now, they were swollen from crying during the reading. As she held David, she looked over at me, and I knew she was looking at me as her ultimate protector. I knew that if I stayed strong, that would hold Nancy together too.

Father Fuller asked Nancy, "Do you, Nancy, in the eyes of God, pass this child to Dion and Carey so that he may be presented into Holy Baptism?" Nancy replied, "I will, with God's help." Nancy passed David to Carey and me, and we passed him to his godparents, Nick and Debbie, who presented him for Holy Baptism. Father Fuller anointed David's head with holy water. David was perfect; no crying, no whimpering.

When the baptism was complete, David was carried by Father Fuller through the church. As he carried David, he exclaimed joyously and with real emotion, "I present to you David Evan, a child of God." There were many quiet tears shed among the guests; no one could help but be moved by the beauty of what had just transpired. We had just moved beyond the technical legalities of adoption; we had come together before God and created a new family. The spirituality in the air was almost palpable, even to the staunchest of skeptics. I knew that we had just been shown what it means to be human.

I took Nancy's arm again, and we left the sanctuary together. As we left, Nancy kissed my cheek and whispered in my ear, "My hollowness is gone."

We gathered with our guests in the hall for the reception. Nancy and her family quickly gravitated to a corner of the room and sat together in a large, comfortable couch. I watched as they settled next to one another; I could see from across the room that they were overwhelmed and needed one another for emotional and moral support. Although the baptism was a breakthrough, and a cathartic and healing event, none of us knew exactly in what direction we were headed. Our relationship was still just beginning, and no one knew for sure how it was going to evolve.

Carey and I walked over to Nancy and her family and told them how special they all were to us. We asked them if they would mind watching over David so that he could rest quietly and we could attend to the other guests. They looked grateful for our request, and we handed David over to Nancy.

Carey went to greet the other guests. I had no intention of straying far from Nancy and her family. I was in my protective mode: It was my duty to protect my family. My biggest fear in planning and holding the baptism was that someone would say something inappropriate to Nancy or her family. Even though the guests were all my friends and family, I was all too aware of how high our emotions were running and how our relationship with Nancy and her family was still not fully understood by anyone else. I was going to see to it that things went smoothly. I stood near Nancy and her family, and as soon as I saw anyone approaching them, I was at their side.

My worry was wasted. There was nothing but positive, warm feedback from everybody. For Nancy, Carey, David, and myself, together as a family, it was our first face-to-face meeting with "the world." We did more than just survive it, we grew, and grew stronger because of it. As the reception progressed, I could sense that we all loosened up just a little and became a little more comfortable with being together in the limelight. After all, everyone who was there was there out of love for this tiny baby boy.

People mingled, munched, chatted, and enjoyed themselves. On a table at the side of the room sat the large cake that Carey had ordered for the occasion. It was decorated with beautiful blue flowers and green leaves. In the center was written, "God Bless David Evan, June 21, 1992."

The baptism left Carey and me feeling very content, very much at peace with things as they were. I don't think we realized, even for all the pain we had endured and had seen Nancy endure, how desperately we needed to bring some kind of resolution to the heartbreak that had marked the weeks following David's birth. We knew our adoption had truly taken place in the church, in front of our friends and family and God, as Nancy had given David to us from the depths of her soul and her love for him. All the legalities that had preceded that time were nothing to us. The state's legal finalization of the adoption, which still lay ahead, was rendered almost insignificant by what we had just accomplished. Together we had made things happen in our own way, a way we could live with.

We woke up the next morning emotionally and physically spent but feeling that something truly spiritual had been accomplished. We spent the day at home, receiving occasional phone calls from friends who wanted to thank us for including them and tell us how inspired they were by what we were doing.

That evening Nancy phoned us. She sounded lighthearted and truly happy. It gave Carey and me such a vicarious sense of relief to know that she was moving past her pain and on to better things. We loved listening to the enthusiasm in her voice. She told us that her family had been talking nonstop about the service and that they had all been deeply moved by it. Her mother and she were even interested in joining their local Episcopal church.

It seemed that the service had turned the tide in many ways. Nancy told us that her mother had suggested that she ask us if it would be all right for them to come to our house for a visit. We were astounded and delighted. We had suggested this idea in previous conversations with Nancy, but Marilou had seemed hesitant, and no visit had ever materialized. Our answer was a resounding yes. She and any members of her family, we told her emphatically, were always welcome at our house.

Nancy's elation was so great that I could hear a tiny warning voice in the back of my mind. Was she *too* excited? I wondered. Was she turning all her focus to this, on us and where David was now, instead of focusing as well on where *she* was headed now? I had become very protective of Nancy and held her in my heart much as I did David. I took it as my duty to protect and care for Carey, David, and Nancy with all that I was worth. Nancy in turn had told me that I had come to be like a father figure to her, so I felt justified now in expressing my concern to her.

"Nancy, I can't tell you how glad I am that this has helped you to work through things," I told her. "All of us needed to find some kind of resolution in our own hearts. That's what this baptism was all about. But I don't want this adoption and all that has happened around it to be the pinnacle or focus of your life."

"What do you mean?" she asked.

"It's been all-consuming for you, and you've handled it unbelievably well, beyond what anybody could ever expect. But please just remember that there are so many things ahead of you, so many really good and wonderful things that are in your future." She listened intently, and I continued. "I guess what I'm saying, is that you should not think of this as your sole purpose in life. Life—God—has much more in store for you."

The phone rang again later that evening, and it turned out to be my godmother, Frannie, who was also a minister. We hadn't talked in a long time, but I had invited her to the baptism, although she had been unable to attend. She apologized for her absence, and I told her we had missed her. As I described the service to her, she told me she was unaware that we had participated in an open adoption. She was very interested in it and wanted me to tell her more about it. To help her to understand the course of events, I read my letter to Bishop Pilla.

"You must be God's messenger to me," she said earnestly.

"You're not going to believe this, but I just got back from counseling a sixteen-year-old girl with an unplanned pregnancy. She's debating what's she going to do, and adoption is an option. Before we left each other we prayed that we would find an answer to her dilemma."

"That's so coincidental it's almost eerie," I told her. "I just told Nancy a few minutes ago on the phone that this adoption is bigger than just us." Frannie asked me if she could give this young girl my telephone number so that she could contact me and find out more about the option of open adoption. Needless to say, I agreed.

When I told Carey about my conversation with Frannie and the fact that I might talk with this young girl, Carey reacted on two levels. First, as David's mother, she was concerned about protecting him. "I don't want David's privacy to be compromised in any way," she told me. "I would rather start out cautiously, and know that whatever role we play in helping other people doesn't invade his right to privacy." I told her I thought that was a wise premise from which to operate. "And," she continued, "I don't ever want David's own sense of identity to become defined by the fact that he was adopted." I agreed with her again.

"But I do feel strongly that we should be advocates for birth families," she told me. "So many people have helped us through all of this, not least of which have been Nancy and her family. The way I see it, our problem was infertility. We wanted a child, and we couldn't have one. Adoption fixed our problem. We have a child now. But what about birth families? Their 'problem' of an unplanned or unwanted pregnancy is hardly fixed by choosing adoption, because they then have to live with the lifelong emotional scars of giving up that child. They're faced with a no-win situation. Their problem doesn't ever truly get solved. We need to help other adoptive parents see that side of the issue and be sensitive to it and open to working with it."

"So you think it's all right for me to have told Frannie that I'd talk with this girl?" I asked Carey. "You're comfortable with that?"

"Yes," she assured me, "as long as David himself remains separate from this or any other work we do on behalf of open adoption. Right now I think we need to protect him, and not become totally consumed with 'the cause.' "

The next time I spoke to Nancy, I told her about my conversation with Frannie and what Carey had said. Nancy and I talked some more about how our adoption meant something to more than just those of us who were immediately involved. We were beginning to clearly see how it could help others by giving them a new alternative to consider. We weren't naive; we knew that not every adoption situation could benefit from openness. But we were learning quickly that there were many birth mothers for whom this was the choice that could see them through an otherwise devastating crisis.

Nancy listened as I told her I was beginning to see that we were part of something really important and that it was an ongoing, dynamic chain reaction. She agreed with me, and we recognized how it gave some perspective to our adoption; it was neither the beginning nor the end of anything. It was part of a more universal happening, an awakening of sorts. Nancy realized, as we spoke, what I had meant when I told her that the adoption should not be considered the central focal point of her life. In her infinite instinctive wisdom and benevolence, she told me, "Please call Frannie back and tell her I would like to talk to this girl as well, because I know exactly what she's feeling right now." I thanked Nancy for her offer and agreed to make another call to Frannie.

CHAPTER

21

One afternoon, not too long after the baptism, I answered the phone to hear Nancy's barely coherent voice on the other end. She was crying and trying to talk to me between sobs. I had a hard time understanding her at first, and my heart raced as I tried to comprehend what was wrong. She finally calmed down enough to tell me that she was at home alone and had just gotten a telephone call from her mother, who was at the hospital. One of Nancy's nephews, a nine-month-old twin, had just died of sudden infant death syndrome. Nancy was beside herself with grief and worry.

As she explained what she had been told, my first reaction was to try to comfort her and say something conciliatory about the death of her nephew. As I spoke, I could tell Nancy was still very agitated and upset. My efforts to make her feel better were having no effect.

When she asked with urgency, "How's David?" the fog suddenly lifted. What an idiot I was! I was so caught up in having the "right" reaction to the news of the death, I hadn't realized that not only was Nancy grieving about her nephew but she was hysterical with worry about David, her son. Her maternal instincts were as strong as any mother's, perhaps even stronger because she wasn't able to be right there with her child as each day of his life came and went. As this realization hit me, a thought flew through my mind: *I still have so much to learn about being a parent.*

Nancy needed to know that her own child was still safe and was being watched over carefully. The first people she had called, she said, were us. She needed reassurance about David's well-being and she needed friends to talk to. I told her David was fine, that he had never been better. When I reassured her that David was fine, healthy, and happy, Nancy was much relieved. I could hear the worry begin to disappear from her voice.

Later Carey and I talked about the phone call with Nancy. We were really shocked that such a tragic situation had happened in her family and were struck by how fortunate we all were that Nancy could immediately alleviate her own worries about her son's well-being. We had never anticipated that such a real-life crisis would be part of our learning process as we gained an increasing appreciation of the benefits of openness. Because she had been able to contact us directly and immediately, Nancy would not have to go on day after day with the seed of worry planted, wondering if her child, related genetically to her nephew who had died, had succumbed to the same sad syndrome.

We realized that there were probably going to be many moments of worry and concern for Nancy, many times when—as a mother—she might need to be reassured that her son was safe and healthy. We loved David with all our hearts, and we could easily put ourselves in her shoes. We would have been unable to cope if we had been forced into a situation where David was taken from our lives and we were left with no way to find out even the smallest piece of information about his well-being. It was a horrible thing even to contemplate. Carey and I began to see fully the degree of daily anguish birth mothers in closed adoptions must suffer. What worry they must feel when another birthday of their child's came; must they not think, "I don't even know where my child is, or if my child is even alive?"

Carey and I vowed we would never let Nancy down and would always make sure she had full access to us and to David, no matter where we were. Our compassion and empathy for Nancy were intense. In fact Carey became as worried about David as Nancy was, and for the next week or so slept with one ear and eye open. If David so much as squeaked or rolled over, Carey was out of our bed and in David's room, checking to be sure that he was all right.

When David was three months old, Carey prepared to start spending some time each week back at the office. She had arranged to do most of her work from home, and every other day or so someone from her office would drop off whatever paperwork she needed. Her department at the hospital had given her a terminal to install at home so that she could hook into the system at the office as easily as if she were on-site. This setup worked well, but she needed to touch base at the office a couple of times a week. With David on a schedule now, it seemed doable.

While this part-time setup worked well for her, Carey had had a difficult time making arrangements with the hospital where she worked to take time off when David was born. She was refused a maternity leave because, they said, she hadn't given birth, and moreover they didn't have a maternity package per se. Carey was furious when she heard this. She told them that just because she hadn't given birth to her baby didn't mean she wasn't the mother of a newborn, who, like all newborns, needed to have his mother with him.

When they refused that argument, she told them she would use her accrued sick time. She wasn't allowed to use sick time, they said, because she wasn't sick. Finally, in anger and desperation

Carey had turned to her doctor to ask his advice, as he was also employed at the same hospital under the same policies. He was as frustrated with her dilemma as she was. He knew as well as Carey did that David needed to have his mother at home with him during those first few weeks.

He wrote a note for her, dictating that she take a leave of absence for mental reasons—that she needed to stay at home with her baby in order to avoid severe mental anguish for both of them. Carey had gone along with the plan, without making any waves, although she didn't agree with the hospital's policy that put her and her doctor in the position of having to resort to such measures. But she knew it was the only way she was going to be allowed to be home with David.

When Carey returned to work, she was determined to confront the injustices of the policy. She spoke with a vice president in the human resources department and complained about the way her situation had been handled. When she was told again that strictly speaking there was no formal maternity-leave policy, she responded, "I realize that. But I should be able to take the time off as an adoptive mother without having to come up with a reason. When you have a baby, it's self-explanatory. I shouldn't have to go to a doctor to get a note just because my baby happens to be adopted. And," she added, "the fact that my doctor had to cite potential mental anguish as a way to get you to let me stay at home with my infant is totally outrageous. I want it removed from my permanent record."

They refused to work with her on the problem and furthermore had no intention of taking it off her record. Carey left the office even more angry than when she had arrived. When she came home that night, she told me how her frustrations had only increased. We knew our hands were tied; there was no way they were going to revise their policy. In the end the most important thing was that Carey had been home with David during his first few weeks at home. Finally we had to chalk it up as another glaring example of the prejudices against and misconceptions about adoption that prevailed in society.

Our original plan for when Carey went back to work had been to put David into the day care at the hospital where her office was. It meant Carey would be able to visit with him at any time during the day. But when one of our good friends and neighbors offered to provide day care for him, we decided that was a better option. We knew Susan would love and care for David as if he were her own, and since she was right across the street from us, it would be very convenient to us all.

We couldn't have been more right. With three children of her own, Susan's house was often filled with other visiting children. David was the center of attention at Susan's from his first day there. He was "adopted" by all the children who frequented Susan's house. There is probably no other child who has been fought over the way David was; everyone wanted to hold him and care for him. Everyone fell in love with him, and Susan's house soon became his home away from home. He became very attached to Susan, too, and like Carey, she could comfort him by just picking him up.

Because Carey was at work only part-time, and my shifts often allowed me to be home while Carey was at work, David was seldom in anyone else's care for long. It was very difficult at first for us to leave him in anyone else's hands, and we each called several times while we were away to check on him. Gradually we became more relaxed about it. One evening shortly after she had returned to work, Carey and I were reflecting on how lucky we were that Susan was able and willing to provide care for David, and we acknowledged how hard it was to be away from him, even just for part of a day. Almost simultaneously we realized that this was in some ways similar to what Nancy had gone through. On a much smaller scale, it gave us insight into how Nancy must have felt when she was trying to make her decision about who would become David's caretakers *for life.*

The baptism had truly been a turning point for all of us. We became united with Nancy as a family. There was a distinct change in our relationship with her; what had been a close and special relationship became even more so. Even the tone of Nancy's voice was different when we talked together. When she called, it was more like she was a daughter calling home than a birth mother calling her child's adoptive parents.

We had continued to urge Nancy to feel free to come visit us anytime. She was very enthusiastic about the idea, but, practically speaking, it was difficult since she still didn't have her driver's license and her home was a good forty minutes from ours. One day in early July, when Nancy and I were on the phone, I reiterated our offer to have her come visit. Nancy thought for a moment and then proposed that she come to visit with her good friend, Tanya. Tanya had her license and had been a strong supporter of Nancy's throughout her pregnancy and the adoption. I told her that of course she could bring Tanya, we would be happy to have both of them as our guests. Nancy was so excited that she hung up and called Tanya immediately. A short while later Nancy called me back and asked if they could come over that afternoon. She really wanted to come see us, and see where David lived and what his bedroom looked like. Needless to say, I gave her the okay to come.

Carey and I could hardly wait for them to arrive. "Your NancyMom is coming," Carey whispered to David as she held him and waited for Nancy's arrival. "You get to see your special NancyMom today." When we saw the car pull into the driveway, we could hardly contain ourselves. As Nancy came through the front door, we hugged one another like long-lost friends. It felt so good to have her with us.

We gave Nancy and Tanya the tour of our house, and Nancy didn't miss a detail. She stopped to look at each framed picture we had of David, picking each up and examining it closely, always with a big smile of approval on her face. As she had requested, we let her take a good long look at David's room. She seemed to want to just take it all in; every detail that was part of his life at home fascinated her. When she saw David, she remarked as she always did at what a beautiful baby he was. She wore her love for him on her sleeve.

It was a luscious, warm day, and we sat on the porch together, chatting and enjoying the fresh air and one another's company. Carey and Nancy sat on the couch with David between them, taking turns at tickling his chin and playing with his small hands. We talked a lot about the baptism and how special it had been.

When she heard that Nancy and Tanya were coming by, Carey had flown into the kitchen and pulled out ingredients that she turned into a delicious lasagna. She knew Nancy loved Italian food, and with her strong maternal instinct Carey wanted to pamper Nancy. We ate a leisurely dinner at the dining-room table, with David in his "David holder," sitting like the king at the head of the table. We talked about anything and everything, trying to learn a lifetime about one another. Nancy asked us who our favorite musical performers were, and when I answered Dan Fogelberg, she said, "Dan *who?*" Her response dated us so obviously that Carey and I burst into laughter. And it certainly then came as no big surprise when neither Carey nor I had ever heard of Nancy's favorite rock group.

Carey and Nancy gave David his bath together after dinner. From downstairs Tanya and I could hear the two of them giggling and gabbing while they got David prepped for the night. I snuck up at one point with the video camera and filmed them as they knelt next to the tub, doting over David. Later that evening Nancy paid Carey the highest compliment when she said to her, "I'm learning so much from you about how to take care of a baby."

As always David began his fussy time at seven o'clock. We could almost set the clocks by him. That night he hit his fussy stage while Nancy was holding him. She tried to comfort him, and when he continued to be cranky, she turned to Carey and said, "Here, I think he needs some mommy love." When Carey held him, he quieted down, and Nancy watched with a look of real peace and contentment as David settled into Carey's arms.

Not wanting to brave the long ride home in the dark, Tanya and Nancy left at about eight o'clock. We said our good-byes with many hugs and kisses. Nancy thanked us over and over again for having her, and we in turn thanked her for coming. It was hard to express to her how good her visit had made us feel. To us she was a very important part of our family.

As we cleaned up the kitchen, Carey and I talked about how comfortable and natural it had felt to have Nancy in our house with us. "I feel like she's my daughter in some ways," Carey told me as she put the leftover lasagna away. "She's still so fragile, she needs to be taken care of. She needs a chance to regain her sense of self. I think part of what she needs is to be able to just watch us be parents to David. Seeing us parenting him helps her to regain her strength, and it helps her to settle into her decision even more. *Her* security in *having* us be David's parents is reinforced by *our* security in *being* his parents." She looked at me. "Do you get what I'm saying?"

"I think so," I answered.

"Nancy needs for us to be strong, self-assured parents to David," Carey continued. "She needs to see that strength in us. That's so important to her. She's confused about the rest of her life—school, things with Todd, work. By being strong in our role as David's parents, we eliminate any confusion she might have about our relationship with him, and with her too."

"I see what you mean. I guess that explains why there was absolutely no sense of competition or jealousy when she was here." Carey nodded in agreement.

Nancy phoned us later that night, before she went to bed. She just wanted to thank us again for having her over. We told her she had to promise us to come again soon. "I promise," she told us happily. "I'll visit again soon. You can count on me."

CHAPTER

22

Nancy's first visit to our house left us all hungry for more. We talked with each other on the phone at least every other day, and Carey and I told her repeatedly, "Next time you come to visit, you have to spend the weekend with us." Nancy couldn't wait to take us up on our invitation. We settled on a mutually convenient weekend in August and began planning.

When the weekend arrived, I drove to pick Nancy up at her house on Friday evening. As soon as I pulled into the driveway, she came bursting out of the front door and tearing down the driveway to greet me, her blue-and-white-striped duffel bag packed and in her hand. I ran into the house to say hi to Marilou and Nancy's little brother, Johnny, and then Nancy and I headed back to our house for our weekend escapade.

We drove and chatted together about our last visit and any news that had happened since then. I asked Nancy how Todd was, and whether he was okay with her coming to spend the weekend with

Carey, David, and me. I knew Todd had been a real source of strength and support for Nancy throughout her pregnancy and the birth of David, but I also knew that he hadn't yet fully come to terms with the extent of the openness we had established.

Nancy confirmed that Todd wasn't quite sure about this whole idea of her taking off for a weekend to be with us. "Well, he has to be special to be this open and to have come this far," I told her. She nodded in agreement, but I could tell that it really didn't matter to her at that moment. She was doing what she believed in, what felt right to her, and that was all that mattered. Nancy was in her own world right now, attending to her own priorities.

As we pulled into the driveway, we could see Carey peering out the window, waiting for us to arrive. "We're going to spoil the heck out of you, you know," I warned her. I knew that Carey had worked to make everything just perfect for Nancy. She had made up the guest room especially with Nancy in mind. She had laid out fresh soap and towels, thrown our frilliest pillows on the bed, arranged a selection of magazines on the nightstand, and topped the bureau with a huge bouquet of fresh flowers. It was as if Nancy were our oldest child returning to us after a summer away at camp or a year at college. This was a *homecoming*.

We went inside and Nancy and Carey greeted each other with bear hugs. Carey showed Nancy to her room, and after plopping her duffel bag on the floor Nancy came back downstairs with us. Carey asked Nancy if she would like to hold David. Nancy took him in her arms and sat down on the living-room couch, occasionally handing him an infant toy or bouncing him very gently on her lap.

As a result of her vocational training in child care, Nancy was very comfortable with babies. Still, Carey noticed that she needed some strong encouragement to feel at ease with handling David. Carey had speculated in private that perhaps Nancy was afraid of becoming too attached to David and that Nancy worried that it might be too painful for her if he fussed when she held him. Carey was very sensitive to Nancy's feelings about David.

Our thoughts turned to dinner, and Nancy told us that she was indeed monstrously hungry. Carey and I had tentatively planned to take Nancy out to eat at our favorite restaurant. But now, as we were gathered together in our house, none of us wanted to leave. It felt too good to just be home together. Since Nancy and I had had a chance to visit on the drive up, I volunteered to go pick something up for dinner so that Carey and Nancy could visit. I drove down the road and got sub sandwiches and chips for the three of us.

When I returned, Nancy and Carey were talking a mile a minute, catching up on everything. David was already in bed for the night. We set the table with our bounty of sandwiches and chips, poured some iced tea, and sat down to eat. Carey suggested we play cards, and we all agreed. She pulled out a deck of cards, and we sat for hours at the table, nibbling, talking, and playing rummy 500.

When we were all tired of cards and had put the deck away, Nancy told us she had something to show us. She ran upstairs and brought down a big yellow and white scrapbook. "I want to show this to you," she said excitedly. "This is David's baby book I've been putting together for myself—for the future."

We sat on the couch, with Nancy between us, the book on her lap, and became totally engrossed in its contents. She had thought of everything; anything she might want to remember or David might want to see or know about in later years was there. There were baby pictures of Nancy and her brothers and sisters. We smiled as we noticed a strong resemblance between Nancy and David, especially in the chin. There were pictures of Nancy when she was pregnant, from early in the pregnancy all the way to the end. Nancy looked gorgeous in every one of them; she typified the beauty of motherhood.

She had saved all her obstetrician's notes, along with her ultrasound pictures. Our profile was in the book, as well as the pictures we had included of Sam and the cats. She had put David's hospital band and his name tag from his hospital bassinet side by side.

There were pictures of her in the hospital after having just given birth to David, looking tired and already a little bit sad and confused. Nancy had arranged everything carefully and attractively, obviously putting much time and thought into the book.

Looking through the book was like opening a Pandora's box of thoughts, memories, and emotions. By the time we had finished with it, all kinds of feelings were churning inside of us again. I realized as I sat there on the couch, with Nancy and Carey right there with me, that this adoption had a life of its own. It was an ongoing, endless, dynamic thing that was going to change its shape and its composition constantly. Just when we thought we had gotten a handle on it and understood its complexities, it would change again, expand, and evoke some new emotion. It was a lifetime journey.

Carey was exhausted. She said good night to both of us and went upstairs. Nancy and I stayed up to talk some more. The late August night had turned cool, so I made a fire in the fireplace, and Nancy and Sam and I sat on the floor in front of it. Nancy sat cross-legged, with Sam's gigantic head resting adoringly in her lap. She was relaxed and comfortable, and we talked more about life in general. As she spoke, Nancy nonchalantly used a derogatory slang phrase that I found to be very offensive. Without thinking I looked her directly in the eye and in a stern voice told her, "Don't you _ever_ use that word in my house." Nancy was taken completely by surprise, and I watched as her eyes filled with tears and she began to cry.

My God, I thought to myself, _I just chewed out the woman who gave me her baby three months ago_. I calmed myself and sat down next to her. "Nancy, honey, our son is sleeping in that room," I said quietly to her, pointing above us, "and he has the rest of his life to learn what it means to hate. One thing I'm sure of is that he's not going to learn to hate in this house."

Nancy looked at me and said, "I wish you had been my father." She explained that the term had been used casually in her household and among her friends, so she had never even given it a second thought. She hadn't realized that it was so offensive and so inappropriate.

Taking her hand in mine, I told her, "Let me tell you the three rules Carey and I live by. These are the three rules of our house: Never hurt, never hit, never hate. It's as simple as that. Anyone in our house has to abide by those rules, or they're asked to leave."

Nancy nodded her head in understanding, and began to talk about our experience in the hospital when the social worker had tried to convince her that Carey and I were there merely to take her baby from her. "I knew how wrong that social worker was then," she said, "and every time I see you and Carey, I know it more and more. This is the way I want my son to be raised. This is the kind of life he should have. I know I did the right thing, because I couldn't give this to him right now. I picked the right parents for him." She paused for a moment and then continued. "And when I have my own children to raise, this is the way I want to raise them."

I was astounded by her maturity, and her ability to assess and process everything that was happening so quickly. She really was wise far beyond her years and her education. And more than that, she had a heart as big as all outdoors.

Carey and I were up bright and early the next morning. Down in the kitchen we drank our morning coffee and talked about how nice it felt to have Nancy staying with us, and about how sweet she was to have shared David's baby book with us. Everything just felt so hopeful and so right that morning; the whole picture was coming into focus for all of us. Nancy slept peacefully upstairs while Carey made fresh cinnamon buns. The aroma filled the house, and to this day the smell of cinnamon brings me back to that first weekend Nancy spent with us.

We had made an appointment to take Nancy with us to have a professional family portrait taken at the photography studio in a local department store. It was getting late in the morning, and we needed to get ourselves together to go. Nancy was still asleep upstairs, so we decided we ought to go up and wake her. Carey,

David, Sam, and I crept into her room like a band of thieves and pounced on her bed. She woke up and smiled an ear-to-ear grin when she saw her greeting committee in bed with her. This wake-up team has become a tradition for the mornings when Nancy is at our house.

Nancy came downstairs in her long nightshirt and sat down at the kitchen table. Carey and I waited on her as if she were royalty, keeping her coffee mug topped off and her plate filled with fresh buns. She lapped it up, laughing at little David's antics and our devotion to her every need. We were all just so obviously happy to be together at last, with no restrictions, no hesitations, no secrets. None of us could stop smiling.

By the time Nancy finished her breakfast, we had to really hustle to make our portrait appointment. Nancy and Carey rushed to get David dressed, and I couldn't help but sit back and watch what a perfect picture they made: David being tended to by both of his mothers. In her rush Carey pulled on David's pants so that the pants legs were pulled up way too high. Carey didn't notice it until Nancy took David's little hand in hers and pointed it at Carey. In a squeaky, baby voice, Nancy served as David's ventriloquist: "Hey you!" she said, pointing David's hand toward Carey, "Hey, *Mom*! Fix my pant legs, would you? I don't want to look like a nerd, you know." It was so funny, Carey and I laughed so hard we had to sit down and pull ourselves together.

Our photo shoot went perfectly. David wore a huge smile the whole time and posed agreeably whenever we shifted his position. We had the photographer take several arrangements, including a portrait of just Nancy and David together, which has been hanging ever since on the wall in David's bedroom. Nancy was so happy and so excited about the whole thing, no one had to ask her to smile—she couldn't *stop* smiling.

When we arrived home that afternoon, we were all tired out and ready to just hang out at home. We decided to take David for a walk in the stroller, and the four of us walked proudly around the block with Sam at our side. As we encountered our neighbors,

Carey and I introduced Nancy to them. "This is Nancy, David's birth mother," we would say with pride. Nancy handled it all with aplomb. She was totally comfortable with everything that was happening. Everyone we introduced her to was gracious, respectful, and receptive. Nancy's dignity was upheld as it deserved to be.

That night our doorbell rang unexpectedly. It was Nick, David's godfather. Debbie was out of town, and Nick knew Nancy was visiting us, so he had driven over to visit with all of us. He came bearing gifts. As soon as he saw Nancy, he handed her a present. Nancy opened it and immediately began to cry tears of appreciation. It was an exquisitely framed photograph of Nancy, Carey, David, and me at the baptism. When Nick saw the tears rolling down Nancy's cheeks, he melted, all six feet three inches of him. He opened his arms and embraced little Nancy in a big bear hug. Carey and I watched in amazement as the two of them broke down in each other's arms. Again, Carey and I knew we could ask for no better godparents for our child, and no better birth mother for our child. We were so blessed.

After Nick left, Carey, Nancy and I played another round of rummy 500. We were tired that night, and all went to bed early. It had been a long, emotional day. I drove Nancy home the next morning, after plenty of promises for another visit soon.

Two weeks after our weekend visit with Nancy, Carey and I attended a Friends of Children meeting. The social workers announced that a date had been set for the annual picnic for adoptive families. It was to be held the last weekend in August, at a community park.

When the FOC meeting adjourned, I went to our social worker, Beth, and asked her, "Is our birth mother invited to this?" Beth rolled her eyes dramatically; she had come to expect the unexpected with us, and we never disappointed her on this count. We had broken every mold the social workers had seen in adoption, and we moved in directions that no one had anticipated. "Sure," she said. "We've been wanting to include birth mothers for a long time, and you guys should probably be the first." She gave us a big smile, and we thanked her.

When we phoned Nancy that night to ask if she wanted to attend the FOC picnic, she told us she would love to come. We decided to make it another excuse for Nancy to spend the weekend at our house.

When the weekend of the picnic arrived, I picked Nancy up at her job at the mall, where she proudly introduced me to her friends and coworkers. She also mentioned that Bob and Lori, our friends from our home-study group, had been at the mall earlier that day and had made a point of coming in to see her. I could see that she was very pleased that we were all able to be so open and involved with one another.

The next morning we did our Nancy wake-up routine, and we all had a leisurely breakfast and spent the morning playing with David. After lunch we started to get ready for the picnic. We had bought steaks, and Carey and Nancy packed them up along with some potato salad and other food, and we headed for the park where the picnic was being held.

The park was swarming with people. There were babies, toddlers, and young children running every which way. Smoke was pouring from the barbecues that were lit and the smell of grilled meat filled the air. We stopped at the registration table and wrote out our name tags and stuck them on. As we walked down the sidewalk, Beth spotted us and came toward us. She greeted us warmly, and looked specifically at Nancy. "How would you like us to refer to you?" she asked kindly, in an effort to acknowledge how special it was to have Nancy as a guest. Nancy giggled and pointed to her name tag. "My name's Nancy, you can call me that!" We all laughed, and the ice was neatly broken.

We wandered into the picnic. There were tables of food, and games and tournaments set up for the children. The playground was packed with kids, and there were parents, social workers, and adoptees everywhere. Carey and I recognized many people from our home-study group and our Friends of Children meetings, and we began to mingle. Nancy went off in her own direction, and I didn't see her again until a while later when she came up to me and whispered sheepishly, "I think I made an 'oops.' " I asked her what "oops" she could have possibly made, and she told me that she had been talking casually with a woman at the picnic. As Nancy mentioned her labor and delivery, the woman looked at her questioningly. Nancy explained that she was a birth mother. The woman was dumbfounded, speechless.

As she finished telling me her "oops" story, Nancy looked at me as if she had done something wrong and was waiting for the fallout. I took her hand in mine. "Nancy," I said to her gently, "don't ever be ashamed of who or what you are. You're part of my family, and I'm so proud of you. You should be proud of yourself too. You're an incredible person, and don't let anyone ever make you think otherwise." Nancy hugged me in relief.

When we got back to our house, Nancy told us she thought she would go home instead of staying over that night. She told us she wanted to get back home and see Todd. We understood; we knew the picnic had been something of an overwhelming experience.

As I drove her home, Nancy opened up to me. "Sometimes it's so hard to see David and then leave him," she said sadly.

I wasn't at all surprised by this. I had actually seen it coming, especially with the encounter Nancy had experienced at the picnic and with Nancy's sudden need to get back to Todd. I knew she was feeling overwhelmed and confused. It seemed only natural, but it was very hard on her. I asked her again what I had asked her some time ago: "Nancy, who is David to you?"

"He's my son," she said very quietly.

"Yep," I said gently, "he's your son. And there's nothing wrong with that, and there's nothing wrong with saying that. I think you should say it more often." I knew that each time she acknowledged out loud that David was her son, it was cathartic for her. "There's also nothing wrong with your loving him, and feeling sad sometimes about being apart from him. That's natural." I knew Nancy needed to let herself be comfortable and at peace with the truth.

Nancy began to cry. "Thank you," she said. "I love you so much." I reached over and took her hand and drove one-handedly until I could feel that Nancy had regained herself.

I thought about how the social workers had been worried by the fact that Nancy was refusing postpartum counseling. But really, I thought, what could strangers provide for her that we couldn't? She didn't need to talk about us with a third party, she could talk about us with us. It was a natural, direct path to healing her wounds. We were at most a phone call away, and we wanted nothing more than to see Nancy happy again.

From the time we met her, Nancy frequently spoke of David's birth father with great sadness, regret, and frustration. The fact that they had created a child together meant something entirely different to each of them. For Nancy this child was sacred. She hadn't planned on a pregnancy or a child, especially from the short-lived relationship they had had, but she was ready to face the responsibility and handle it as best she could. She and David's birth father were unable to agree on a course of action, so Nancy was forced to handle the pregnancy and birth without any input or support from him. She harbored great resentment because of this, and she carried it with her like an actual weight on her shoulders.

One day shortly after the picnic Nancy phoned and told me out of the blue that she had phoned David's birth father to lay her feelings on the line. She had told him she was angry with him for many reasons, not least of which was that she felt the way he presented the history of their relationship to the social workers wasn't exactly accurate. She was angry about his lack of support of her decision and his ability to wash his hands of the situation. When she was done telling him of the anger she had been carrying around, she finished the conversation by telling him point-blank, "I forgive you."

With that Nancy released her anger, closed a chapter in her life, and took charge of her feelings once again. I told her I was extremely proud of her for what she had done, that it was a very brave and mature thing to do. I could hear in her voice that by confronting him she had gained instant emotional freedom. She was taking all the right steps toward getting stronger and wiser and standing on her own two feet.

As we continued our conversation, Nancy confided in me that her biggest fear in undertaking this open adoption was what she was going to say to David if he asked her about his birth father. Because of the openness in our adoption and the role Nancy would play in David's life, we all knew he would come to understand why Nancy hadn't been able to raise him herself. But, Nancy repeated, she was really worried about what to tell David if he pushed for information about his birth father. Carey and I suspected that this weighed heavily on her mind and had given it much thought.

I told Nancy, "If David asks you about his birth father, you just tell him to take that question to his parents. We'll handle it from there." My response gave Nancy an instant release from this worry she had been grappling with for so long. It took the entire problem off her shoulders. She was very satisfied with my plan, and trusted Carey and me implicitly. As we said good-bye, I realized that between Nancy's phone call to David's birth father and my plan to relieve her of the burden of telling David about him, we had just cleared a huge hurdle that had been standing in the path of Nancy's progress. An old proverb came into my head: When the student is ready, the teacher appears.

CHAPTER

23

Fall of 1992 arrived. We all seemed to be doing well, settling into our own routines, accomplishing what we each needed to accomplish. David was six months old and growing by leaps and bounds. He had blossomed into a cuddly, chunky little bundle of smiles and thick shiny black hair. Carey and I were the typical first-time parents, in awe of every new noise, motion, or expression our son made and recording it all on film for posterity. Naturally we felt David was gifted in all aspects of babyhood, far beyond his peers.

He had just mastered sitting up by himself, something Carey attributed not just to his obvious intelligence and determination but also to the balance he was afforded by his generous girth. He was on his way to crawling and spent much time on the living-room floor on "Lamby," a lambswool throw that Carey's mother—who was known to David as Mamie—had given him as an newborn.

Carey would plop David down on Lamby, place "George" the stuffed caterpiller within his grasp, and prop several colorful board books in his view. "He's an avid reader," Carey would joke as she made what she called his "reading selections for the day" and placed them around him. He really did seem to love books, and when packing his diaper bag for an outing, books were third on the list only after food and diapers.

Without question eating was David's forte. Carey always said that for David eating was a total-body experience. He didn't just eat his food, he lived in it. By the end of a meal his food covered him from head to toe. It was between his fingers, in his hair, in his nose, on his eyelids, in his eyebrows, in the creases of his neck, down deep in his diaper—it was *everywhere*, and he didn't seem to mind it a bit. We had finally learned to strip him down to his diaper before putting him in his high chair for ease of cleanup afterward.

David positively adored table food and at six months, with barely a tooth to his name, would no longer have anything to do with mushy baby food. He was indignant if anything pureed or creamed was put in front of him. He went straight for the real stuff, and he was definitely a three-square-meals-a-day-plus-snacks kind of guy. Like me, eating was his passion, something his roly-poly physique clearly attested to.

At the end of September Carey had a small half-year birthday party for David. We invited our closest friends and family. Carey cooked David's favorite dinner—spaghetti with meat sauce—and for dessert she baked a rich chocolate cake with chocolate fudge icing. In honor of the half-year milestone he had crossed, Carey presented David with half of the cake to tackle himself. Never one to be intimidated by a generous portion of food, David dove right into his half-cake and shoveled it by the fistful toward his mouth while all the adults looked on and laughed. He managed to squirrel away quite an impressive portion of his half-cake, and to this day Carey swears that it was then that he became the chocoholic that he is today.

In our neighborhood Halloween merited a celebration of a caliber approaching that of Christmas. As soon as we passed the midway mark of October, the decorations went up and the plotting and planning began. Parents worked diligently on perfecting their children's costumes, and many created costumes for themselves, which they wore as they handed out treats or escorted their kids from door to door. It was like one giant party as the night wore on. Carey and I had always enjoyed exchanging silly pranks with one of our neighbors. She had a life-size dummy with a pumpkin for a head, which she usually sat outside her front door. Carey had started a tradition of sneaking over at night and moving Mr. Pumpkin Man to a new location, such as up in a tree or in the basketball net. Halloween was always fun.

But this year was different. Better. Now we had David. Carey's holiday spirits had returned in force. One gorgeous fall weekend in October, when there was an unmistakable crispness to the air, we put on our winter jackets, bundled David up, and drove to the pumpkin sale at a local church.

"I've always wanted to do the pumpkin thing," Carey told me as I parked the car, "and this year we're going to do it."

"The pumpkin thing?" I asked her with raised eyebrows.

"The pumpkin thing," she confirmed. "I always count the pumpkins on the front steps of each house. A lot of people have a pumpkin for each person in the household. Tell me you've never noticed that."

"I've never noticed that," I told her.

"Well, it's true. And we've always had just one giant pumpkin. We've never done the pumpkin thing. But this year we're going to have one for you, one for me, and one for David."

"Oh, I see where this is going," I chuckled. "We're a three-pumpkin family at last. I think it's a great idea," I told her.

The church lawn was covered with pumpkins of every shape and size. Carey took David out of the stroller and carried him among the pumpkins. I was assigned collection duty. As Carey found three perfect pumpkins, I gathered them and brought them to the sales table to pay for them: one large pumpkin, one medium pumpkin, and one small pumpkin.

When we got home, David went down for his nap and Carey set to work carving. When she was done, we had three very wicked-looking pumpkins for our front steps. Carey placed them out on the stoop with great satisfaction.

The next morning when I went out to get the newspaper, I took a glance at our pumpkin family and burst into laughter. I ran and got Carey to show her the metamorphosis one of our pumpkins had undergone. When she saw what had happened, she, too, laughed long and hard. David's little minipumpkin was sporting a crown of black construction paper, cut into pointy spikes to mimic David's own thick, black tresses which always stood straight up no matter how hard Carey tried to slick them down. Our neighbor had apparently found a new and innovative retaliation for Carey's Mr. Pumpkin Man antics.

Halloween was over, Thanksgiving lay ahead. Carey's holiday spirits continued to soar as we headed toward winter. I was quickly and happily becoming accustomed to being a father. David was healthy and flourishing. We were still in close touch with Nancy, and she, too, seemed to be doing well.

Then one evening in mid-November Nancy phoned me and, sounding almost too scared to speak, said, "You're going to be very upset with me."

I responded, "I don't think there's a lot that you could do that would make me upset."

Nancy proceeded to tell me, clearly expecting a severe reaction from me, that she had dropped out of school. Instead of being angry, I told her, "That doesn't surprise me. When you gave David up for adoption, you made the most adult decision you could have made. Now, back in school, you're expected to follow the rules, including asking permission to go to the bathroom. You've moved beyond that level, and I'm not surprised that you gave up on it."

Nancy was silent, surprised by my calm reaction. I continued. "I have to tell you this, Nancy. You're not a kid anymore. Having a child and carrying out the decision you made was a very mature thing to do, and it made you even more mature than you already were. You've been through something that has made you wise beyond your years. You probably look at the kids at school and see them and what they're doing as childish."

Nancy was amazed that I could see her situation from her vantage point so clearly. There was almost audible relief on her end. "But, Nancy, I want you to promise me something."

"What?"

"I want you to get yourself enrolled at night school. It would be destructive for you not to finish your education. You need to go to school and get your diploma. You need to do that for yourself."

She quickly agreed to my request, and then opened up about why going back to school had been so difficult for her. She described the peer pressure she felt from classmates who thought poorly of her for relinquishing her child. It had gone from bad— when she had been pregnant at school and planning to give David up for adoption—to worse, now that he had been born and she had given him up to us.

Many of her classmates were really quite cruel to her. They would chastise her not only behind her back but to her face as well, telling her they couldn't believe she was receiving training to become a professional in child care but had given away her own baby. They continued to gossip about the fact that the baby wasn't Todd's, and even though Nancy was always very forthright in telling them that they didn't know the whole story (and often explaining in complete honesty that she had been date-raped), Nancy was understandably being worn down by the abuse from her peers.

In addition it was really hard, she told me, to face other teenage mothers with their children, let alone to do her vocational training in the child-care facility where she had to come face-to-face with both the mothers and the infants. She told me, though, that she knew that she did the right thing when she saw what kind of life these other children were being given by their young mothers. "Those kids have no kind of life that I would ever wish for a child of mine. Their fathers aren't around at all, and the mothers aren't around enough. I know I did the best thing for David by giving him parents like you," she said.

Within a month Nancy was attending night school in the evenings, and working full-time at the mall during the day. She had regained her sense of purpose and focus and was functioning very well. She began to dream of us and David frequently, and the dreams were always happy ones, often involving us traveling. I took these dreams for granted, and it wasn't until I mentioned them in passing to a social worker at a Friends of Children meeting that I realized how extraordinary Nancy's dreams were. The social worker told me that almost always birth mothers had disturbing, sad dreams or nightmares about their children for at least the first year following relinquishment. Apparently our openness had a clinically therapeutic effect.

We got a call from Nan Lahr in mid-November telling us that a date for our finalization hearing had been set by the probate court. We were scheduled to appear on December 28th. When we shared the news with Nancy, she was quite excited and asked if she could attend the hearing with us. This seemed only natural to us, as we were now a family unit and had gone through all the other steps of the adoption with one another's support.

Our social workers requested that prior to the finalization hearing, they meet with Carey and me to review our adoption experience. We met with them in early December in the very room where we had first met Nancy. The meeting was a long one, in which they asked us to detail our experience and provide them with our opinions and constructive criticism regarding the process. We were a precedent of openness for them, and they wanted to learn everything they possibly could from what we had experienced.

We complied with their request for information and told them that the real problem was that there were too many people involved. We explained what the repercussions had been for us, that we hadn't been able to be there for the birth of our son as Nancy had requested. The effect of so many social workers involved in one case, we said, was that "the left hand didn't know what the right hand was doing." The result, we told them, could be quite devastating to those in the adoption triad. We suggested that perhaps one social worker could represent both sides of the adoption, as an open adoption really represented people working openly toward one common goal. We acknowledged that a birth mother needed an advocate, but given the intrinsic values of an open adoption, we thought one social worker would serve the purpose better than three or four.

As we left the meeting, I offhandedly told them, "Oh, by the way, Nancy's going to be at the finalization hearing." Their reaction astounded us. They told us they weren't at all sure of how the court would respond to such a request because it was quite unusual. Carey and I had the distinct impression we were being told that Nancy would probably not be allowed into the hearing.

Carey and I were surprised by this reaction. As we drove home, we tried to comprehend why or how Nancy could possibly be refused attendance at the hearing. We had been told that we could invite friends and family to the finalization hearing, and Nancy was both to us. We concluded that if this turned out to be the case, it would be totally unacceptable to us, and we would fight it all the way.

We felt with all our hearts that Nancy deserved to see this adoption through to the last step. She had never asked anything of us and had always given freely of herself. We felt that if she wanted to attend the hearing, it was the very least she deserved. We hoped that word would come back to us that there was no problem and that we could proceed as we planned.

Several days passed, and Nan Lahr called to tell us that the agency had spoken to the court administration and that they felt the idea was received coolly. Still, she told us, she thought that our request was being given consideration and that we should take a wait-and-see attitude. She reminded us of how we were really a first with the extent of openness we had achieved in our adoption. We were moving through uncharted waters, she reminded us, and we should be careful not to rock the boat.

Carey and I had been told what to do too many times by all the "authorities" involved in the adoption process. We had come way too far to take a step backward. We vowed that Nancy was going to walk into that courtroom with us, or else we weren't going to walk in at all. Nan Lahr's best advice, she told us, was to bring Nancy with us to the hearing, but to be prepared for the possibility that she might have to stay outside in the hallway for the proceedings. Grudgingly we decided we would follow this advice in the hope that we'd run into the best-case scenario.

Every year Carey prepared a huge Thanksgiving feast and we opened our doors to friends and family. This year, with David as our star attraction, there wasn't an empty seat in the house. Our large dining room table was filled to capacity. Nick and Debbie, ever the doting godparents, came to share our bounty instead of doing their usual family dinner. Carey's extended family along with Kit, and Kit's sister, Bethie, were there with us as always. David sat in his high chair, stripped down to his diaper, enjoying the endless attention he was getting as well as his first full-blown turkey dinner, complete with stuffing, peas, creamed onions, and candied sweet potatoes . . . and then, of course, home-baked pumpkin and apple pies for dessert.

As David squealed in delight over his tray of food, Carey asked me to say a prayer of thanks. Those of us around the table joined hands and bowed our heads. What would normally have sufficed for a Thanksgiving prayer was nowhere near adequate for this Thanksgiving, blessed as our lives were by David, Nancy, and our friends and families. Before I could get my first few words out, my eyes filled with tears and my voice cracked. Carey squeezed my hand. I looked over at David sitting in his glory in his high chair. I regained my composure, said a quick grace, and the festivities began.

Christmas 1992 was upon us. Our house looked like it belonged on the December page of a Norman Rockwell calendar. Carey had always been a Christmas fanatic, but this year, inspired by the presence of David, she had more spirit than Mrs. Claus herself.

In addition to our own household holiday spirit, friends stopped by nearly every day, laden with gifts—mostly for David—and holiday goodies. They also brought what ended up amounting to an impressive collection and variety of "baby's first Christmas" ornaments for the tree. Between her precious David and the almost continual company of friends and relatives, Carey was in seventh heaven.

Carey, always ultraorganized, had sent out our Christmas cards, each complete with a professionally done wallet-size photo of David, at the beginning of December. She had decided well before December that our decorating theme of the season would be red bows and small white lights. We shopped early and nearly bought out the supply of each at the local home-supply warehouse.

By the second week of December our Christmas lights were up and done to perfection on our evergreen bushes outside. Carey meticulously tied countless red bows on the dogwood tree and the firebush in our front yard. She draped a garland of fresh ever-greens around the outside of our front door and decorated it with white lights and red bows. A large, fragrant evergreen wreath adorned with a big red bow hung on the front door.

Our fireplace mantel was bedecked with greens and a nativity scene, and our stockings were indeed hung with care in anticipa-tion of old Saint Nicholas. Nick and Debbie had selected a special stocking for David, which had front and center stage on the man-tel. It had a little stuffed dog poking its head out of the top of the stocking, and Nick and Debbie had filled it to overflowing with toys and goodies for their godson.

The Christmas tree stood in the corner of the living room, cov-ered from top to bottom with the delicate wooden ornaments Carey had collected over the years as well as the growing assort-ment of "David's first Christmas" ornaments. We had spent an entire day decorating the tree, while David sat on Lamby, trans-fixed by what we were doing. It wasn't until the next day, after our long labor of love in dressing the tree, that he showed his true interest in what we had accomplished. Carey turned on the twin-kling Christmas tree lights and plopped David down on Lamby, fully expecting him to gaze in amazement at the exquisite tree as he had done the day before.

But David had a different plan. It wasn't enough just to look at the ornaments. No, he had decided he needed to perform hands-on exploratory surgery of this perfectly decorated tree. As soon as Carey went into the kitchen to pour herself a cup of coffee, David was headed on all fours for the tree. By the time Carey came back, he had removed several ornaments, broken a couple more, and was debating which small delicacy was to be his next victim. Pa-rental Christmas lesson number one was quickly learned: All tree ornaments must be hung at least three feet from the ground. By the time I came back from work that afternoon, our now top-heavy tree was practically bending over from the weight of all the ornaments Carey had crowded together out of David's reach.

Even without the ornaments to tackle, David was fascinated with the Christmas tree. He quickly learned that he could roll himself under the tree and gain a unique perspective of the branches and the lights that illuminated it. He was like an auto mechanic sliding underneath a car. He would worm his way under the lowest branches and lie, perfectly contented, with his little legs protruding from underneath the tree.

Carey had started her Christmas shopping in early October. Naturally David was the focus of her efforts. She was in paradise, shopping at long last for her own child's first Christmas gifts. Carey believed in buying children gifts they could enjoy, so David's gifts from us were all toys, in every shape, size, purpose, color, make, and model. Each item Carey bought was dutifully logged in her gift book, wrapped to perfection, and then stored in the guest room. The bed was soon overflowing with brightly wrapped packages, and piles began to spring up on the floor.

We spent Christmas Eve at Mamie's house, joined as always by the rest of Carey's family and Kit, Bethie, and assorted members of their family. Mamie made her traditional seafood casserole dinner, with fresh fruit and sorbet for dessert. We made it an early evening, wanting to get David back home and into his crib so that he would be rested for his first Christmas. Kit and Bethie came back with us to our house to spend the night so that they could be there for David's first Christmas morning.

Carey and I woke up early on Christmas, as excited as if *we* were the kids waiting to see what Santa had brought. Kit and Bethie were up soon after us. David, too young to know better, slept in while Carey and I put the finishing touches on the presents pile under the tree, brewed a pot of coffee, and chatted with Kit and Bethie.

After David woke up, we brought him down to the living room and he sat on the floor with his morning bottle, surveying the mountains of packages that had appeared since he was last in the room. He obviously didn't know what to make of the whole scene, but he was very patient as we helped him unwrap present after present. We knew we had to keep the pace up or it would be New Year's by the time the last gift was unwrapped. David barely had time to look at one present before we were urging him to open the next, and he certainly didn't grasp what was going on. But that didn't matter to us. It was Christmas, and we were with our son. Nothing could be better.

When the last present was opened, Carey prepared a fabulous breakfast of scrambled eggs, bacon, french toast, fruit, and coffee for all of us. David joined eagerly in the feeding frenzy, undaunted by the overwhelming celebration he had just endured in the living room. He was in wonderful spirits.

As soon as our leisurely breakfast was over, we put David down for a nap while we cleaned up the kitchen and living room, and then changed out of our pajamas and into some holiday duds. When David woke up, we all piled into the car and headed back to Mamie's for another round of gift exchanging.

With the morning's practice he had had, David was like an old pro now at this game of gift opening. He knew to let us do the work opening his gifts for him while he delighted in crawling among the reams of wrapping paper that accumulated on the floor. He was as happy as a dog in a bone factory as he crawled through the paper, grabbing at it and tearing pieces of it when the mood hit him. He didn't even mind when Carey, in keeping with her decorating theme of the season, stuck a large red gift bow on top of his head. He was having the time of his life scrambling through the Christmas paper, and we were having the time of our lives just watching him.

Our adoption-finalization hearing was to be held three days after Christmas, on the twenty-eighth. We had made a plan with Nancy that she should come to stay with us the night before the finalization so that we could all proceed to the courthouse together in the morning.

Marilou had extended an invitation to us to have dinner at the house when we were to pick Nancy up on the twenty-seventh. We happily accepted and arrived very late in the afternoon with a small bag of gifts for Nancy and her family. We were so happy to see Nancy and Marilou again, and exchanged joyous holiday greetings as we stepped inside the house. Nancy's brother, Johnny, was there, too, as were Vickie and Nancy's stepfather, Don, and we were greeted warmly by them as well.

Marilou had thrown a holiday party on Christmas Eve, and the house was decorated from stem to stern with every conceivable kind of Christmas ornament. David's eyes were as big as saucers as he saw the lights and mechanical Christmas figurines that Marilou had scattered heavily throughout the house. Marilou took our coats and then ushered us into the kitchen, where she had laid out a huge buffet of delicious party leftovers. She gave us plates and told us to help ourselves to the feast. She took David and sat with him on her lap while we got our food. Marilou's home cooking was irresistible, and our plates were piled high by the time we took our seats back at the kitchen table.

While the rest of us ate and talked, Grammy Lou kept David in her lap and lovingly fed him samplings of all the different foods she had prepared. She was so happy to be able to hold him and talk with him, and he was perfectly content to sit with her for a while. When he finally did get a little antsy, Marilou simply let him crawl down out of her lap and work his way around the kitchen, exploring every nook and cranny as he went. Marilou was a natural at being a grandmother.

After dinner and dessert we retreated to the living room, where we exchanged our Christmas gifts. Carey had chosen some special photographs of David and had framed some for Nancy and some for Marilou. They were received with much genuine appreciation. Carey had also gone to the bookstore at the teaching hospital where she worked, and bought a thick, navy-blue cotton sweatshirt for Nancy. Nancy, who practically lived in oversized, comfortable sweatshirts, loved the gift.

Marilou and Nancy had each picked out a special gift for David. Nancy gave him a stuffed Sesame Street Cookie Monster, because, she told us, Cookie Monster had been her favorite character as a child. Marilou gave David a big, snuggly teddy bear along with a special card with a gift check enclosed. He happily played with his two new toys while we finished up our visit.

As we got ready to leave, Marilou urged us to take good care of Nancy at the hearing the next morning. "Look out for my Nancy," she told us, "I don't want her to be hurt anymore."

We knew Marilou was very protective of her children and was very concerned that Nancy be treated respectfully and kindly by anyone we might encounter at the hearing. Little did she know that I was equally protective of Nancy. "Don't worry, Marilou," I told her. "If anyone so much as looks at Nancy the wrong way, they'll be sorry they ever crossed paths with me. We'll take good care of her." My word was good enough for her, and she escorted us to the door, gave us each a hug and a kiss, and we were on our way home.

When we arrived back at our house, we were all pretty tired and filled to the gills with Marilou's holiday cooking. After moving the Christmas gifts out of the guest room the night before, Carey had freshened the room for Nancy's arrival. Nancy put her overnight bag down in the room, kicked her shoes off, then helped Carey bathe David and put him to bed.

After he was down, Nancy and Carey compared ideas on what they were going to wear to the hearing. Nancy had brought several different outfits, and Carey had put out several outfits that she was debating wearing for the occasion. Like long-lost buddies, Nancy and Carey went back and forth between the guest room and our bedroom, helping each other make a wardrobe selection while they chatted about the holidays and what they thought the hearing would be like. I poked my head into the room from time to time and joined in the conversations. We were all tired, though, and decided to hit the hay on the early side since we had such a big day ahead of us.

In the morning we greeted Nancy, as had become our tradition, with all of us—Sam included—piling boisterously onto her bed to wake her up. We all had an unspoken sense of the resolution we were about to undertake.

December 28, 1992, we arrived at the courthouse for our finalization hearing, hoping for the best, but prepared for anything. We found out that the judge who was supposed to hear our case was ill and that our case was going to be heard by a court administrator, who openly invited Nancy into the court. Our spirits soared, and we walked into the courtroom together, with David squirming happily in Carey's arms. The Clerk of Courts approached us and asked us if we would like her to videotape the proceedings, as she happened to have the equipment set up anyway. We thought about it for a moment and then told her we would all appreciate it very much.

Not only was Nancy invited into the courtroom but she was sworn in along with Carey and me. We sat together in front of the judge's bench awaiting the culmination of months and months of emotional ups and downs, heartaches, and happiness. The court administrator looked directly at Nancy and asked her, "Do you understand what's going on here?" and Nancy replied unhesitatingly, "Yes."

As the proceedings took place, I heard the distant sound of a train roaring down the tracks. It struck me as perfectly symbolic; we in fact were moving forward, farther and farther, faster and faster, with ever-increasing confidence, down the path we had chosen. My eyes stung with tears as I thought of this and looked at my wife, my son, and our friend and birth mother.

The hearing lasted all of fifteen minutes, and our adoption was final. More than the finalization itself, the importance of the hearing was that we entered the room as a family and left the room as a family. Nothing and no one could take that away from us now.

When the proceedings were over, we got ready to take a few snapshots for posterity. The Clerk of Courts suggested that we pose behind the judge's desk and that she would take the pictures. We gratefully took her up on her offer. We sat David in the judge's seat, with the three of us standing next to him. David ended up finalizing his own adoption by grabbing the judge's gavel from the table in front of him and sticking it into his mouth, leaving his trademark drool behind.

As David's first birthday approached, he seemed suddenly to pass a slew of major developmental milestones. Neither Carey nor I had ever before fully comprehended the excitement and pride felt by a parent as a child conquers a challenge. We were constantly amazed by David's accomplishments, large or small. As 1993 began, our video camera seemed to be constantly focused on him for fear of missing the opportunity to record his latest greatest achievement.

One weekend afternoon in January Carey was attempting to change David's diaper as he lay squiggling on the floor in his room. I stood in the doorway, camcorder in hand filming the diaper-change scene while Carey grew increasingly frustrated with David's wiggle-worm antics. Suddenly David stopped still, looked toward the door, pointed his finger, and said "Kitty!" as clear as a bell. Carey and I followed his gaze and saw that one of our cats had pranced quietly into the room.

Carey looked as if she had just witnessed the Second Coming. "Did you hear that?" she said loudly and proudly. "Did you *hear* that? He said 'kitty'! He said his first real word! He said 'kitty'! He's talking! Can you believe it, Dion? He said 'kitty' and we got it on tape! Wow! His first real word was *kitty*!" She scooped David into her arms and hugged him tightly. "Yes, David, you're right," she told him as she smooched him all over his face. "That's a kitty. What a smart boy you are! Mommy has such a smart little David!"

David, a keen diplomat even at the tender age of ten months, sensed that he had hit upon a gold mine and began repeating "kitty" while alternately pointing at the cat and looking at us for approval. Carey was ecstatic, and I was practically jumping up and down as I kept the film rolling. You would have thought our son had just recited Einstein's theory of relativity.

Little did we know that soon he was going to one-up himself by passing another milestone. One day in late February I was at work and was on the phone talking to Carey. She was puttering in the kitchen while David was furniture-cruising from chair to chair around the dining-room table. In midsentence, Carey let out a shriek.

"What's wrong?" I asked in terror.

"Nothing!" she told me. "You'll never believe what just happened!"

"What happened?" I asked her, still concerned.

"I was just standing in the doorway to the dining room watching David furniture-walk around the table, when he suddenly stopped and took about five steps right toward me. Five *real walking* steps!!" Carey was so excited she could hardly contain herself. "As soon as he realized I was watching, he lost his balance and sat down. I can't believe it! He's walking! Life as we know it has ended!"

I was as excited as she was, but disappointed that I hadn't been there to witness my son's first real steps. Carey spent the rest of the afternoon encouraging David to repeat his walking performance. He obliged and by the time I got home from work, he happily gave me a demonstration of his new abilities.

I had my chance at witnessing another of David's firsts a couple of weeks later. David and I were hanging out in the living room together one lazy morning, just the boys. We were having a grand old time doing not much of anything. Carey had gone to the store for groceries.

While David practiced his new walking skills, I went to the front door to let Sam in. He was nowhere in sight, so I whistled for him. He didn't appear, so I whistled again. Finally he came loping around the corner and up to the door. He followed me back inside and lay down on the living-room floor. David took one look at Sam, pursed his lips, and let out a whistle identical to the one I had just used to call for Sam. My jaw dropped.

"David Evan!" I said. "Did I just hear what I think I heard? You just whistled, little man! That's incredible!" David looked nonchalantly at me, then back at Sam and let out another adult-size whistle. I was dumbfounded. I whistled again, and then told David, "Now you try it." Sure enough, David echoed my whistle right away. I was astounded. "No one's going to believe me!" I told him. "You'll probably never do this again in your life."

But when Carey got home, I put David to the test. "Watch this, hon," I told Carey. "Watch what your son can do. You're not going to believe it." I looked at David. "Dave, where's Sam?" I asked him. "We need Sam. Whistle for Sam, Dave." I whistled once to remind him, and lo and behold, he let out a whistle identical to mine. Carey looked like she had seen a ghost.

"Oh my gosh," she said slowly. "He whistled. That's amazing! Did you teach him to do that?" I told her that he had just sponta- neously mimicked me and that he got it right the very first time. Carey was as amazed as I had been when I first heard it. It was the funniest thing to see this munchkin boy purse his little lips and emit a man-size whistle, complete with a wavering intonation. Neither Carey nor I had ever seen anything like it.

"He's a prodigy," Carey said, taking him into her arms. "He's just a budding genius! I've said it all along!" David looked her right back in the eye and let out another whistle. Carey started laughing and couldn't stop. "You crazy man!" Carey said, tickling him under his arms. "You are such a silly boy! You can walk, you can talk, and you can whistle. What a showstopper you are!" David dissolved into laughter as Carey tickled him and laughed until her ribs hurt.

On March 31, 1993, our finalization was three months behind us, and David's first birthday was upon us. Carey and I had decided that David's birthday would be celebrated in two installments. The first party would be on the thirty-first, and would be for his little friends and playmates. We would have a party for our families and Nancy's family on April 3rd.

Nancy came to our house the day before David's family birthday party to help Carey with the preparations. She and Carey had decided Nancy should spend the night so that she could be there to help with preparations first thing in the morning. David was always very happy to see Nancy and would eagerly lunge into her arms. Carey and I had noticed early on that David seemed somehow to sense that Nancy was someone very important in his life. He was more at ease with her than with other friends of ours and watched her very intently when she was around. And while Carey was inarguably his first love, he also seemed to enjoy being close to Nancy. So as soon as Nancy arrived to help with the party, David angled for her arms.

"You love your NancyMom, don't you, pumpkin?" Carey said as she handed David to Nancy. "And you know what?" she asked him. "I know your NancyMom loves you too. And she's going to help Mommy with your birthday party. Hooray! It's going to be so much fun!" No one needed to convince David. He was one big ear-to-ear grin as he basked in the attention given him by his mom and his NancyMom.

Nancy and Carey soon got down to business. They made a beautiful chocolate sheet cake that smelled heavenly and looked like it would feed an army. Then they decorated the house with balloons and streamers and Sesame Street party accessories. David showed off his ever-improving walking, talking, and whistling skills and followed Nancy and Carey everywhere they went. Nancy was as impressed by his performances as Carey and I, and constantly told him how special he was.

Our families and friends and Nancy's family arrived in droves, with present after present and hug after hug for David. Carey had picked up buckets of gourmet fried chicken and pasta salad from the deli, and served it buffet-style with green salad and bread. Everyone filled their plates and mingled while they ate. The celebration was uninhibited, and for the first time there wasn't even the slightest sense of discomfort on anyone's part. David belonged to us all, and we were all there to celebrate the first year of his remarkable life.

David handled it all with aplomb. He cruised among the guests, happily allowing himself to be picked up and adored by anyone so inclined. He didn't get the least bit cranky or irritated by the large crowd that had assembled. He made out like a bandit with birthday gifts. Debbie and Nick had brought him a shiny new tricycle and safety helmet. Nick, an avid cyclist, promised David his own personal bike-riding lessons. He and Debbie plunked David on the seat and took him, his feet dangling inches above the pedals, for several rides through the living room and dining room.

Bethie and Kit had bought him a wonderful wagon. He loved the whole notion of having a special little sitting-spot-on-wheels. They piled it high with throw pillows, tossed Lamby in, and pulled David around and around the house while he sat regally and patiently in his cushioned throne.

Grammy Lou gave him a cross made out of wooden letter blocks, which read, "I love Jesus, Jesus loves me." David took to it immediately. He loved shaking and rattling it, and was infuriated several days later when Carey insisted that we hang it on the wall in his room. Only later did he realize that he could simply take it down off the peg when he wanted to play with it.

Nancy had bought him outfit after outfit of darling clothes. It was obvious she had undertaken a world-class shopping spree for David. Each outfit was cuter than the last. Then she gave him the most special present of all: a scrapbook filled with pictures of his birth family, dating all the way back to a picture of Marilou when she was pregnant with Nancy. It had dozens and dozens of family photos, including one of herself when she was about seven years old, dancing in her Cookie Monster T-shirt. "See that?" Nancy said as she held David in her lap and pointed to herself in the picture. "That's me! That's your NancyMom when she was little. I loved to dance. Grammy Lou used to call me DancyNancy." David seemed to understand what she was saying and looked closely at the pictures in the book.

Carey and Nancy put the giant birthday cake on the table and lit the big blue candle, which was shaped like the number one. The walls nearly shook as all of David's guests sang a rousing version of "Happy Birthday." Carey cut pieces for everyone, Nancy added the ice cream, and I helped to pass out the servings. David, of course, got the first giant piece, which he dove into and ate with zest in his high chair, pausing only to let out his trademark whistle each time Sam cruised by.

CHAPTER

24

In October 1993, when David was one and a half years old, Carey and I were surprised to get a phone call from the head of the Adoption Network asking us if we would be interested in being interviewed by the crew of *60 Minutes* for a segment they were going to do on adoption. Carey and I eagerly agreed. We thought, optimistically, that what we had achieved with our adoption was so important that it should serve as an example to inspire others. Who better, we thought, than *60 Minutes* to help disseminate our message?

We were told when and where to appear. On the designated date Nancy, Carey, David, and I dressed ourselves up and headed to a church on the west side of Cleveland, where the filming was going to be done. When we pulled into the parking lot, we were amazed to see how many cars were there and that there were many people coming and going from the church. It definitely looked like there was a happening taking place.

When we walked into the room and saw the number of people there—hundreds—I turned to Carey and told her, "I don't think it's us they really want to talk to." There were lots of social workers and lots of adoptive parents, birth parents, and children. We found seats in the large circle of chairs, and as we sat down, we noticed that Leslie Stahl was seated in a chair in the center of the circle. She told us that we were each to stand up, introduce ourselves, and talk off-the-cuff about our individual adoption experience.

I had never seen anything like this, and I was pretty fascinated by the whole thing. Carey was taking everything in, and Nancy was clinging to my side as if she were looking for a wing to take cover under. The cameras started rolling, and each group of people stood up and introduced themselves and spoke about their situation. Most of them were too nervous to go into much detail, so the filming went quickly and soon it was our turn.

We stood up, and as I got a little way into our story, I could see the producers motion to the crew to focus all the cameras on me. I continued talking, and the film kept rolling, and in my peripheral vision I could see more than a few people in the audience sniffling and wiping tears from their eyes. I told our story in colorful detail, and when I was finished, I was pleased with the job I had done. I felt I had told our story honestly and compellingly.

After the meeting the show's producer approached me and asked for more details about our experience. I was more than willing to talk with her, thinking it would further our cause. I told her what she wanted to know, and we seemed to really hit it off. I asked her if our interview would be included in the show, and she diplomatically told me that she didn't know how it would end up being edited.

Carey, Nancy, and I all felt good about how we had presented our story, and—believing in the value of the lessons we had learned and now exemplified—we felt for sure that we would get some airtime. We strongly believed that our story would have a widespread, positive impact if given the right platform. We waited month after month for that segment to be aired, and finally one night it came on. Carey and I were glued to the set, eager to see the final product. When the piece was over, we burst out laughing. The focus of the piece was not at all what we had understood it to be. Instead of being about open adoption, it was about a woman who had used fraud and illegal means to conduct searches for adoptees and birth families. Furthermore the only sign of us in the film was a split-second shot of the back of my head. Other than that we might as well have been on Mars the day they filmed.

We got a good laugh out of the way the *60 Minutes* interview turned out, but it also made us a bit more skeptical of the press. We continued to receive occasional calls from various media, but we decided to keep our story to ourselves until we felt the time and the means were right.

Fall turned into winter. Another year had passed. David was almost two years old and was really coming into his own. He was beginning to put small sentences together and was already showing his passion for fire trucks and any other vehicle with sirens. Carey was really excited for this Christmas, as we knew David would be much more aware of what was really going on.

Nancy told us in excitement about the annual Christmas Eve party thrown for friends and family by her mother. It was quite a shindig, according to Nancy, and we were not only invited but expected to attend this year. We eagerly accepted the invitation.

Christmas Eve arrived, and we headed for Nancy's house, a few small gifts for her family packed in a Christmas shopping bag. We were totally unprepared for the scope and magnitude of the party. Outside, the house, trees, and yard were illuminated by strings and strings of colorful Christmas lights. Cars filled the driveway and lined the street. As we made our way up the walk, we could hear the buzz of people talking against a cheerful background of Christmas music ringing from the house.

As soon as we walked in, we were the center of attention. Marilou hugged all three of us, and we were ushered through the crowd, with Marilou performing our introduction over and over: "This is Nancy's baby, David, and these are his parents, Carey and Dion." For the most part we were met with smiles of recognition and heartfelt hugs. Only a few people were baffled by this unique introduction.

The house was packed with people, food, presents, and decorations. The high-volume Christmas music and animated conversation made it almost impossible to hear us talking to one another. There were two Christmas trees decorated almost to the point of collapse; mechanical Santa and Mrs. Clauses were everywhere. Christmas teddy bears were perched on each step of the stairway leading to the second floor. It was a happy, joyous sensory overload. Extra tables had been strategically set up throughout the house and were loaded edge to edge with Marilou's delicious home-cooked treats. There were hams and turkeys, roast beef, three kinds of homemade pierogis, and a gigantic shrimp cocktail. There were salads, breads, cheeses of all kinds, and condiments too numerous to mention. The dessert tables were a dieter's nightmare. Marilou must have been cooking round the clock for weeks.

Everyone was in the Christmas spirit. Nancy and her sister, dressed to the nines, danced with joy and abandon to the music as they prepared food out in the kitchen. Carey and I watched them with grins on our faces.

David, whose presence had been eagerly anticipated by everyone, was held and hugged and passed around from person to person. His feet barely hit the floor, and he was constantly being given a present to open. All of Nancy's family, it seemed, had bought and wrapped something for him. By the end of the evening he had twelve new emergency-vehicle toys to his name, sirens howling.

When he wasn't being held or lavished with Christmas gifts, David, feeling quite at ease in his Grammy Lou's house, was ambling hither and yon. He wandered into the kitchen, and in an effort to keep up with him, Carey and I were one step behind, trying to prevent him from removing everything from inside Grammy Lou's kitchen cabinets. As we pulled him back from one of the bigger cabinets, Grammy Lou stopped us and said, "Let him go at it! That's his cupboard, and he can mess it up as much as he wants to." Then, kneeling down to David, she told him, "From now on this will be your cabinet to play in whenever you're at Grammy Lou's house."

By the end of the evening we were all exhausted from eating and celebrating. We got ready for the long drive home and said our fond farewells to all the guests. Grammy Lou looked very sad at our departure and hugged us long and hard, with tears streaming down her face. We promised her that David would be back soon to play in his cupboard, and we climbed into the car and drove home.

In January 1994 we got a phone call from Nancy that was really an engagement announcement. She and Todd were engaged, she told us brightly, with a spring 1995 wedding planned. We were the third people with whom she shared her good news. First, she told us, she had called her mother, then Todd's mother, and then us. We were flattered that we ranked at the top of her list, alongside parents and parents-in-law.

Carey and I were really delighted for Nancy, as this signaled to us a step forward for her. Todd had been a real source of support and love for her through all her recent hard times. We congratulated Nancy from the bottom of our hearts and told her we knew she and Todd would be really happy together. We gave her our fondest wishes and best luck, and of course Carey offered to help with all the planning that was going to have to happen. Together

Carey and Nancy ended up spending many hours poring over bridal magazines and wedding planners, scheming and planning what would work best, from colors and flowers to who would be invited.

Nancy's relationship with her father had always been strained at best. They saw each other very rarely. Nancy doubted very much whether her father would even attend the wedding. With the uncertainty of her relationship with her father, Nancy invited me to give her away, and I was proud and honored to accept. She asked David, too, to be in the wedding, and he of course agreed without understanding what he was agreeing to!

About a week later Nancy called me back and told me, with genuine surprise, that her father seemed to be planning on attending the wedding after all. I had a hunch that David's birth and the adoption might have been an inspiration for him to rekindle his connection with her. The last time he had seen Nancy was the day she delivered David, and then it was only for a few minutes. "D, I hate to do this, I feel really bad about it," she said sweetly, "but I have to unask you to walk me down the aisle." I could tell that she felt awkward about it.

"Nancy, don't give it a second thought," I reassured her. "I think it's only right and appropriate that your dad walk you down the aisle and give you away to Todd. I'm sure it's going to be a very difficult, emotional thing for him. Who knows better than you and me and Carey what it means to give a child away in love to someone else? Let him have the honor, he deserves it. If I were your father, I'd want to walk with you down that aisle."

Nancy sounded very relieved by my response, but still sorry that the arrangements had to change. "Thanks, D," she told me. "I still want you to be a part of the ceremony. Would you be willing to do a reading for me?"

I told her absolutely, that I was ready and willing to help her and be a part of the wedding in whatever way I could, even if she decided she just wanted me to do the party cleanup! She laughed at this and told me that what was important to her was that Carey,

David, and I be there with her as she took this next step. "We wouldn't miss it for the world," I assured her.

In April 1994 Nancy made another announcement. This time she told us that she was pregnant. We were all surprised, but we could see the happiness and joy on Nancy's face when she told us, and we rejoiced with her. David, we said happily, would soon have a brother or sister to play with!

Carey and I talked privately about this new "development" in Nancy's life. Following David's birth, she had matured and healed beyond anyone's wildest dreams. We knew that in the short time that had passed, she had come a long, long way. But we had learned in our adoption-study classes that birth mothers frequently go on to have another child within a few years of a relinquishment, often as a subconscious way of trying to fill the emptiness with which they are left.

We questioned whether this was the case with Nancy and whether she would be okay with it when it became a more obvious reality. The bottom line was, we believed, that this emptiness that was felt by so many birth mothers had—for Nancy—been alleviated if not resolved by the openness of our adoption. We also knew that Nancy had been born to be a "mommy." She had often mentioned how much she looked forward to having a family of her own with someone she loved. That hadn't been the case with David's birth father, but we knew she and Todd loved each other deeply.

So although we had a tiny element of concern for Nancy, given her youth and the giant responsibility she would be undertaking, we thought it was probably going to work out well for her and Todd. This baby, we told her enthusiastically, would have a great set of parents in Nancy and Todd. They loved each other and, we believed, they could handle being parents.

Carey and I also thought about how the birth and presence of this baby would affect David. We saw it as nothing but positive. Having struggled for so long to become parents in the first place, we had no way of predicting whether we would ever be parents to another child, but we both believed that siblings were important to any child. We were ecstatic to know that David was going to have a brother or sister just two and a half years younger than himself.

Because our adoption was so open, we weren't concerned about whether David would be confused by the fact that Nancy had relinquished him and gone on to have and keep another baby. We felt that if we were always completely open and honest with him, David would grow up understanding that Nancy had always loved him and done her very best for him, as had we. Some people might consider this a simplistic point of view, but sometimes the simpler, the better.

Soon after learning of Nancy's pregnancy, Carey tried to subtly introduce the concept to David. He seemed unconcerned, and being as young as he was, we didn't expect much more reaction than we got from him. Carey had always made a point of explaining to David the relationship between him, Nancy, Carey, and myself. As his ability to understand expanded, Carey elaborated more. She told David that his NancyMom had carried him in her tummy *just for us* so that we could have a very wonderful baby to love. Later she introduced the idea that she couldn't carry a baby in her own tummy, which was why it was so special that NancyMom had carried David in her tummy for us. Now she told David that NancyMom was carrying another special baby, who was going to be his brother, but who would belong to NancyMom and Todd.

Nancy and Todd's wedding date was moved to June 1994, and between Grammy Lou, Carey, Nancy, and her two sisters they were able to put together a lovely wedding ceremony quickly and efficiently. The day of the wedding was warm and sunny and filled with promise. Carey and I proudly dressed two-year-old David for his important wedding appearance. He wore little blue shorts with suspenders, and a white dress shirt with a bow tie. He looked too cute for words, and he was feeling awfully excited and important.

We were in charge of picking up the food, which was being prepared by Marilou and Nancy's favorite restaurant just down the street from us. We piled tray after tray into our van and drove to the wedding with the tempting aroma of warm Italian food filling the car.

The ceremony was going to be held outside at Grammy Lou's house. We arrived a couple of hours early to help with the food setup and to pitch in and help in any other way we could. The yard was decorated beautifully and festively for the occasion. There were tables covered with white tablecloths set up in the front yard, and bunches of pink, white, and blue balloons anchored strategically everywhere. Todd was standing in the driveway talking with a group of his friends. When we greeted him, he was uncharacteristically talkative and animated. It was easy to see that he was having a classic case of the prewedding jitters.

We headed straight into the house to find Nancy. She was upstairs in her bedroom—her room from childhood—getting dressed. She was a nervous wreck, but she looked gorgeous. When David saw her, he stared at her as though he were looking at a princess. We hugged her and congratulated her and told her we were there and were ready and willing to help her in any way we could. She thanked us and told David how handsome he was looking that day. He grinned happily at her approval; he was sensing his own importance in this event. Nancy had her mother and sisters in the room with her, so we left her to finish getting ready.

Carey went to help get the food unpacked and set up. David and I found some cookies and juice and sat down at a table for a little pre-ceremony snack. As I sat there, Nancy's sister, Jeannie, came up to me and told me, with a sense of disbelief, that her father was there at the house, that he had indeed come to the wedding.

"I don't want him meeting his grandson for the first time in front of all these people," I told her. "I want to go find him and introduce myself and David." She told me that he was inside in the study. I scooped up David and made my way into the house. I found him, as Jeannie had said, in the study. I walked in, closed the door behind me, and said, "Hi, I'm Dion Howells, and this is my son and your grandson, David."

I had taken him totally off guard. He was stunned. He looked at David and then at me and told me, "I had no idea you were going to be here." I realized at that moment that he truly had no grasp of what was going on with Nancy or how far she had come. It was almost as if after two-plus years, he was confronting a truth that had been too much for him to face up to when he first heard about it.

"This is your grandpa, David," I said. Then I looked at Nancy's father and asked him, "You don't mind that I call you that, do you?"

"Of course not," he said strongly. "I *am* his grandpa."

David looked right at him and decided he should introduce himself. "Hi, I'm David," he said boldly.

"I know you are," his grandfather said with a twinge of revelation in his voice. "And I just have to tell you that I think you look very handsome in your party clothes," he said. "You certainly are quite a grown-up young man." I was astounded at the grandfatherly-ness that had already taken over. David was as happy as he could be, and played in the room for a few more minutes while conversing nonchalantly with his newfound grandpa. David dismissed the meeting by announcing, "I need to go get a cookie."

Before we left the room, Nancy's father asked me if we might exchange telephone numbers. He told me he would like to join in our open relationship in any way he could. I told him I would be happy to exchange phone numbers with him. He held on tight to that number, and in fact invited us to dinner not a week later.

An announcement was made that the ceremony was about to begin. We were sent to the backyard, where everyone stood in wait. Nancy appeared in her mother's colorful flower garden, seemingly out of nowhere. Standing in the sunshine next to her father, Nancy looked more radiant than ever in her long white gown and lace veil. She walked toward the guests, her arm hooked in her father's. David and his cousin Ashley were a few steps behind her. When David saw Carey in the audience, he abandoned his duty and ran to her.

The officiating judge welcomed the guests to this momentous occasion and invited me to begin my reading. I read the poem Nancy had picked and took my place back in the line of attendants. The ceremony took about five minutes, and Nancy and Todd were pronounced husband and wife. The celebration began.

When we went to congratulate Nancy and Todd, Nancy made a point of introducing us to the judge. "I'd like you to meet my son, David, and his adoptive parents, Carey and Dion," she told the judge. He shook our hands and then realized what Nancy had just said. "Say that again?" he asked. I spent a few minutes with him, telling him of our adoption experience. He was flabbergasted but impressed. "That's phenomenal," he told me. "And it's definitely a first for me."

The celebration was a typical Marilou event. There were people and food everywhere, with music filling the air. Kids were racing around in every direction, and spirits were flying high. David made everyone laugh when he crawled into the center of a balloon display and walked around the party hidden in the middle of it.

By late evening it was clear that the party was turning into a "younger generation" party. As our wedding gift we had arranged for Nancy and Todd to have the honeymoon suite at one of the nicest hotels in downtown Cleveland. We took our leave, giving Nancy and Todd each a big hug and a kiss. We told them we loved them and to have a great time. David gave NancyMom a big kiss good-bye, and we headed for home.

Two weeks following their wedding we had Nancy and Todd over to our house for dinner. Carey prepared a huge dish of lasagna and we all ate and gabbed until we were too full to move. Nancy and Todd were relaxed and happy in their new roles as husband and wife. David was completely at ease with both of them.

Before they left, Carey and I told them that we would like to give them David's nursery furniture as our baby gift. Nancy and Todd were really touched by this and thanked us profusely. Carey told them that she had also saved all of David's clothes and that she was going to give them to Nancy for her baby, who, it turned out, was a boy who would be named Corey. Without having to say as much, we all appreciated how meaningful it would be to have Nancy's soon-to-be-born second son sleeping in the crib of his older brother, David, and wearing David's clothes. As we had realized many times before in this adoption, what goes around comes around.

CHAPTER

25

Later that month, in June 1994, Carey and I were contacted by our social worker at Lake County Catholic Service Bureau. She asked us if we were interested in pursuing a second adoption, because she had a young birth mother who was looking for adoptive parents. We fit what she was looking for exactly, she told us.

Her call took us by surprise, and we had to do some fast thinking and quick self-examinations, as the baby was due quite soon. It didn't take us long to reach a decision. We decided, for several reasons, that we were not going to undertake this adoption.

First and foremost the memory of Nancy's pain in saying what she thought was a final good-bye to David was still fresh in our memories. We knew we would never be able to forget the tragedy of human emotion that we had been a part of. We knew we never wanted to have to be part of, or witness to, anything of that kind again.

I found it hard to imagine bringing another child into the picture, simply because I loved David so strongly, and so singularly, that I felt complete. He and Carey were my world now, my life. I didn't want or need to add anyone else to the picture. There had been a time when I could have lived without any children at all. Now I knew I couldn't live without David; I loved him more than life itself. To bring another child into our family now meant to me that I would have to siphon off some of the time and attention I so relished giving to David. I told Carey I felt our family was complete as it was.

Carey felt strongly that if we undertook another adoption and were unable to achieve this kind of openness again, it would be an unfair disadvantage for David's potential sibling. We felt that we couldn't take the risk of putting a second child into a situation where he or she would have to struggle with his or her identity more than David did. We were also realistic enough to know that our open adoption was a successful one. We knew there were no guarantees of each open adoption turning out so well.

Our family had become more than just Carey and me. Our actions would affect David profoundly, and his welfare was paramount to a large circle of family beyond just the two of us. If we were to undertake another adoption, it would affect an enormous number of people, including Nancy.

We discussed the potential adoption with Nancy. We were still very committed to honoring her expectations of us as David's parents. Her reservations echoed our own almost exactly.

Our answer, we told Beth, was no. The irony of the situation was not lost on us. We would never forget the years we had spent praying that we would become parents and then the months wishing that we would be chosen for an adoption. A call like this would have—and had—meant our dreams were coming true. But we had been on the inside now, and we had seen the most complex and potentially devastating emotions that were part of any mother giving up her child. We knew we had found the only path that would work for us in an adoption situation. We had gone down it once already, naively at first, and then with greater and greater pain and awareness, and finally we had achieved resolution. We didn't think we had it in us to face all of that again, with the ever-present risk that it might blow up in our faces.

We were able to move past the whole thing without any second thoughts or regrets. We wished the birth mother all the best, and we knew that there were countless other couples out there who would be waiting for a call just like the one we had gotten. We knew Beth would see to it that that baby found the right parents and the right situation, as she had helped us to find our own perfect family.

The leaves were beginning to show signs of turning color. There was that certain fall crispness in the air in the mornings and evenings. It was hard to believe that David was soon going to be three years old. Time was flying.

In early October we attended a surprise birthday party at Grammy Lou's house for Nancy's stepfather, Don. By this time Nancy was just a few weeks away from her due date. Carey and I had talked more and more about the baby to David as Nancy's due date approached. When asked whether he hoped for a baby girl or a baby boy, he made no bones about the fact that he wanted "a baby brodder."

We arrived at the party and greeted our very pregnant Nancy with hugs. David took one look at her and for the first time he really seemed to register the fact that there was indeed something in that round belly of hers. "My baby's in there?" he asked her as he pointed, the tip of his chunky little index finger resting directly on Nancy's stomach. NancyMom told him yes, that's where his baby was. David put both his hands on her stomach, stood on his tiptoes, and planted a kiss right in the center of her belly. "Oh, you sweet boy," Nancy told David, "your baby loved that kiss from you."

Carey watched with interest and reminded David, "That's

where you came from, too, David. You were in NancyMom's tummy, too, before you were born."

David looked a bit skeptical, so Nancy tried to help him understand. "That's right, David. You were in there, and boy-oh-boy did you used to turn around and roll over in there and kick me with those little feet of yours." David lit up like a Christmas tree. He was obviously delighted to hear a story about himself to match that of his "baby brodder."

A couple of days later, David was at home with Carey playing with toys up in his bedroom when he turned to her and out of the blue announced to her, "Mommy, I was in *your* tummy."

Carey, taken by surprise, answered quickly, "No, sweetie, you were in your NancyMom's tummy."

"But I *want* to be in your tummy," David said earnestly.

Carey's heart ached to know that this was something she would never be able to give him, the security of knowing that he had been a physical part of her at one time. She had always been sad about this irony of adoption, that she loved him as much as if he had come from her body, even though he hadn't. When she sensed that David was also saddened by this, she tried hard to explain the facts to him to help ease his sorrow.

"I know, David," she said gently. "I know you want to be in my tummy. And *I* wish you could have been in my tummy too. But I've never had a baby in my tummy, and I never will. I just can't have a baby in there. That's the way God made me." David listened intently. "But," Carey continued, pulling David onto her lap and hugging him tightly, "if I *could* have a baby in my tummy, *you* would be the baby I'd want to have there."

A few days afterward Carey wheeled David down the road in his wagon to visit a neighbor who had just had her second child, a boy. David keenly observed the new baby and his older sibling. When Carey held the baby, David watched her closely, with more than just a hint of jealousy in his expression.

On the wagon ride back home David needed to get something straight with Carey: "I'm going to have a baby brodder too," he said to Carey. Carey confirmed that indeed he was going to have a baby brother soon. "And he's in NancyMom's tummy, right?" Carey confirmed this too. "But he'll still be my brodder?" Carey told him yes again. "But he's not going to *live* with me, right?" David asked.

Carey suddenly saw where this line of questioning was headed and answered him that his brother would be living at NancyMom and Todd's house, not at David's house. That was all he needed to hear. David rolled his big green eyes in relief and responded, "Okay. *That's* good."

CHAPTER

26

Sunday evening, October 29, 1994. Carey, David, and I were relaxed in front of the television in the family room. It was a cool fall night. David and Carey had just finished perfecting David's Halloween costume, and David was in his pajamas, headed to bed in just a few minutes. The telephone rang, and Carey answered it. It was a definite déjà vu. In her sparkling voice of happiness and anticipation Nancy told us she was in labor and was headed to the hospital. We told her one of us would be there as soon as possible. When we hung up, we were momentarily dazed with excitement and memories. Nancy was in labor! Baby Corey was on the way! And this time we were going to be right there with her; we would be welcome participants in this miraculous event.

Carey turned to David and told him that NancyMom was on her way to the hospital to have his baby brother. David, loving Nancy with all his heart and having awaited the birth of his brother for what must have seemed to him like forever, was ready to pull his jacket on and hit the road. "I'm going to go!" he declared loudly. Carey explained to him that she and David needed to stay home and that I would go to the hospital to see if NancyMom needed any help from us. If she did, we told David, I would telephone home to Carey and David.

This plan sounded agreeable to David, but, he said, he wanted me to bring a present to NancyMom and his baby brother. He took us to his playroom and looked around at his toys. He found a picture of Cookie Monster that he had recently colored with gusto. He picked it up and handed it to me and made me promise to give it directly to Nancy and Corey. I smiled at his thought process, and at the fact that unbeknownst to little David, Cookie Monster had been Nancy's favorite Sesame Street character as a child.

This time I knew the way to the hospital like the back of my hand. I knew I didn't have to rush, and I knew that I was going to walk into a happy scene and be welcomed with open arms. This ride to the hospital was a happy one.

The labor and delivery rooms had been moved since David's birth two and a half years ago, so I had to ask directions to Nancy's room. I walked through her door and saw her sitting up in her bed, beaming, smiling at the sight of me, just as when Carey and I had arrived for David's birth. Todd stood at the side of her bed, his face glowing with pride and happiness. He had the television turned on, a Cleveland Browns football game broadcasting its comforting sounds of Saturday night football throughout the room. Todd's mother, Genny, sat in a chair. Marilou and Don apparently hadn't arrived yet.

I gave Nancy a big hug. I was already feeling my emotions welling up inside of me, and I knew I didn't need to say anything at all to Nancy about what this imminent miracle meant to me and to all of us. She knew just by looking at my face.

"Here," I said, handing her David's masterpiece. "David wants you to have this with you when you deliver his baby brother." She took it from me and smiled broadly. "Cookie Monster is David's proxy, so to speak," I told her. "David's here in spirit, although he told us in no uncertain terms that he wanted to come with me." Nancy laughed.

Todd and his mother were getting hungry and were talking about going to get something to eat from the cafeteria. Todd was worried about leaving Nancy, though, and was debating whether or not to go. This time I knew better than to leave the room. I was going to stay by Nancy's side come hell or high water. "Here," I said, pulling my beeper from inside my pocket. "If it beeps and you get a nine-one-one message, get yourself up here fast. Otherwise relax and enjoy your meal. I'll take good care of your wonderful wife."

Todd and his mother left, and while I was making sure Nancy was comfortable, a look of worry flashed quickly across her face. I could read her like a book.

"What's wrong?" I asked her.

"Nothing," she said.

"Tell me what's wrong, Nancy," I said firmly.

"It's just that"—she paused—"it's just that I hope I'm going to be a good mother," she said.

I squeezed her hand and looked right into her big beautiful eyes. "Nancy, my love, you already are a good mom. You've already given birth to two incredibly special families, and that's something not many people can say. You are a wonderful mom, in every sense of the word."

"Thanks, D," she said quietly. "I guess I just needed to hear it from you before this little guy makes his way into the world."

I told her I needed to call home to report to Carey and David what was going on. Nancy got on the phone to talk to Carey, and when Carey asked how she was doing, Nancy looked down at my hand holding hers and giggled, "I'm in good hands."

As soon as we hung up the phone, the nurse came in to check Nancy and told her that she thought it was time for them to break Nancy's water. The doctor appeared a few minutes later, right after Todd and Genny came back. I offered to leave, but Nancy told me to stay. I stood and held Nancy's left hand and Todd stood and held Nancy's right hand while the doctor broke her water. He told us her contractions should pick up soon.

Marilou and Don were the next to come through Nancy's door. It was starting to look like a family reunion. Marilou couldn't find a hand of Nancy's to hold, so she settled for massaging her feet, which relaxed her enormously. Marilou told Nancy that she looked radiant and that everything was going to be fine. "It looks like you're in good hands," she said, pointing to Todd's and mine, and Nancy giggled and looked at me to emphasize how much she and her mother thought alike.

Marilou and Don decided to go home and wait for Nancy to call them when she wanted them to come back. Like the rest of us they were expecting Nancy to have a repeat performance of the twenty-two-hour labor she had had with David. Nancy surprised us all. Her labor progressed very quickly. In less than six hours she was ready to push baby Corey out into the big, wide world. I left the room so that she and Todd could share this miracle privately.

Genny and I waited outside the door to Nancy's room, and a short while later the nurse came out and told us we could go back inside. Nancy looked exhausted, but she had a giant Cheshire-cat grin on her face. In her arms she held the tiny swaddled baby Corey. Todd stood next to her bed, looking overwhelmed. "Would you like to hold your grandson?" Nancy asked Genny, and Todd took Corey and handed him to Genny.

After a few minutes Nancy looked at me. "Would you like to hold him, D?" I was a pro by now, and there was no hesitation whatsoever as I reached out my arms for him. I looked down at his tiny little face and remembered as if it were yesterday holding a newborn David in my arms, feeling awkward, confused, and overwhelmed. Although they were half brothers, David and Corey looked nothing alike. Corey had blond hair and fair skin, while David had had his shiny black hair and olive skin from the moment he was born. Corey looked like Todd; he was definitely and obviously Nancy and Todd's child. This felt right, as if everything had fallen into its rightful place. It felt miraculous.

I looked back at Nancy and could see the yearning in her eyes; she needed to hold her baby. She needed to hold Corey, and feel herself to be a whole person, and feel the wholeness of her new family. I remembered how Carey and I had discussed Nancy's second pregnancy when she announced it to us and how we had said that she was meant to be a mom. We had talked about how Nancy's love for her children was as strong as any of life's forces. It was obvious to me now, watching her with Corey, that she was in fact totally prepared to move on to this new phase of her life. She was whole again.

I left for home at two-thirty A.M. When I tiptoed into our bedroom, Carey sat bolt upright in bed and asked me to give her all the details of the evening. We talked for a long while about Corey's birth and what now lay ahead.

In the morning when David jumped onto our bed, I told him, "Hey, pal! Guess what? You've got a baby brother! Baby Corey was born last night!" David bounced with anticipation. "Would you like to go to the hospital to see him?"

David was thrilled at the prospect. "Yes! Yes!" he answered, and headed immediately to the playroom to pack a bag of toys to bring to his new brother.

At the hospital David ran into Nancy's room and jumped onto her bed and gave her a big hug and a kiss. Todd stood at the side of Nancy's bed eating some hash browns. "What you eating?" David asked him. Todd's paternal instincts had definitely kicked in. He grinned at David, showed him the potatoes, and offered to share them with him.

David climbed down from Nancy's bed and went over to the bassinet where Corey lay sleeping. He reached over the edge and touched Corey's hand. Then he got his toy bag and one by one pulled out the toy fire engines and firemen and held them up for his new baby brother to see. "Look! This is a fire truck," he said

—

softly, "and this is a fireman." And then in a very loving, authoritative voice, "I'm going to teach you to be a fireman."

Nancy assumed her new role as a full-time mother with ease and eagerness. She loved being a mother, there were no two ways about it. Todd and Nancy had dated since they were in junior high school, and Nancy had long dreamed of the day when she would marry him and they would begin their family together. Now Nancy was completely devoted not only to Todd but to Corey too. Carey and I often talked about how having another son must feel to Nancy. This time everything was going to be so different.

Carey and Nancy now had a whole new bond: motherhood. It was a strong and constant bond, that resulted in many, many phone calls between them. Carey was like a support and help hotline for Nancy, especially since Corey and David had many similarities in personality and idiosyncrasies. We all used to laugh about the fact that during those first few months Nancy would inevitably call Carey before she would call the pediatrician. Carey happily walked Nancy through making adjustments to solve feeding problems, sleeping schedules, and so forth. I really enjoyed listening in on Carey's end of their phone conversations. They were so much happier than the conversations we had all shared when Nancy was just postpartum with David. Nancy was exuberant in her new role, and relished every moment she had with Corey. Nancy was at last fulfilled.

We could see, as she moved into her new role, that Nancy had really healed. This was evident even before Corey was born. She would openly compare this pregnancy to her "David pregnancy." When people would ask Nancy if this child that she was expecting was her first, she would forthrightly tell them no, it was her second son. When people would question her further about how her first son was taking the impending birth of his brother, she would tell them without a second thought that he was excited about it. She was very confident now about her relationship with David, and moreover she was very proud of it.

The first few months following Corey's birth were very busy ones for Todd and Nancy. Two weeks after having Corey, Nancy and Todd moved into their first purchased home. Nancy had to settle into a new house while settling into motherhood. She did both with her usual energy and focus.

Christmas that year was an event with a capital *E*. There was so much for Nancy and her family to celebrate. Every Christmas one of the traditional gifts among Nancy's family was framed pictures of the children and adults. This year Carey had a wonderful idea. She suggested that she, Nancy, and Vickie have professional portraits done of their children together for Marilou. Nancy and Vickie loved the idea. For Nancy especially this was a very special undertaking: Here she was, at last, with *her baby*, born out of the love between her and her husband, Todd.

The picture-taking adventure was a lot of fun. The mothers dressed the kids in black, white, and red, so they looked not only cute but coordinated with one another. The children behaved perfectly, and the shoot was done in ten minutes with outstanding results. The biggest challenge was handling the curiosity of the photographer, who kept trying to get Carey, Vickie, and Nancy to elucidate on how everyone was related to one another.

When the proofs were done, the mothers chose their favorite picture—the one where the four children were sitting closest together—and ordered an eight-by-ten-inch copy for Marilou. Carey was in charge of finding a special frame and having it matted and finished. Amid the traditional Christmas Eve hoopla, Nancy, Carey, and Vickie presented Grammy Lou with this marvelous gift. Grammy Lou was overwhelmed with emotion as she looked at the bright, smiling faces of her four grandchildren posing together.

Perhaps the best part of the Christmas Eve party that year was that Corey was the center of attention. Nancy was just beaming with pride over his popularity. Nancy had dressed Corey for the party in a bright red Santa shirt that his aunty Kit had given him. He looked adorable, and even David kept his eye on Corey. With all the wrapping paper, food, and people filling the house, David would ask with regularity, "Where's Corey?" as though he was afraid his baby brother might get lost in the hubbub.

When Nancy and Todd asked us to be Corey's godparents, we accepted with pleasure. Nancy and Todd thanked us and told us that they felt relieved knowing we had this commitment between one another. "This way," Nancy told us, "if anything were to happen to Todd and me, we know there's an unbreakable bond between the boys. I know they'll always have each other."

Corey's baptism was held on February 12, 1995, during a regular Sunday service, with the full congregation in attendance. David was in happy, fiery spirits that day; nothing could stand in his way of enjoying this special event with his baby brother. As we sat waiting for the baptismal service to begin, David made continual social visits to the various family members he spotted in the pews nearby. First he was off to visit Aunt Vickie, whose lap he sat in for a few minutes while conversing animatedly with her. Then it was back to Carey, and moments later, off to sit with Grammy Lou. While the regular service progressed, David visited many familiar laps.

When the baptism was performed, Carey, David, and I stood with Nancy and Todd as Corey was anointed. David, having noticed that several other babies were upset and crying, duly noted his baby brother's exemplary behavior to those around him: "Him being good!" he told us. "Him not cry!"

Corey wore the same baptismal gown that David had worn for his baptism. The gown was an heirloom treasure in Carey's family. As the gown traveled back and forth from one family member to another, each child's name and christening date was entered on the top of the box. Now the boys' names appeared right next to each other: "David Evan Howells, 6/21/92; Corey Alan Wiltrout, 2/12/95."

Following the service we all attended the church's coffee hour. It gave us a chance to come together and reflect a little on how far we had come. Nancy had her own important observations and insights, and Carey and I listened in fascination as she talked about how Corey and David were so much a part of her, and so much a part of each other. "Now that I have Corey," she told us, "not a day goes by that I don't think of David. It's not that I'm thinking about what I'm missing, it's that through Corey I'm able to love David more and more every day, even though I'm not with him. I never imagined that could be possible."

Carey and I thought about what Nancy was saying. It was a very profound and complex thought. We remembered again the social workers telling our home-study class, almost as a warning, that many birth mothers got pregnant again within a couple of years after relinquishing a child. They seemed to imply that it oftentimes was a birth mother's way of trying to replace her child or fill the emptiness she felt.

As we listened to what Nancy said, we realized beyond any doubt that for Nancy, Corey was far from a replacement. He was a separate, distinct part of Nancy's life. She loved him for who he was and for who she was to him. But her incredible depths of emotion and insight allowed her to use her love for Corey as a healthy conduit for coming to terms with the loss she had suffered when she gave up David. As she grew to love Corey more with each day she spent with him, she was able to love David more each day even though she wasn't with him.

Then to our amazement Nancy went on to tell us more. "I love having David's crib for Corey. It seems to still hold David's spirit.

I feel his presence every time I lay Corey down in it. I can't explain it," she said almost shyly. "I just feel David there." I gave her a hug and told her she didn't have to explain it because Carey and I knew just what she meant.

Corey's baptism service was performed by Cleveland Episcopal Bishop Grew. Bishop Grew greeted us, and after our introductions I fell into telling him the bigger picture of our family. I've never seen a member of the clergy at a loss for words, but the bishop was momentarily speechless when he heard how Nancy and we had come together through the openness of our adoption of David. The bishop was astounded and wanted to hear everything I could tell him about our experience.

He asked me if I would mind letting him see a written copy of the "Baptism of Passage" because, he said, it had great religious significance. I happily agreed to share it with him, and he gave me his business card so that I could send it to his office. It has since been submitted for liturgical review for possible inclusion in the Anglican *Common Prayer Book*.

Marilou threw a party at her house following the coffee hour. It was a typical Marilou wingding, a joyous celebration, a delicious feast. Our togetherness was becoming a comfortable tradition.

A month after the baptism Corey and David had their own private party at our house, their first brother-and-brother sleep-over. While Todd and Nancy took a one-night vacation, Corey stayed with us. David was delighted to have the chance to be the big brother. He would retrieve diapers and changes of outfits for Corey and deliver them to Carey regardless of whether or not she requested them. Carey would hold the two boys in her lap so that David could help Carey give the baby his bottle. Determined to keep his little brother happy and amused, David rounded up all of his toys that he felt qualified as "baby toys" and made a neat little pile of them for his baby brother to play with and bring home with him. When it was time for dinner, David pleaded with Carey to allow him to be the one to spoonfeed Corey his baby cereal; Carey acquiesced.

When Nancy and Todd returned to get Corey, Nancy greeted him as if they had been separated for a year instead of a night. As happy as Corey had been with Carey, he was clearly elated to be with his mother again. I watched closely as Nancy talked with Carey about how nice it had been to get away for an evening and how much she appreciated our care of Corey. As she and Carey talked, David busied himself making sure the toys he had picked out for Corey were in the pile as they should be, ready to go home to his little brother's house. I watched the smile of contentment on Nancy's face as she held a chunky, peaceful Corey in her arms and watched a busy, happy David getting things in order. From the look on her face she was in heaven.

CHAPTER

27

As David's fourth birthday approached, another chapter of our story revealed itself. On a cold March afternoon in 1996 I was downstairs in David's rec room enjoying a game of "good guys and bad guys" with David. The phone rang and I answered it as I finished an attack on David's "best bad guy."

It was Nancy on the phone. Immediately I knew something was wrong. Her voice didn't have its usual fortitude or cheerfulness. She sounded lost and confused. I asked her what was the matter. Her answer left me momentarily breathless.

"I found out last night that David's birth father died in August 1994," she said quietly.

I was stunned. I actually had to stop to repeat the words to myself to let the full impact of what she had said hit me. *David's birth father was dead.* It was a possibility I hadn't even considered. It seemed unfathomable. We had not had any contact with Jim whatsoever, yet we had taken his existence completely for granted.

Nancy continued by telling me that she had crossed paths with Jim's younger brother in a restaurant the night before. Recognizing him, she had introduced herself to him by saying, "Hi, I'm Nancy. I know your brother, Jim." The brother, she told me, had responded by saying, "You *used* to know my brother. He died two years ago in a motorcycle accident."

Nancy had been shocked when she heard this. Jim's brother went on to show Nancy the photograph of David that Nancy had given to Jim. His brother had taken the photo from Jim's property after his death and now carried it with him in his wallet.

I searched for something fatherly to say to Nancy, but I was still too stunned to think clearly. "Are you all right?" I asked her.

"Yes," she said, "but I'm not really sure what I'm feeling."

I could well imagine what she meant by this. My own emotions were whirling and blurry, so I could see how Nancy must be totally bewildered and unsure of her own reaction. The only advice I could think to offer was to say that regardless of who Jim was or what he represented to us, he deserved our prayers. "And," I added, "in David, Jim has certainly left behind one incredible legacy."

Nancy and I spoke in short, confused snippets for a few minutes longer and then hung up, each needing to digest further the news of this turn of events. When Carey came home a short time later, I told her about my call from Nancy. "My poor David," was Carey's immediate response, as her first reaction was to view Jim's death as a huge loss for David. However, together we faced the dilemma of not knowing quite how to label, sort through, or handle our emotions. We knew where to "put" the emotions of losing a friend or a loved one, but this was a very different kind of loss.

Telling David about his birth father's death, as it turned out, was easier than anyone could have predicted. David had been insisting for quite some time that his "first father," as he sometimes referred to Jim, was dead and was an angel now. Now, with the knowledge of Jim's death and David's previous insistence about his birth father being dead, I was left to ponder the old adage of truth being stranger than fiction. A few days after the phone call from Nancy, David brought up the topic of his first father in passing.

Seizing the opportunity, I acknowledged for the first time that indeed his first father had died. "You know, pal," I told David quietly, "it turns out that you've been right about your birth father. He did die, and he is an angel."

David turned to me and nonchalantly replied, "I know that, Dad. And he likes you, my daddy, and he's happy that you say prayers for him." And with that the subject was closed.

Of all of us it is perhaps David who reaps the greatest rewards of Nancy's love. On the morning of his fourth birthday I asked him, "Who are the most important women in your life?" He told me without hesitation, "My mommy and my NancyMom." I suggested to him that he and I should go out and get a gift for each of them to celebrate his birthday, since they were so important to him. He told me he thought that was a great idea, and when I asked him what he thought we should get for them, he responded with an emphatic "Flowers!" So off to the florist we went. David picked out red carnations for each of his moms and then he added a white carnation to NancyMom's in honor of his baby brother, Corey.

Together, our family, David's birth family, and our extended families have seen what can be achieved through unconditional love. We have seen the rich rewards of uncontested love, living without doubt or fear for what the future holds. Our families mesh together easily and serve as a simple example of what honesty and love can accomplish.

On a larger scale, our extended family has taught me that, given a chance, our society can heal our pain and we can grow toward healthier, more uplifting relationships with one another. Fear, jealousy, hatred, and secrecy are what inevitably lead to failure, even if it takes years for them to manifest.

Both Nancy and Carey are truly the heroines of David's story. They have led us to the success and heights of happiness that we enjoy. They are two mothers who have never been afraid of each other, but have made their purpose in life to give completely of themselves to their son, David Evan Howells.

Perhaps it is David himself who has best defined what his family is to him. One day not too long after his fourth birthday, David was upstairs in his bedroom sharing his new toys with his best friend, Claire. Carey was downstairs in the kitchen preparing lunch. From where she was working, she could hear the conversation between David and Claire.

"Is that your real mom?" she heard Claire ask David. Carey knew that Claire must be referring to the photograph of David and Nancy that hung on his wall.

"Nooooo," David responded, "That's my NancyMom. My *real* mom's down there in the kitchen."

EPILOGUE

As our story has unfolded, Carey, Nancy, and I have been asked with increasing frequency to share our thoughts and experiences as guest speakers at adoption conferences, adoptive parents groups, meetings of adoption professionals, television shows on adoption, and university social work classes. Our first hurdle when we speak is to try to define to our audience what *open adoption* really is. We have found that it's easier to define *closed adoption* than *open adoption*. Traditional closed adoption involves placing a child with someone other than his or her birth family and sealing all identifying records. It is the type of adoption most of us think of when we think of adoption. It is the kind that has, in the past, been shrouded with secrecy and reticence. Today there is a movement toward being more open *about* adoption, but *open adoption* is still in its embryonic stage.

Some professionals define *open adoption* as an adoption in which there is limited to full knowledge of an adoptee's lineage and heritage in some form. For Carey, Nancy, and myself, the definition of *open adoption* is less clinical. For us, it is an empowerment issue. The openness of our adoption has transferred control of our child's destiny from social workers and the court systems to us. Openness has allowed us to independently establish an adoption and parenting (which is not to say coparenting) plan that is in our estimation ethically and morally acceptable. It is up to us to decide what is in the best interest of our child and act upon that decision.

Carey and I have been sadly surprised by the negative reaction open adoption and our story have received from both the pro-life and pro-choice factions. We mistakenly believed that open adoption would be perceived as an acceptable fourth option, one that clearly did not go against the basic premise of either set of beliefs. In contacting major national concerns for both pro-life and pro-choice, I was received with not only a lack of support but in some cases downright anger and opposition.

One pro-choice representative told me I was trying to detract from women's issues with a new twist on halting a woman's right to have an abortion. One pro-life representative told me that while adoption is a good thing, open adoption creates the potential for emotional child abuse. Clearly neither side is stopping to really consider the issue. Open adoption does not take sides. It merely presents another alternative that poses no threat to either side's cause.

Open adoption is clearly not the only healthy way to adopt, just as it is clearly not the solution for every unplanned pregnancy. The bottom line is that in the past, unplanned or unwanted pregnancies have faced three outcomes: the mother or the child's family keeping the baby and raising it as best she or they can given the circumstances; putting the child up for a traditional closed adoption; and abortion. Open adoption is an emerging fourth alternative that must be considered by anyone involved in any way in adoption or pregnancy counseling.

Anyone involved in adoption should feel morally obligated to elevate this option to at least the level of the existing three. This point was made painfully clear to me on Easter Sunday of 1995. My minister approached me after the service, asked me how this book was coming along, and expressed his hope that it would be available soon. He went on to tell me that in the previous year, he had counseled three pregnant teenagers. Of the three, two had decided on abortion, and the last had decided to keep her baby. "I can't imagine what each of them would have done if I could have handed them your book and asked them to read it before making their decision," he told me.

As I listened to him, I was filled with great sadness and frustration. I remembered our Nancy telling us that as she had gone from church to church and agency to agency in an attempt to find the right adoption situation for her unborn child, she had truly believed that no one wanted her child under the circumstances by which she wanted to relinquish him. She could not have been more misled.

Anyone who has ever felt the ache of the unfulfilled desire to have a child knows what I mean when I say that the skeptics often fail to realize that birth mothers and adoptive parents enter into an adoption with a mutual driving force: love for a child. How many prospective adoptive parents would turn away from a birth mother who, out of pure love for her child, wanted to meet them and maintain some degree of knowledge of her child? Very few, I believe.

Along with the rest of the nation, and the world in fact, Carey and I have watched as several unsuccessful open adoptions have received widespread attention. Who can forget the tragedy of the Jessica DeBoer story? What real-life story has ever tugged at the heart of a nation like the story of Jessica, a three-year-old girl who was returned by the courts to the birth mother who had relinquished her newborn daughter to the couple of her choice in what promised to be a rewarding open adoption?

The pain the DeBoers felt and continue to feel cannot be imagined by any of us who have not been faced with the exact same circumstances. We have seen this type of tragedy replayed several times as adopted children have been ousted from their families and returned to birth parents. The emotion evoked in all of us as we witness these melodramas is very real to each of us, however removed we are from the real-life story. The result is that many of us have become terrified not just of open adoption but of adoption of any kind. It puts our hearts on the line. We feel we could better live with unrequited love than the remote chance that an adoption might not work out in the end.

I urge you not to turn away from open adoption or adoption in general out of fear. Instead, tap into the emotion you feel and realize that it is in many ways an inverted mirror-image of the emotion felt by a birth mother as she carries through the difficult decision to surrender her child to someone else. Use that insight to expand your compassion and empathy, and to open your mind and heart to all the emotions and dynamics at work in an adoption situation. Combine that insight and emotion with your best judgment to determine whether any adoption situation you might encounter would benefit by openness. Be willing to test the waters, but be prepared to take things slowly and carefully.

Open adoption, as Carey frequently says when she lectures, is not for the faint of heart. She has described the open-adoption experience as one of the most bittersweet processes a human being can live through. While you are taking things into your control, you have to accept that ironically they are also somewhat out of your control because you are choosing to respect and honor the needs of a birth family as well as your own needs. If you require close control and predictability in order to function in a positive way, then quite possibly open adoption is not for you. If your need for control brings out a tendency toward jealousy or insecurity, then open adoption would probably not work for you.

But remember that even in a traditional, closed adoption, there is the risk of loss and unpredictable outcomes. We have good friends who were blessed with a child they adopted in a closed adoption that happened quickly and smoothly. Within the next three years they were contacted again two times with the news that they had been chosen by a birth mother for a traditional, closed adoption. Both times the adoptions fell through at the last minute because the birth mother changed her mind. They were not spared the ensuing pain of loss simply because they hadn't met the birth mother. Their loss was as deep and real as if they had already met the birth mother and held the baby in their arms.

These friends have gone on to have a successful pregnancy and birth of a child. They are now working to help their adopted son understand that he was adopted and what adoption really means. They themselves are in fact still realizing the ramifications of adoption and the drawbacks of not knowing everything there is to know about their child's heritage. They are quickly discovering that a child's insight is very deep, and the probing questions are there from the beginning. To answer a five-year-old's "If I didn't come from your tummy, then whose tummy did I come from?" with a final "I don't know," leaves not only the child but the adoptive parents feeling confused and dissatisfied and more than a bit sad.

In the course of our adoption, Carey had one friend at work who was particularly sensitive and sympathetic to what we were going through. Unable to have children, she was an adoptive mother of two. With great patience and compassion, she served as a sounding board for Carey through the ups and downs we faced. She laughed and cried with Carey. She offered to read a prayer at David's baptism, and we happily took her up on her offer.

Following the baptism, she bravely informed her family that twenty-six years ago, she had given a baby up for adoption. Only her parents and her husband had ever been told this. She had struggled greatly and in large part alone with the secrecy and intense pain of having given up her child. Inspired by our story, she searched for and found her daughter, as well as her daughter's two children. Her daughter was thrilled; she too had struggled with what she *didn't* know. They have gone on to enjoy a very close relationship, and both have experienced a healing as a result of their reunion. When she talks of her experience, our friend's eyes inevitably fill with tears and she always says, "I couldn't have done it without David." Open adoption teaches us that we can be free to better handle not only our future and the future of our children but the past as well.

Our friends Bob and Lori from our home-study group have enjoyed the benefits of an increasingly open adoption in their relationship with the birth mother of the first child they adopted. We have had the pleasure of meeting the birth mother of Bob and Lori's son. However, when they were contacted about a second adoption, it involved a different birth mother and very different circumstances. This time around, the birth mother chose to meet Bob and Lori once face-to-face, agreed to the adoption, but then requested that further contact be avoided. She was already raising two children and felt that she needed to keep her focus and attention there. Lori has submitted letters and photographs of their child to the adoption agency so the birth mother can pick them up and be updated on the well-being of her birth child. So far, the birth mother has chosen not to receive these communications.

The truth is, open adoption has to be considered on a case-by-case basis. It has to fit the personalities, beliefs, and motives of both the birth family and the adoptive family. For us, it was the only way. It has allowed us not only to have the son we so love, but for us and him to be proud and certain of how and why he came into our lives.

For anyone else interested in exploring the option of open adoption, I urge you to begin by educating yourself. Get involved with a local nonprofit adoption support group. Contact the major adoption organizations in our country. Network. Ask questions. Learn about all aspects of adoption, and then look into your own heart and decide if open adoption is the best choice for you. If it is, stand behind your conviction all the way. Don't mistakenly believe that just because something has been done one way in the past, it is unchangeable. Carey, Nancy, and I learned that we could create our own standards and rules. You can too.

Bringing forward the issues involved in adoption through *The Story of David* leaves us with a challenge: to address those issues in the best possible way. We must prepare, through education, anyone involved in adoption for the human issues, the emotions. Anything beyond that is secondary and usually subject to the law. Anyone entering an adoption process without preparation and education on the human issues will be blind-sided, perhaps with devastating and permanent results. It is worth the time and effort to understand and respect that we are all people, all humans, with wants and needs. We must not be so quick to close the door on one another. Leaving it open—even if it's just a crack—allows us the air we need to live. We can then take our time to find the balance we need.

The Story of David is the story of one open adoption. I cannot pretend that it provides every answer or every solution to every adoption question or issue. I cannot even pretend that we ourselves knew at the outset what we would accomplish or how we would accomplish it. It has been a process of trial and error that we believe has resulted in an overall story of success. It is my hope that it can help impart to others some of the important lessons my family and I have learned over the past five years, and that it can serve as a springboard for others to dive into their own story with some confidence.

When I look at my son, I see a child who is a rare and beautiful mosaic, an exquisite composite of influences and independence. His impish smile, green eyes, and energy are his birth mother's. His olive skin and black shiny hair are his birth father's. The way he loves to hug and snuggle, his love for books, his enjoyment of quiet time and his contemplative moods all come from Carey, his mother. His sense of humor, his appetite, his zest for life, and his hardheadedness are from me, his dad. The rest is David, all David, original and unfettered.

When I look at my son, I see a child who has been given the room, the openness, to know who he is, and to blossom into a unique and special person: David Evan Howells.

Adoptive Families of America provides information and problem-solving assistance about the challenges of adoption to prospective adoptive families and members of adoptive families. They are a most helpful group of people who can help you negotiate the complicated avenues of the adoption process, whichever process you choose to pursue—domestic, private, or international.

Many of their services are free.

TOLL-FREE NUMBER: 1-800-372-3300
FAX: 1-612-645-0055
ADDRESS: Adoptive Families of America
2309 Como Avenue
St. Paul, MN 55108